P9-DFV-882

Antiquing New York

Antiquing New York

The Guide to the Antique Dealers of New York City, Upstate New York, and Long Island

John L. Michel
Barbara N. Michel

Columbia University Press *New York*

No representation is made that this guide is absolutely accurate and complete. Errors and omissions may occur within the body of this publication. The editors and the publisher do not assume and thereby disclaim any liability to any party for any loss or damage regardless if errors or omissions result from negligence, accident, or any other cause.

Columbia University Press
New York Chichester, West Sussex
Copyright © 1995 Columbia University Press
All rights reserved
Library of Congress Cataloging-in-Publication Data

Michel, John L.
Antiquing New York : the guide to the antique dealers of New York / John L. Michel, Barbara N. Michel.
p. cm.
Includes index.
ISBN 0-231-10012-4 (cloth); ISBN 0-231-10013-2 (paper)
1. Antique dealers—New york (State)—Directories. I. Michel, Barbara N. II. Title.
NK 1127.M55 1995
381'.457451'025747—dc20 CIP

Casebound editions of Columbia University Press books are Smyth-sewn and printed on permanent and durable acid-free paper.

Printed in the United States of America
c 10 9 8 7 6 5 4 3 2 1
p 10 9 8 7 6 5 4 3 2 1

This book is dedicated to

Libbie and Jay

Jack, Bob, and Cliff

Contents

Preface

This antique guide is a result of our own experiences as antiquers. In New England and other areas, there is an abundance of comprehensive state guides published by dealer associations and private individuals which report the location and give a description of most antique shops. In New York, however, we discovered that a comprehensive state-wide guide did not exist. After a weekend of antiquing in the state, it was frustrating to learn that a town we had bypassed on a limited-access highway had seven or eight shops. Perhaps more frustrating was having to manipulate several local guides and tourist booklets in order not to bypass that town and those shops. We hope that this comprehensive statewide guide will end these frustrations for our readers and contribute to enjoyable and rewarding days of antiquing.

Another reason for compiling this guide is to show that not only is New York State an abundant source of antiques because of its history but also that the entire state is an excellent source of *quality* antiques and collectibles. Not only Manhattan but areas such as Marathon, Beacon, Cold Spring, Westchester, and Long Island offer high-quality antiques.

The task of assembling the material became a project that took on a life of its own. While we felt at times that we should have considered the enormity of the state before we undertook this task, with the encouragement of friends and dealers we continued to compile information. Our method was to write to all the antique dealers whose names we were able to uncover and ask them to complete a form that asked for a description of their shop, areas of specialization, the price range of their merchandise, and whether or not they accepted credit cards. If the form was not returned within several weeks, we made a follow-up call to see if it had either not arrived or was just slowly working its way to the top of the "things to do" pile. To make the guide as comprehensive as possible, we asked each dealer to name two other dealers who should be in the guide. Not only did most dealers comply but many also sent us additional information. There were dealers who, for various reasons, did not want to be in the guide or, despite a telephone call or two, never returned the form. We apologize to those dealers we missed. Since the guide will be updated they can be considered for listing in the next edition. There is information on the last page as to how to apply for a listing in the guide; there is no charge for this listing.

Although our names appear as the authors of this book, there are several individuals at Columbia University Press who proved to be of enormous help and encouragement. John Moore, Kate Wittenberg, and Jennifer Crewe gave their unqualified support for this project. Kate's suggestion that we should do the guide was the primary catalyst for finally undertaking this project. Leslie Bialler deserves special thanks. He was responsible for setting up the computer programs that made this all work, he was able to find what disappeared when we touched a wrong key, and he gave of his time unselfishly. Ruth Lilienstein not only provided the graphics for this guide but subtle pressure to get it done. Mark Saunders, the National Sales Manager for Columbia University Press, made several helpful suggestions to improve the presentation of material. And, Anne McCoy, Audrey Smith, and Teresa Bonner made sure that in the end it all came out right.

Finally, we would like to thank our parents, Gladys Clifford and Murray Weinberg, and say to them—"Yes, it is finally done!"

JLM
BNM
January 1995

How to Use this Guide

This guide is divided into three geographic regions: New York City, Long Island, and Upstate New York. An **Antique Street Guide**, a quick reference to dealers by street, is included at the beginning of the section for both Manhattan and Brooklyn. Each of the three geographic regions is self-contained; that is all of the information for that region is contained directly in that section. At the end of the guide, there is a general index to all of the dealers and multidealer shops.

For New York City, the dealers in the boroughs of Queens, Staten Island, Brooklyn, and The Bronx are listed alphabetically borough-wide. Because of the number of dealers in Manhattan and the natural and human-made geographic peculiarities, the listing is broken into geographic areas: SOHO, Greenwich Village/Chelsea, Eastside, and Westside. Dealers are listed alphabetically within each geographic area. Also, one can quickly reference how many dealers are on a particular street or in geographic sections by using the **Antique Street Guide**. Plus, there are maps for SOHO and Greenwich Village.

The Upstate New York and Long Island sections are presented in similar fashion. Towns are listed alphabetically. Dealers and multidealer shops are listed alphabetically within a town by using the first letter that appears in the first word of the business name but excluding *a*, *an*, and *the* from the alphabetizing format. For example Anne McCoy Antiques would, because of the "A," in Anne, come before Connie Aranosian Antiques. In the Upstate New York section because of local custom or proximity, some towns have been combined under one heading. Antique shops in Bouckville and Madison have been combined under Madison-

Bouckville. And, all of the towns with the last word Chatham have been combined under Chatham.

Following the listing of dealers in each geographic area are listings of dealers by specialty area and by services. For example, if you are interested in yellow ware, you would look under that category in **Specialty Areas** to find the names of dealers who usually stock an above-average selection. Or, if you are interested in having an item appraised, repaired, or refinished, you would look under those categories in the **Services Section**.

The information provided for each dealer is the same: name, business address, telephone and fax numbers, general description of the merchandise offered for sale with areas of specialization, services offered, price range, and whether or not credit cards are accepted. If any information is missing, the dealer either did not include it or did not want it listed. In several instances, dealers did not return the forms until the guide was in proofs; we included them in a section entitled **Last Minute Replies** which appears before the general index. None of the dealers in this section are listed in **Specialty Areas** or the **Services Section**.

FINAL WORD: The antique business is like any other. Each year, more than a few shops open while others close their doors. Without a doubt several shops listed in this guide will no longer exist by the time you are using the guide, so if you are traveling a distance for one specific shop, it is best to call ahead. Also, although dealers aim to keep to the hours announced, there are times when auctions, shows, and buying trips cause a change in their normal schedules. Again, if the shop is out of your way, you should call ahead.

ABBREVIATIONS:
MD: Multidealer Shop
Credit Cards:
MC: MasterCard
O: Optima
V: Visa
D: Discover
AMEX: American Express
DC: Diners Club
Price Range:
Dollar signs, ranging from one to five, are used as a general guide to the prices of the merchandise a dealer stocks. For example, two dollar signs ($$) mean that a collector will find merchandise costing up to $5,000.

Five dollar signs ($$$$$) should be taken to mean that one should expect to find some but not all merchandise priced above $15,000.

$ 0–$1,000
$$ 0–$5,000
$$$ 0–$10,000
$$$$ 0–$15,000
$$$$$ 15,000+

Antiquing New York

New York City

MANHATTAN

ANTIQUE STREET GUIDE

The format for the Manhattan **Antique Street Guide** is presented in walking tour fashion, with the assumption that one is walking from north to south (uptown to downtown). Thus, listings for 96th Street appear before those for 86th Street, which in turn appear before those for 72nd Street and so on. On each street, antique shops are listed running east to west. One can start on the East Side of Manhattan and walk to the West Side without missing a shop. From 59th Street and above, this pattern is broken by Central Park. Getting to the shops on the West Side will require walking through the park—a bucolic diversion from Manhattan's concrete and glass best done only during the day. As one walks west from the East Side, street numbers decrease until one reaches Fifth Avenue. From that point, numbers start to increase as one continues to walk west. Avenues which run north to south are divided into three geographic categories: (1) 61st Street and above, (2) 60th Street to 42nd Street, and (3) 42nd Street to Houston Street. For convenience, Broadway, which bisects the borough at an angle from northwest to southeast, is listed under avenues and the geographic location of named streets is given.Unfortunately, this grid pattern breaks down in Greenwich Village and to some extent in SOHO, the area south of Houston Street. Bleecker Street runs at an angle through The Village. And, West 11th Street and West 4th Street do intersect! City planners are still trying to find out what happened to the other streets. Maps are provided for both areas.

NUMBERED STREETS

87th Street, East

165 David George Antiques, p. 31

86th Street, East

12 Joseph G. Gerena Fine Art, p. 37
12 Jeffrey Myers, Ltd, p. 36

12	Robert M. Peters/Arctic Fine Arts, p. 42
12	Arlene Berman Fine Arts, p. 28

80th Street, East

236	Jean Hoffman & Jana Starr Antiques, p. 36
24	Shepard Gallery, p. 43
21	Bernard & S. Dean Levy, Inc., p. 30

79th Street, East

325	Renate Halpern Galleries, Inc., p. 42

78th Street, East

450A	Ages Past Antiques, p. 28
450B	Yew Tree House Antiques, p. 44
265	Frog Alley Antiques, p. 34
264	Alan M. Goffman, p. 28
200	Americana Blue, p. 28

77th Street, East

18	American Illustrators Gallery, p. 28

76th Street, East

30	David A. Schorsch, Inc., p. 32

75th Street, East

418	Treillage, Ltd., p. 44

74th Street, East

506	Judith & James Milne, Inc., p. 37
167	Karen Warshaw Ltd, p. 37
19	Cora Ginsburg, Inc., p. 31
19	Leigh Keno American Antiques, p. 38

72nd Street, East

255	John Rosselli Ltd, p. 37

71st Street, East

242	Newman's Collectibles, p. 41
151	Paul Steinhacker - Primitive & Asiatic Art, p. 42

70th Street, East

152	Linda Morgan Antiques, p. 38
21	Hirschl & Adler Galleries Inc., p. 35

68th Street, East
18 Margot Johnson, Inc., p. 39

65th Street, East
130 1/4 Bizarre Bazaar Ltd., p. 30
19 Rita Ford Music Boxes Inc., p. 42

64th Street, West
20 The Emporium, Ltd., p. 61

63rd Street, East
305 Yale R. Burge Antiques, Inc., p. 44

62nd Street, East
315 Marvin Alexander Inc., p. 40
315 Objets Plus, Inc., p. 41
315 Old Versailles, 3rd floor, p. 41
315 Chrystian Aubussin Inc., p. 31

61st Street, East
305 Art Trading (U.S.) Ltd., p. 29
305 Georgian Manor Antiques, Inc., p. 34
153 Throckmorton Fine Art, Inc., p. 44

60th Street, East
250 Jean Karajian Gallery, p. 48
247 Proctor Galleries, p. 50
243 Nicholas Antiques, p. 49
238 Federico Carrera, p. 47
235 A. Smith Antiques, Ltd., p. 46
213 Gardner & Barr, Inc., p.47
210 Paris To Province, p. 50
209 Earle D.Vandekar of Knightsbridge, Inc., p. 47
207 Suchow & Seigel Antiques, p. 51

59th Street, East
328 Schmul Meier, Inc., p. 51
328 Suttonbridge, p. 51

57 Street, East
225 Roger Gross Ltd., p. 51
104 S.J. Shrubsole, Corp., p. 51
44 Dalva Brothers, Inc., p. 46

41 J.J. Lally & Co., p. 48
11 James II Galleries, Ltd, 4th floor, p. 48

56th Street, East
60 I. Freeman & Son, Inc., p. 48
12 Ralph M. Chait Galleries, Inc., p. 50

53rd Street, East
425 Newell Art Galleries, Inc., p. 49

37th Street, East
201 Treasures From The Past, p. 59

35th Street, East
121 Pantry & Hearth, p. 58

34th Street, West
440 Constantine Kollitus, p. 65

31st Street, East
201 City East Antiques Center , p. 53

25th Street, West
110 Chelsea Antiques Building, p. 65

24th Street, East
305 Bruce Gimelson, p. 53

24th Street, West
111 A. Goldstein, Wrought in America, Inc. , p. 64
514 John Koch Antiques, p. 66

21st Street, West
54 Acanthus Books, p. 64

20th Street, West
6 Wendover's LTD of England, p. 66

18th Street, West
7 Metropolis Collection, p. 66

15th Street, West
344 John Charles & Co., p. 66

13th Street, East

143 Dullsville, Inc., p. 54
64 Antiques By Patrick, p. 53
55 Victor Carl Antiques, p. 60
32 Waves, p. 60

12th Street, East

47 Howard Kaplan Bath Shop, p. 56
37 Kentshire Galleries, Ltd., p. 57
8 Renee Antiques Inc., p. 58

11th Street, East

80 Kensington Place Antiques, p. 57
72 J. Garvin Mecking, Inc., p. 56
67 Roger Appleyard Ltd., p. 59
67 Roland's Antiques, p. 59
61 H. M. Luther Inc., p. 54
58 Paramount Antiques, Inc, p. 58
55 Eastside Antiques, p. 54

10th Street, East

53 Martell Antiques, p. 57
43 Reymer-Jourdon Antiques, p. 59
36 Maison Gerard, p. 57
30 L'Epoque Antiques, p. 57
28 Tudor Rose Antiques, p. 59
29 Karl Kemp and Assoc. Ltd. Antiques, p. 56

10th Street, West

277 Paper Moons, p. 26

NAMED AND NUMBERED AVENUES, PLACES AND SQUARES

Amsterdam Avenue (61st Street and Above)

500 Better Times Antiques, Inc., p. 61

Broadway (61st and Above)

2244 Gallery II Collections, p. 62

Broadway (42nd Street to Houston)

836 David Seidenberg, p. 53
836 Hyde Park Antiques, p. 56
833 Universe Antiques, p. 60

831	Howard Kaplan Antiques, p. 55
830	Philip Colleck, p. 58
827	Howard Kaplan Antiques, p. 55
815	Abe's Antiques, p. 53
814	Midtown Antiques, Inc., p. 57
813	Florence Sack Ltd., p. 54
812	Turbulence, p. 60
808	Agostino Antiques, Ltd., p. 53
799	Far Eastern Antiques & Arts, Inc., p. 54
799	Flores & Iva Antiques, p. 54

Broadway (Below Houston)

594	American Primitive Gallery, p. 12

Central Park, West

230	Allan Daniel, p. 61
230	Kendra Krienke, p. 62

Columbus Avenue, West Side

556	Welcome Home Antiques, p. 63
550	The Golden Treasury, p. 62
505	Alice's Antiques, p. 61
380	Alice Underground, p. 61
282	La Belle Epoque Vintage Posters, Inc., p. 63

East End Avenue

10	Zane Moss Antiques, p. 45

First Avenue (60th Street to 42nd Street)

899	Charles P. Rogers Brass & Iron Bed Co., p. 46

First Avenue (42nd Street to Houston)

156	A Repeat Performance, p. 59

Fifth Avenue (60th Street to 42nd Street)

781	A La Vieille Russie, Inc., p. 46
725	Norman Crider Antiques, 5th floor, p. 49
724	The Garden Antiquary, p. 47
576	Aaron's Antiques, p. 46

First Avenue (61st Street and Above)

1101	Darrow's Fun Antiques & Collectibles, p. 31

Lexington Avenue (61st Street and Above)

1349 Charlotte F. Safir, p. 30
1218 The Lands Beyond, p. 37
1210 Japan Gallery, p. 36
1193 Hubert des Forges, Inc., p. 35
1187 F.H. Coins & Collectibles, Ltd., p. 33
1120 North Star Galleries, p. 41
1102 Sylvia Pines-Uniques, p. 43
1036 J. Dixon Prentice, Antiques, p. 35
1028 Pimlico Way/Amdier Antiques, p. 42
988 Ellen Berenson Antiques, p. 32
980 Lenox Court Antiques, p. 38
978 L'Art De Vivre, p. 37
941 S. Wyler Inc., p. 43

Lexington Avenue (42nd Street to Houston Street)

150 The Old Print Shop, Inc., p. 57

Madison Avenue (61st Street and Above)

1262 Frank S. Miele Gallery, p. 34
1242 Art of the Past, p. 29
1131 Fanelli Antique Timepieces, Ltd., p. 33
1131 Marie E. Betteley, p. 40
1122 Malvina L. Solomon, Inc., p. 39
1095 Guild Antiques II, p. 35
1089 Guild Antiques II, p. 35
1086 Art Asia, Inc., p. 29
1082 Burlington Antiques Toys, p. 30
1045 Smith Gallery, p. 43
1040 E & J Frankel, Ltd., p. 32
1015 Linda Horn Antiques, p. 38
994 Edith Weber & Assoc., Inc., p. 32
989 Kenneth W. Rendell Gallery, Inc., p. 37
969 Godel & Co. Fine Art, p. 34
967 Leo Kaplan Ltd, p. 38
965A Leo Kaplan Modern, p. 38
962 Florian Papp, Inc., p. 34
948 Antiquarium Fine Ancient Arts Gallery, Ltd., p. 28
942 Stair & Company, p. 43
927 Gemini Antiques Ltd., p. 34
878 20th Century Antiques, Ltd., p. 44

University Place
50 Fishera & Perkins, p. 24

West End Avenue (61st Street and Above)
565 Diane Gerardi's Vintage Jewelry, p. 61

York Avenue (61st Street and Above)
1675 D.T.L. Trading, p. 31
1577 C.M. Leonard Antiques, p. 31
1525 Eli Wilner & Company, p. 31

NAMED STREETS

Bleecker Street (Greenwich Village)
413 Hamilton-Hyre, Ltd., p. 24
390 Susan Parrish, p. 27
382 Old Japan Inc., p. 26
374 American Folk Art Gallery, p. 22
370 Distinctive Furnishings, p. 23
344 Niall Smith Antiques, p. 26
335 Dorothy's Closet, p. 23
322 Renee Kerne Antiques, p. 26
321 1/2 The Antique Buff, p. 22
283 Second Childhood, p. 26
270 Star Struck, Ltd., p. 26
175 Gallery II Collections, p. 24

Broome Street (SOHO)
470A Le Monde Des Kilims, p. 16
465 Atelier, p. 12

Greene Street (SOHO)
125 Back Pages Antiques, p. 12
110 Twin Fires, p. 19
57 Les 2 Iles, p. 16

Greenwich Street (Greenwich Village)
43 Star Struck, Ltd., p. 26

Grove Street (Greenwich Village)
61 Jane Werner-Ayre Asian Fine Art, p. 24

Hudson Street (SOHO)
535 Panache Antique Clothing, p. 18
502 Lucy Ann Folk Art & Antique Quilts, p. 25

Jane Street (Greenwich Village)
74 Kelter-Malcé, p. 24

LaFayette Street (SOHO)
345 Elan Antiques, p. 15
290 Rooms & Gardens, p. 19
285 Urban Archaeology, p. 20
281 Brian Windsor Art, Antiques, p. 13
280 280 Modern, p. 20
276 Coming To America, p. 14
275 Lost City Arts, p. 17
270 Secondhand Rose, p. 19
231 Chameleon, p. 13

MacDougal Street (Greenwich Village)
108 Den of Antiquity, p. 23

Mercer Street (SOHO)
77 Michael Carey, p. 17
71 Pine Country Antiques Inc., p. 19

Mott Street (SOHO)
280 Forthright Furniture, p. 15

Perry Street (Greenwich Village)
117 El Ombu, p. 24
41 Antiquarius, Ltd., p. 22
41 Thomas, p. 27

Prince Street (SOHO)
181 Mood Indigo, p. 17

Spring Street (SOHO)
151 E. Buk, p. 14
134 Peter-Roberts Antiques, Inc., p. 18
114 First Peoples Gallery, p. 15
106 Jacques Carcanagues, Inc., p. 16
96 Illustration House, Inc., p. 16

Sullivan Street (SOHO)

79	Beyond the Bosphorus, p. 12

Thompson Street (SOHO)

150	Eileen Lane Antiques, p. 15
120	Kimono House, p. 25
80	Bertha Black Antiques, p. 12
69	Classic Toys, p. 13
68	Lyme Regis, Ltd., p. 17

University Place (Chelsea)

91	Palace Galleries, Inc., p. 26
81	Artisans Antiques, p. 22
50	Fichera & Perkins Antiques, p. 24

West Houston (SOHO/Greenwich Village)

116	Cobweb, p. 13

Wooster Street (SOHO)

152	Ricco/Maresca Gallery, p. 19
131	Home Town, p. 16
120	T&K French Antiques, Inc., p. 19
117	Gallery 532 SOHO, p. 15
100	c.i.t.e., p. 13
86	Wooster Gallery, p. 21
83	Fred Silberman Co., p. 15
63	Objects & Images, p. 17

West Broadway (SOHO)

436	Antique Addiction, p. 12

Soho

American Primitive Gallery
594 Broadway, 2nd floor (10012)
(212) 966-1530
(212) 343-0272 fax
Hours: Mon–Sat, 11–6 but closed weekends during July & August

This gallery features exciting and eclectic offerings of 19th and 20th century folk art, Outsider Art, Self-Taught Art, American Indian art, early utilitarian objects, and unusual Americana. Also available is a complete museum quality mounting service for antiques and sculpture on bases of wood, metal, or plastic. There is also a prop rental service. PR: $$$$$. CC: AMEX.

Antique Addiction
436 West Broadway (10012)
(212) 925-6342
(718) 287-5738 fax
Hours: Daily 11–7

In addition to its diverse collection of estate and costume jewelry, this shop also offers an interesting selection of cufflinks, Bakelite, cameras, eyeglasses, lighters, and other smoking accessories. CC: MC, V, AMEX.

Atelier
465 Broome Street (10013)
(212) 925-3820
Hours: Mon–Fri, 11–7; Sat–Sun, 12–6 or by appointment

This dealer stocks 18th and 19th century furniture and such accessories as tapestries, sculptures, and screens. PR: $$$. CC: No.

Back Pages Antiques
125 Greene Street (10012)
(212) 460-5998
Hours: Mon–Fri, 9–6; Sat, 11–6; Sun, 12–6

Back Pages features Americana that was produced when fun was a nickel. Wurlitzer jukeboxes, slot and sodapop machines, penny arcade and gambling machines, and various sports related games fill this shop. They restore and service everything that they sell. PR: $200+. CC: No.

Bertha Black Antiques
80 Thompson Street (10012)
(212) 966-7116
Hours: Wed–Sat, 2–7 or by appointment

This charming shop specializes in folk art, painted furniture, American glass, English ceramics, antique textiles, and pillows made from vintage fabric. An extensive collection of religious art including Spanish colonial, European sculpture, and fine retablos is available. PR: $$. CC: AMEX.

Beyond The Bosphorus
79 Sullivan Street (10012)
(212) 219-8275
Hours: Tues–Sat, 12–6

Established in 1986, this shop

contains handmade tribal/ nomadic rugs, featuring Turkish kilims. New, antique, and semi-antique kilims in a variety of designs including stylized florals and geometrics in colors ranging from rich dark blues, browns, and reds to teal, terra cotta, and rose in room sizes to mats and runners are available. A large selection of kilim pillows in sizes from 8"x8" to 2'x3' are also offered. PR: Rugs, $$; Pillows, $. CC: MC, V, AMEX.

Brian Windsor Art, Antiques, and Garden Furnishings
281 Lafayette Street (10012)
(212) 274-0411
(212) 941-8005 fax
Hours: Daily 12–6

This shop contains an eclectic mixture of decorative home and garden furnishings, Americana, folk art, and architectural ornaments from the past to the present. CC: AMEX.

Chameleon
231 Lafayette Street (10012)
(212) 343-9197
Hours: Mon–Fri, 11–8; Sat–Sun, 12–7

Chameleon offers a selection of furniture and accessories that ranges from Mission to Moderne to mahogany. Many of the items are reflective of the season, such as urns and garden furniture in the spring. PR: $$$. CC: MC, V.

c.i.t.e.
100 Wooster Street (10012)
(212) 431-7272
(212) 226-6507 fax
Hours: Mon–Sat, 11–7; Sun 12–6

This shop offers an interesting and eclectic assortment of distressed antiques, architectural ornamentations, collectibles, and accessories. Display materials and prop rentals are available. CC: MC, V, AMEX.

Classic Toys
69 Thompson Street (10012)
(212) 941-9129
Hours: Tues–Sat, 12–6:30

This shop carries New York City's largest range of old toy cars and vehicles and one of the largest selections of old toy soldiers and farm and zoo animals. In addition there is a constantly changing general stock of old toys such as Britains, Marx, Dimestore, Dinky, Corgi, Star Wars, GI Joe, and more. PR: $$. CC: MC, V, AMEX, DC, CB.

Cobweb
116 West Houston (10012)
(212) 505-1558
Hours: Mon–Fri, 12–7; Sat, 12–5; Sun closed

In more than 10,000 square feet of show space, one will find country, formal, and ethnic furniture and accessories from Morocco, Egypt, France, Argentina, The Philippines, and

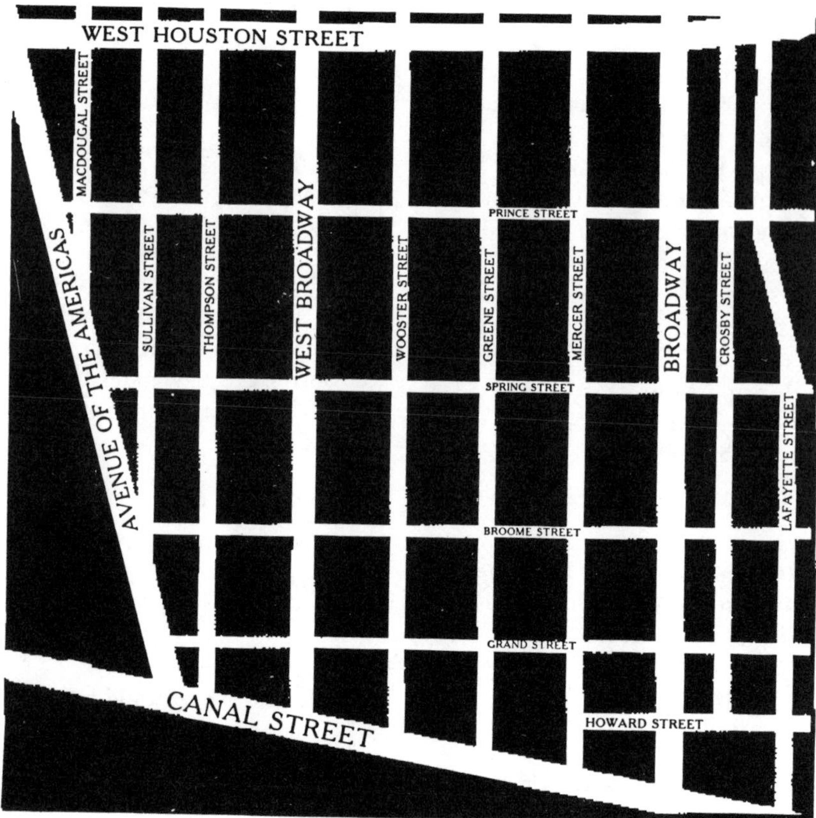

Soho

Indonesia. Tables and chairs (café, garden, and dining), benches, beds, chandeliers (many for candles), lanterns, pedestals, plantstands, cupboards, armoires, doors, gates, clay vessels, kilims, and much more are available. PR: $$. CC: MC, V, AMEX.

Coming To America
276 Lafayette Street (10012)
(212) 343-2968
Hours: Daily 11–6

Painted country furniture, folk art, architectural ornaments, trade signs, English-style down-filled upholstered furniture, painted gameboard tables, paintings, mirrors, rugs, quilts, lamps, and shades are offered. This interesting shop is well worth a visit. PR: $$$. CC: AMEX.

E. Buk
151 Spring Street (10012)
(212) 226-6891
(212) 316-3100 fax
Hours: Daily by appointment

This dealer specializes in scientific, industrial, and technological artifacts, instruments, tools, machines, devices, equipment, and accessories. Fine and unusual furniture and accessories, architectural renderings, and American folk art are also offered.

Eileen Lane Antiques

150 Thompson Street (10012)
(212) 475-2988
Hours: Daily 11–7

Established in 1981, this shop specializes in Swedish and Austrian furniture from the Biedermeier, Art Deco, and Jugendstil periods. In addition, one of the largest selections of alabaster chandeliers is offered. Prop rentals are available. PR: $$$. CC: MC, V, AMEX, DC, CB.

Elan Antiques

345 Lafayette Street (10012)
(212) 529-2724
Hours: Mon–Sat, 1–7;
Sun, 12–6

Celebrating 20th century design, this shop offers American furniture, Italian Art Glass, and Mission oak to the 1960s. Consignments are accepted. Prop rentals are available. CC: MC, V, AMEX.

First Peoples Gallery

114 Spring Street (10012)
(212) 343-0166
(212) 343-0167 fax
Hours: Tues–Sun, 11–6

This gallery specializes in original native art in the contemporary and traditional forms. The gallery represents well-known sculptures, painters, carvers, textiles, and designer jewelry. In addition, the gallery carries 11th century pottery from Socorro, New Mexico and old pawn jewelry. CC: MC, V, AMEX, D, DC.

Forthright Furniture

280 Mott Street (10012)
(212) 334-8291
Hours: Tues–Sun, 11–8

Tucked away in Little Italy, this shop specializes in furniture from the American Arts & Crafts Movement (Mission Furniture). CC: No.

Fred Silberman Company

83 Wooster Street (10012)
(212) 925-9470
Hours: Mon–Sat, 11–6:30

In more than 4,000 square feet, one will find Italian furniture, lighting, glass, and ceramics from 1920 to 1950. In addition there is a selection of Hagenauer sculpture in all sizes plus American, Austrian, and French pottery. CC: All.

Gallery 532 SOHO

117 Wooster Street (10012)
(212) 219-1327
Hours: Tues–Sun, 12–6:30

This gallery specializes in original American Arts & Crafts furniture; antique lighting by Handel, Tiffany and others; American Art Pottery; and related accessories. In addition, interesting furniture from all periods is carried. CC: MC, V, AMEX, D.

Home Town
131 Wooster Street (10012)
(212) 674-5770
Hours: Tues–Sat, 11–7

Home Town specializes in authentic painted antique furniture, folk art, architectural banks, tramp art, doorstops, children's toys, gameboards, wooden signs, and unusual decorative accessories. Appraisals, a finders service, and prop rentals are available. CC: MC, V, AMEX.

Illustration House, Inc.
96 Spring Street, 7th floor (10012)
(212) 966-9444
Hours: Tues–Sat, 10:30–5:30

A unique gallery devoted solely to exhibiting and selling original paintings and drawings by America's greatest illustrators. Auctions of illustrative and comic art are held annually in May and November. The proprietors are the foremost experts in the field having authored several books on the subject and lectured at museums and educational institutions; they publish **The Illustration Collector**. Appraisals and research are done. PR: $$$$$. CC: MC, V.

Jacques Carcanagues Inc.
106 Spring Street (10012)
(212) 925-8110
(212) 274-8780 fax
Hours: Daily 11:30–7

This shop carries articles ranging from furniture to Santos. Specialty areas include Tribal Arts from Asia (India, Nepal, Thailand, Burma, and Korea) and items from The Philippines, Morocco, Guatemala, and Panama plus an extensive jewelry collection from these countries. PR: $$. CC: MC, V, AMEX, D.

Le Monde Des Kilims/ Martman, Inc.
470A Broome Street (10013)
(800) 4-kilims
(212) 431-9016 fax
Hours: Daily 11–7

This business specializes in the finest antique and decorative kilims and pillows. Elegant home furnishings are also created by upholstering European antique or turn of the century furniture with the very finest kilims. Oriental rug repair, restoration, and cleaning as well as appraisals are available. PR: $$$$$. CC: MC, V, AMEX, D, CB.

Les 2 Iles
57 Greene Street (10012)
(212) 276-9281
(212) 966-7921 fax
Hours: Mon–Fri, 11–6; Sat–Sun, 12–6

This shop specializes in 18th and

19th century furniture from Provence: formal and country pieces, mirrors, decorative lamps, and other interesting accessories. Custom made leather for desks and furniture repair and restoration are available. CC: MC, V, AMEX.

Lost City Arts
275 Lafayette Street (10012)
(212) 941-8025
Hours: Mon–Fri, 10–6;
Sat–Sun, 12–6

This funky and eclectic shop is one of the most interesting antique emporiums in the city. Americana from the 1920s to the 1950s such as electric advertising and architectural antiques plus furniture and lighting from the Art Deco period to the 1950s are only some of the items that can be found in this shop. CC: MC, V, AMEX.

Lyme Regis, Ltd.
68 Thompson Street (10012)
(212) 334-2110
Hours: Wed–Sun, 1–7; call for summer hours

Established in 1983, this antique shop offers an unusual and eclectic presentation of 18th and 19th century small decorative objects, textiles, paintings, pottery, and jewelry from England and Scotland. PR: $45+. CC: MC, V, AMEX.

Michael Carey
77 Mercer Street (10012)
(212) 226-3710
(212) 226-4059 fax
Hours: Tues–Sat, 11–6 or by appointment

This dealer is noted for stocking fine pieces from the Arts and Crafts Movement (1900-1915). Furniture conservation and restoration and appraisals are done. CC: No.

Mood Indigo
181 Prince Street (10012)
(212) 254-1176
Hours: Tues–Sat, 12–7;
Sun–Mon, 11–6

In addition to specializing in Fiestaware, Russel Wright, 1939 New York World's Fair, and Art Deco accessories, this shop also offers a fabulous selection of novelty salt & pepper shakers from the 1940s and 1950s, cookie jars, and cocktail shakers. Mail order is available. CC: MC, V, AMEX.

Objects and Images
63 Wooster Street (10012)
(212) 431-1000
Hours: Tues–Fri, 12–6:30;
Sat–Sun, 11–6:30

This shop offers fine reproductions—decoratives, pottery including Raku, and paintings that are original style reproductions of the old masters. PR: $$. CC: MC, V, AMEX.

Hessian Soldier Whirligig, 33 inches with blade in upright position, 1870s–1880s. *(Courtesy American Primitive Gallery, New York City—Steve Tucker photographer)*

Panache Antique Clothing
525 Hudson Street (10014)
(212) 242-5115
Hours: Mon—Sat, 12—7; Sun, 1–6

Panache, an original turn of the century storefront, is lavishly but neatly stocked with women's gabardine suits and coats; 1920s to 1950s dresses, separates, scarves, gloves, hats, and never-worn shoes; Victorian lingerie and handbags; and a selection of costume jewelry that includes Bakelite and Mexican silver. For the men, gabardine and Hawaiian shirts, scarves, ties, suits, and jackets are available. Quilts, drapes, tablecloths linens, and hatboxes are also for sale. PR: $. CC: MC, V, AMEX.

Peter-Roberts Antiques, Inc.
134 Spring Street (10012)
(212) 226-4777
(212) 431-6417 fax
Hours: Mon–Sat, 11–7; Sun, 12–6

Specializing in the finest furniture, pottery, lighting, rugs, and accessories of The American Arts and Crafts Period, these dealers offer the work of Gustav Stickley, his brothers, Limbert, Roycroft, and other important designers of the period. Definitely worth a visit. PR: $$$$$. CC: No.

Ricco/Maresca Gallery

152 Wooster Street (10012)
(212) 780-0071
(212) 780-0076 fax
Hours: Tues–Fri, 10–6; Sat, 11–6

This gallery offers the work of masters of American Self-Taught and Outsider Art such as William Hawkins and Bill Traylor.

Pine Country Antiques, Inc.

71 Mercer Street (10012)
(212) 274-9663
(212) 226-0940 fax
Hours: Daily 11–6

In addition to offering European and American pine furniture, this shop has custom reproduction furniture. Restoration and refinishing in a variety of paint finishes are available. All work is guaranteed. PR: $$$$. CC: No.

Rooms & Gardens

290 Lafayette Street (10012)
(212) 431-1297
Hours: Mon–Sat, 11–6

In addition to specializing in French and American garden furniture and 19th century French country and Parisian home furnishings, this shop also contains a wide variety of one of a kind antique home accessories and 19th century French oil paintings. CC: MC, V, AMEX.

Secondhand Rose

270 Lafayette Street (10012)
(212) 431-7673
Hours: Mon–Fri, 10–6;
Sat–Sun, 12–6

This shop displays 19th and 20th century decorative arts with an emphasis on one of a kind, exotic, and unusual pieces. The largest collection in the world of original wallpapers dating from the turn of the century is in stock. Prop rentals and movie services are available. PR: Middle-Expensive. CC: AMEX.

T & K French Antiques, Inc.

120 Wooster Street (10012)
(212) 219-2472
(212) 925-4876 fax
Hours: Tues–Fri, 11–6:30; Sat, 11–6;
Sun, 12–5

These dealers offer 18th and 19th century French furniture, unusual and decorative accessories, and the famous original French Rattan Café chairs by Drucker. PR: $$$$$. CC: MC, V, AMEX.

Twin Fires

110 Greene Street (10012)
(212) 343-2322
(212) 343-0990 fax
Hours: Tues–Sat, 11–6; Sun, 12–5

This business specializes in

Daniel Chester French, Spirit of Life, 1914. Bronze, dark brown patina, 49 1/4 inches high. *(Courtesy Hirschl & Adler Galleries, New York City)*

antique and reproduction pine furniture from England and Europe. Tables, armoires, dressers, hutches, cupboards, and settles are only some of the pieces that one will discover. Accessories and gifts are also stocked. Customizing and design services are available. PR: $$$. CC: MC, V.

280 Modern
280 Lafayette Street (10012)
(212) 941-5825
(212) 274-1612 fax
Hours: Mon–Sat, 11–7

The shop offers 20th century Decorative Arts, particularly lighting and furniture, and tribal arts. PR: $$$. CC: All major.

Urban Archaeology
285 Lafayette Street (10012)
(212) 431-6969
(212) 941-1918 fax
Hours: Mon–Fri, 8–6, Sat, 10–4 (closed Saturday during July and August)

Urban Archaeology is one of the country's leading architectural salvage and restoration companies. Their 54,000 square foot gallery houses an extensive collection of antiques and architectural elements from the turn of the century onward, including such things as interior and exterior lighting, bathroom fixtures and plumbing, display cases, hardware, interior and exterior doorways, mantels, garden furniture, and the like. Prop rentals and lamp repair and restoration services are available. PR: $$$$$. CC: MC, V, AMEX.

Wooster Gallery
86 Wooster Street (10012)
(212) 219-2190
(212) 941-6678 fax
Hours: Mon–Sat, 10:30–6:60;
Sun, 12–6

This gallery specializes in French Art Deco furniture, furnishings, lighting, and objects. CC: AMEX.

Greenwich Village/Chelsea

American Folk Art Gallery
274 Bleecker Street (10014)
(212) 366-6566
(607) 68702786 fax
Hours: Winter: Tues—Sat, 12-8; Sun, 11-?; Mon, usually Summer: Tues–Sat, 12-7; Sun, 11-5; Mon, usually

This dealer specializes in folk art, painted furniture, hooked rugs, quilts, architectural items, stoneware, wrought and cast iron, baskets, treeware, and country decorations, Prop rentals can be arranged. Consignments are accepted. Research, authentication, and a finders service are available. PR: $$. CC: MC, V, AMEX, DC.

Antiquarius Ltd.
41 Perry Street (10014)
(212) 647-0008
(212) 647-0333 fax
Hours: Daily 1–8

Located between 7th Avenue and West 4th Street, this shop contains 18th, 19th, and 20th century furniture, paintings, silver, porcelain, sculpture, and decorative arts. Although primarily dealing to the trade, the public is welcome. Consignments are accepted. Appraisals are given. CC: No.

Antique Buff, The
321 1/2 Bleecker Street (10014)
(212) 243-7144
Hours: Mon–Sat, 12–7

Established in 1977 and offering quality merchandise from Victorian times through the 1950s, this dealer emphasizes estate jewelry; cameo broches; a full array of rings, especially engagement and wedding bands; earrings; bracelets; and necklaces.

Artisan Antiques
81 University Place (10003)
(212) 751-5214
(212) 353-3970 fax
Hours: Mon–Fri, 10–6

This importer offers French Art Deco furniture and decorations with a focus on lighting including chandeliers, sconces, and lamps by Lalique, Muller, Salsino, and others. Period iron work and leather chairs are also stocked. CC: AMEX.

Barry of Chelsea Antiques
154 9th Avenue (10011)
(212) 242-2666
Hours: Tues–Fri, 12–7;
Sat–Sun, 12–6

This shop sells restored vintage desk, table, and floor lamps; chandeliers; sconces; globes; ceiling fixtures; and other lighting devices from the 1880s to the 1930s. If you are looking for an extensive and interesting selection of lighting fixtures and devices, this is the shop to visit. PR: $$. CC: MC, V, AMEX.

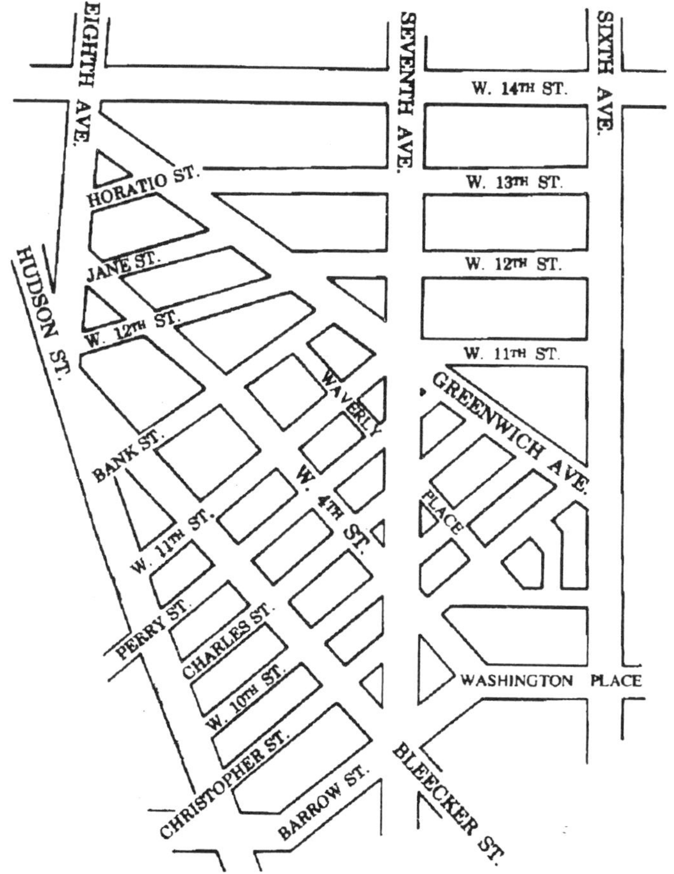

Greenwich Village

Den of Antiquity
108 MacDougal Street (10013)
(212) 475-6888
Hours: Tues–Sat, 4:30–10:30

This dealer specializes in antique jewelry and anything small and irresistible—masks, silver, Orientalia, and the like. PR: $$. CC: All.

Distinctive Furnishings
370 Bleecker Street (10014)
(212) 255-2476
Hours: Daily 12–7

This shop is filled with 19th and early 20th century American, English, and French antiques and accessories. Here one will discover furniture, lamps, statues, pictures, oil paintings, mirrors, candleabrum, silverplate, trunks, candle holders, and chandeliers. PR: $$. CC: MC, V, AMEX.

Dorothy's Closet
335 Bleecker Street (10014)
(212) 206-6414
Hours: Mon–Sat, 11–7; Sun, 11–6

This shop carries quality vintage

clothing and accessories ranging from the 1930s to the 1950s. In addition, there is a wide range of textiles, 1930s to 1940s drapes, and costume jewelry. PR: $. CC: MC, V, AMEX.

El Ombu
117 Perry Street (10014)
(212) 633-8663
(212) 633-8663 fax
Hours: Mon–Fri, 12–9; Sat & Sun 11–5

In addition to Argentine furniture, this shop contains a full range of silverware and decorative items from Argentine artisans to complement an Argentine country look. CC: No.

Fichera & Perkins Antiques
50 University Place (10003)
(212) 533-1430
Hours: Mon–Sat, 10:30–7

Since 1970, these dealers have been offering a large selection of gold and silver vintage jewelry in addition to Art Nouveau and Art Deco glass and lamps. CC: MC, V, AMEX.

Gallery II Collections
175 Bleecker Street (10012)
(212) 777-3350
Hours: Mon–Sat, 1–10; Sun, 1–9

Established in 1980, this gallery specializes in fine Victorian and Art Deco jewelry. A large selection of wedding bands from the 1800s through the 1950s and platinum Deco diamond engagement rings is stocked. Gallery II Collections is also located at 2244 Broadway. PR: $$. CC: MC, V, AMEX.

Hamilton-Hyre, Ltd.
413 Bleecker Street (10014)
(212) 989-4509
(212) 989-4509 fax
Hours: Mon–Fri, 12–7; Sat, 12–6

This popular source for decorators and dealers offers an eclectic collection of European and American antiques and decorations such as faux bamboo furniture, lighting, mirrors, and paintings.

Jane Werner-Aye Asian Fine Art & Appraisals
61 Grove Street (10014)
(212) 989-1829
Hours: By appointment

Specializing in Indian, Tibetan, and Southeast Asian antiques, art, and artifacts, this dealer offers an outstanding collection of bronzes, thankas, ritual objects, furniture, antique carpets, masks, paintings, and more. Appraisal and restoration services are available. PR: $$$$$. CC: No.

Kelter Malcé
74 Jane Street (10014)
(212) 675-7380
Hours: By appointment only

Displayed in room settings, these

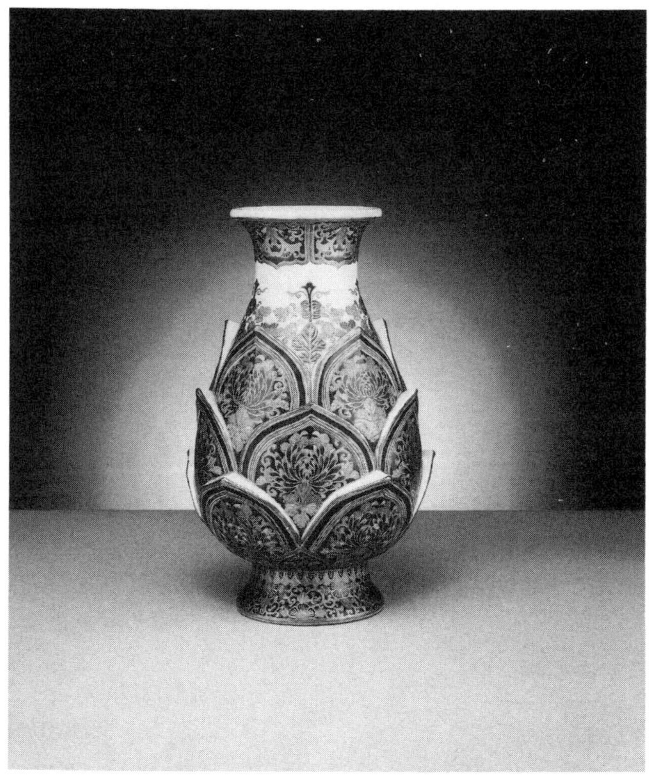

Satsuma lotus-form vase decorated in gosu blue and colored enamels. Signed "KEIDO" with Shimazu mon. Height 15'. EDO Period. *(Courtesy of Flying Cranes Ltd., New York City)*

dealers specialize in American furniture in original paint and condition, folk art, quilts, hooked rugs, sports memorabilia, and decorative smalls to furnish corporate environments and homes. CC: MC, V, AMEX.

Kimono House
120 Thompson Street (10012)
(212) 966-5936
Hours: Tues–Sun, 12–7

This shop contains old kimonos and rare Japanese textiles. PR: $. CC: MC, V, AMEX.

Lucy Anna Folk Art & Antique Quilts
502 Hudson Street (10014)
(212) 645-9463
Hours: Tues–Sat, 12–7; Sun, 12–6

Antique patchwork and applique quilts from the 1880s to the Depression era, stuffed barnyard animals, pillows, handmade dolls from around the country, and Teddy Bears and collectibles made from quilts, chenille, and vintage textiles fill this charming shop. PR: $. CC: MC, V, AMEX, O.

Niall Smith Antiques

344 Bleecker Street (10014)
(212) 255-0660
Hours: Mon–Sat, 11–6

In business for 21 years, this dealer offers English, Irish, and Continental furniture and objects in the Neoclassical taste. CC: No.

Old Japan Inc.

382 Bleecker Street (10014)
(212) 633-0922
Hours: Wed–Sun, 12–7; Mon–Tues by appointment

Established in 1990, this shop contains Japanese antiques, folk art, jewelry boxes, and dolls. PR: $50+. CC: MC, V, AMEX, D.

Palace Galleries

91 University Place (10003)
(212) 221-8800
(212) 228-0137 fax
Hours: Mon–Fri, 9:30–5

This business offers antiquities, bronzes, Continental furniture, and paintings. PR: $$$$$. CC: No.

Paper Moons

277 West 10th Street, PH-H (10014)
(212) 243-1007
(212) 243-0747 fax
Hours: By appointment only

These dealers specialize in tramp art and unusual folk art items from small and whimsical to large and formal. Whether you're interested in a tramp art frame or case piece, Paper Moons is worth a call. Decorating services are also available. CC: No.

Rene Kerne Antiques

322 Bleecker Street (10014)
(212) 727-3455
Hours: Fri & Sat, 2–9; Sun, Mon, & Thur, 2–7; Tues & Wed by chance or appointment

Art Deco, Retro, and items from the 1950s fill this shop. One will always find electric fans, glass (Czechoslovakian, Italian, and American), cuff links, costume jewelry, purses, vintage clothing, salt & pepper shakers, and collectibles. CC: MC, V, AMEX.

Second Childhood

283 Bleecker Street (10014)
(212) 989-6140
Hours: Mon–Sat, 11–6

Established in 1969, this shop specializes in antique and collectible toys—cast iron toys, tin wind-ups, banks, soldiers, comic character items, doll house furniture and miniatures, and movie posters. PR: $$. CC: MC, V, AMEX, D.

Star Struck, Ltd.

43 Greenwich Avenue (10014) and 270 Bleecker Street (10014)
(212) 691-5357, 366-9826 (Bleecker Street)
Hours: Mon–Sat, 11–8; Sun, 12–7

This shop has vintage clothing from the 1930s, 1940s, 1950s, and 1960s. Vintage jeans, jean jackets and vests, Tux wear, leather jackets, ladies' dresses, blouses, and jackets, and men's shirts, sweaters, and pants are always in stock. CC: MC, V, AMEX, D.

Susan Parrish

390 Bleecker Street (10014)
(212) 645-5020
Hours: Tues–Sat, 12–6 or by chance or appointment

This dealer is known for authentic, unadulterated antiques. Her shop is filled with antique quilts, folk art, Americana, textiles, vintage table cloths, antique Navaho weavings, 19th and early 20th century paintings, and painted furniture, mostly from the 19th century. CC: MC, V, AMEX, D.

Thomas

41 Perry Street (10014)
(212) 675-7296
Hours: Daily 1:30–8:30

This is not your usual antique shop. It is stocked with an eclectic mix of furniture, lighting fixtures, lamps, paintings, prints, decorative accessories from the 19th century to the 1970s. CC: No.

61st Street and Above, East Side

Ages Past Antiques
450A East 78th Street (10021)
(212) 628-0725
Hours: Mon–Sat, 11–5:30

Located in a 19th century wooden clapboard building, this charming shop offers a fine collection of 19th century English pottery—Staffordshire figures, blue and white transfer ware, and a good selection of pink, copper, and silver resist luster. One will also find an interesting variety of English Royal items.CC: AMEX.

Alan M. Goffman
264 East 78th Street (10021)
(212) 517-8192
Hours: Anytime by appointment

Doing business since 1974, this dealer specializes in paintings, watercolors, and drawings from the "Golden Age" of American Illustration, 1880-1940. Folk art and 19th century glass Hyacinth vases are also offered.

American Hurrah Antiques
766 Madison Avenue (10021)
(212) 535-1930
(212) 249-9718 fax
Hours: Tues–Sat, 11–6 but closed Saturday during June, July, and August

These dealers ofer the highest quality quilts, American Indian arts, country furniture, hooked rugs, weathervanes, folk paintings, and sculpture. CC: No.

American Illustrators Gallery
18 East 77th Street (10021)
(212) 744-5190
(212) 744-0128 fax
Hours: Tues–Fri, 12–5 and by appointment

This business features works by American illustrators of the "Golden Age": Norman Rockwell, Maxfield Parrish, Howard Pyle, N. C. Wyeth and the Brandywine School, H. C. Christy, C. D. Gibson, John Falter, and others. CC: No.

Antiquarium Fine Ancient Arts Gallery, Ltd.
948 Madison Avenue (10021)
(212) 734-9776
(212) 879-9362 fax
Hours: Tues–Fri, 10–5:30; Sat, 10–5 except closed Sat during August

Established in 1979, this business specializes in museum quality Classical, Egyptian, and Near Eastern antiquities, ancient glass, and ancient jewelry. Each piece is accompanied by a certificate of authenticity and documentation. PR: $$$$$. CC: MC, V, AMEX, DC.

Arlene Berman Fine Arts
12 East 86th Street (10028)
(212) 472-0115
Hours: By appointment

Specializing in paintings of the

Magnificent Hochat pastoral group known as Der Schlummer der Schaferin or The Sleeping Shepardess, modelled by Laurentius Russinger, iron red wheel mark, German, circa 1765. *(Courtesy of James M. Labaugh, White Plains)*

WPA Period as well as the 1930s-1940s, this dealer offers a fine selection that is affordable for the beginning collector. PR: $$$.

Art Asia, Inc.
1806 Madison Avenue (10028)
(212) 249-7250
(212) 249-7267 fax
Hours: Mon–Sat, 10:30–6:30; Sun, 12–6

This shop contains Oriental arts, a selection of Japanese woodblock prints, and Southeast and East Asian sculpture and ceramics. Designer costume jewelry and costume jewelry by local American designers are also carried. CC: MC, V, AMEX, D, DC.

Art of the Past
1242 Madison Avenue (10128)
(212) 860-7070
(212) 876-5373
Hours: Mon-Sat, 10–6

Representing more than 2,000 years of Asian culture, this business offers paintings, stone sculptures, bronzes, jewelry, and other works of art from India, Tibet, Nepal, and Southeast Asia. PR: $$$$$. CC: MC, V, AMEX, DC.

Art Trading (U.S.) Ltd.
305 East 61st Street (10021)
(212) 557-1038 fax
Hours: By appointment only and shows

This dealer offers a fine collection of English, European, and

Chinese pottery and porcelain of the 17th, 18th, and early 19th century with particular expertise in 18th century English pottery. PR: $200+. CC: No.

Bernard & S. Dean Levy, Inc.
24 East 84th Street (10028)
(212) 628-7088
(212) 628-7489 fax
Hours: Mon–Sat, 10–5:30

Fifteen galleries of American colonial and Federal furniture, paintings, silver, brassware, and ceramics from 1650 to 1830 are appropriately presented in a five-story townhouse, located one block from The Metropolitan Museum of Art. PR: $$$$$. CC: No.

Bizarre Bazaar Ltd.
130 1/4 East 65th Street (10021)
(212) 517-2100
(212) 517-2283 fax
Hours: Mon–Sat, 11–6 but call to confirm

Situated in a beautiful landmark building, this shop is filled to the brim with exquisite selections of early 20th century smalls, antique toys, and museum-quality models of aviation and automobilia. Also, one of the finest and largest selections of antique artists' mannequins is offered. A finder's service is available. PR: $$$$$. CC: MC, V, AMEX, D.

Burlington Antique Toys
1082 Madison Avenue (10028)
(212) 861-9708
(212) 249-3502 fax
Hours: Mon–Sat, 10–6

Considered to be one of the city's leading toy stores, this shop offers toy soldiers (both antique and current production), a wide selection of die cast cars, and tin toys. PR: $$. CC: MC, V, AMEX.

C.M. Leonard Antiques
1577 York Avenue (10028)
(212) 861-6821
Hours: Tues, Wed, & Thur, 11–5 and by appointment

French and English furniture from the 18th and 19th century, paintings, silver, porcelain, and decorative smalls are offered. PR: $$$. CC: MC, V, AMEX.

Charlotte F. Safir
1349 Lexington Avenue, 9–B (10128)
(212) 534-7933
Hours: None, mail order only

This mail order book search service deals in out of print and hard to find books. Although cookbooks and children's books are a specialty, and extensive network means that books in any category can be found. The search service is free and there are no obligations. Plus, prices are reasonable. CC: No.

Chinese Porcelain Company, The
822 Madison Avenue (10021)
(212) 628-4101
(212) 794-4896
Hours: Mon–Fri, 10–5:30; Sat, 11–4

In addition to Oriental ceramics and works of art, this business also offers Ancient southeast Asian and Indian sculpture. CC: AMEX.

Chrystian Aubusson Inc.
315 East 62nd Street (10021)
(212) 755-2432
Hours: 9:30–5

French furniture and antiques and French and English accessories fill this shop. A large collection of lamps—pottery, porcelain, glass, and metal—is featured. PR: $$$$$. CC: No.

Cora Ginsburg, Inc.
19 East 74th Street, 3rd floor (10021)
(212) 744-1352
(212) 879-1601 fax
Hours: Mon–Fri by appointment

This dealer specializes in antique textiles, needlework, decorations, costumes, and costume accessories. CC: AMEX.

D.T.L. Trading
1675 York Avenue (10128)
(212) 722-8400
(212) 534-1234 fax

This private dealer with a showroom offers one of the largest collections of Rene Laliquye Art Glass. PR: $500+. CC: No.

Darrow's Fun Antiques & Collectibles
1101 First Avenue (10021)
(212) 838-0730
(212) 838-3617 fax
Hours: Mon–Fri, 11:30–7;
Sat, 11:30–4; Sun by appointment

This unique establishment is dedicated strictly to antique toys and memorabilia: animation cels, tin wind-ups and battery toys, celluloid toys, cars and trucks, neon and sundry advertising signs, political buttons and memorabilia, coin ops, jukeboxes, toy soldiers, wood and plastic model kits, GI Joe, Barbie, Star Wars, and Trek toys, and much, much more. PR: $$$. CC: MC, V, AMEX, D.

David George Antiques
165 East 87th Street (10128)
(212) 860-3034
Hours: Mon–Sat, 10–6

This warm and cozy shop with a continental flavor contains English furniture, lamps, tables, textiles, prints, books, and Chinese and Japanese porcelains. The Basement Shop, an annex four doors down, contains an eclectic mix of furniture and accessories. CC: MC, V, AMEX.

David A. Schorsch, Inc.
30 East 76th Street,
Suite 11-A (10021)
(212) 439-6100
(212) 439-6170
Hours: Daily 11–6 and by appointment

This private gallery in the heart of Manhattan's Museum Mile, within walking distance of the Metropolitan and Whitney Museums, specializes in the highest quality folk art, Americana, and both Shaker and American furniture. Consignments are accepted. Appraisals and authentication services are available. PR: $$$$$. CC: No.

E & J Frankel, Ltd.
1040 Madison Avenue (10021)
(212) 879-5733
(212) 879-1998 fax
Hours: Mon–Sat, 10–5:30

Specializing in Chinese works of art from Neolithic through the 18th century, these dealers offer an extensive collection of ceramics, jade, paintings, sculpture, and decorative arts, as well as Japanese art. An appraisal service is available. PR: $$$$$. CC: MC, V, DC.

Edith Weber & Assoc., Inc.
994 Madison Avenue (10021-1834)
(212) 570-9668
(212) 570-9668 fax
Hours: Mon–Sat, 11–5:30; Sun & holidays closed

This shop offers an excellent selection of fine antique jewelry of the Georgian, Victorian, Art Nouveau, Edwardian, and Art Deco periods, and historical jewelry belonging to individuals such as Washington, Lafayette, Queen Victoria, and Napoleon. Collectible period jewelry by renowned jewelers such as Tiffany, Cartier, Lalique, Van Cleffs, and David Webb is also available. PR: $300+. CC: MC, V, AMEX.

Eli Wilner & Company
1525 York Avenue (10028)
(212) 744-6421
(212) 628-0264 fax
Hours: Mon–Fri, 9:30–5:30

In addition to offering the finest quality period frames and hand crafted replica frames, Eli Wilner & Company offers period frame restoration and picture hanging services. Lectures, publications, exhibitions, and research are also done. PR: $$$$$. CC: MC, V, AMEX.

Ellen Berenson Antiques
988 Lexington Avenue (10021)
(212) 288-5302
(212) 288-5302 fax
Hours: Mon–Fri, 10:30–6:30; Sat, 11–6

In addition to period furniture, painted furniture, and excellent 19th and early 20th century furniture in the style of 18th century French, Italian, Continental, and English furniture, paintings,

Gustav Stickley Settle, ca. 1912. *(Courtesy Peter-Roberts Antiques, New York City)*

chandeliers, lamps, and decorative arts—all very sophisticated and of excellent quality—fill this shop. PR: $$$$. CC: MC, V, AMEX.

Evergreen Antiques
1249 3rd Avenue (10021)
(212) 744-5664
(212) 744-5666 fax
Hours: Mon–Fri, 11–7; Sat, 11–6

This shop offers a fine selection of 19th century European furniture and accessories—Biedermeier, Neoclassical, and Scandinavian country. CC: MC, V, AMEX.

F.H. Coins & Collectibles, Ltd.
1187 Lexington Avenue (10028)
(212) 737-5256
Hours: Mon–Fri, 10:30–6; Sat, 12–5; Sun by appointment

Established inthe 1978, this shop specializes in English, German, and Eastern European porcelain; Bacarrat, Steuben, and Lalique crystal; sterling silver; and U.S. coins. Repair and restoration work for porcelain is available. Appraisals for coins and stamps is done. PR: $$$. CC: No.

Fanelli Antique Timepieces, Ltd.
1131 Madison Avenue (10028)
(212) 517-2300
Hours: Mon–Fri, 10–6; Sat 11–5

Fine antique timepieces, including a large selection of carriage clocks, skeleton clocks, and rare American tall case clocks, are offered. Vintage wristwatches, pocket watches, and estate and Russian jewelry are also available. Single items and entire estates are purchased; consignments are accepted. Clock repair and restoration services, as well as prop rentals, are offered.
PR: $300+. CC: MC, V, AMEX.

Florian Papp, Inc.
962 Madison Avenue (10021)
(212) 288-6770
(212) 517-6965 fax

Florian Papp specializes in very fine English and European furniture. They represent innovative designs which were recognized by contemporaries of the 18th and 19th centuries and have remained appealing to the 20th century eye. PR: $$$$$. CC: No.

Frank J. Miele Gallery
1262 Madison Avenue (10128)
(212) 876-5775
Hours: Tues–Fri, 11–6; Sat, 10–5

This gallery features a fine selection of works which includes paintings, sculpture, pottery, and furniture by self-taught American artists of the 19th and 20th century. PR: $$$. CC: MC, V, AMEX.

Frog Alley Antiques
265 East 78th Street (10021)
(212) 734-7388
Hours: Tues–Wed, 12–7:30; Thur–Sat, 12–5

This shop contains a funky and eclectic collection of furniture from the 1920s on, costume jewelry, collectibles, and glassware, especially from the Depression era. PR: Moderate. CC: All.

Gem Antiques
1088 Madison Avenue (10028)
(212) 535-7399
(212) 249-7267 fax
Hours: Mon–Sat, 10:30–5:30

This small, friendly shop caters to both beginning and advanced collectors by offering an in-depth selection of both American and European Art Pottery, paperweights, porcelain, and pottery. PR: $$$$. CC: MC, V, AMEX, DC.

Gemini Antiques Ltd.
927 Madison Avenue (10021)
(212) 734-3261
Hours: Mon–Fri, 11–5

Located on the second floor, this gallery specializes in mechanical banks, toys, folk art, and Americana. PR: $$$$$. CC: No.

Georgian Manor Antiques, Inc.
305 East 61st Street (10021)
(212) 593-2520
Hours: Mon–Fri, 10–4:30

This dealer offers the finest quality antique English and Continental furniture, paintings, porcelain, and glass. PR: $$$$$. CC: No.

Godel & Co. Fine Art
969 Madison Avenue (10021)
(212) 288-7272
(212) 288-0304 fax
Hours: Mon–Sat, 10–6

This fine art gallery deals in American works of art from the

19th and 20th century. An in-house framing service specializes in period and reproduction frames. PR: $$$$$. CC: No.

Guild Antiques II

1089 & 1095 Madison Avenue (10028)
(212) 472-0830, 717-1810
Hours: Mon–Sat, 10–5

In two large stores, one will find an excellent selection of 18th and 19th century English furniture, Chinese Export Porcelain, and related accessories. CC: MC, V.

Hirschl & Adler Galleries, Inc.

21 East 70th Street (10021)
(212) 535-8810
(212) 772-7237 fax
Hours: Labor Day to Memorial Day: Tues–Fri, 9:30–5:15; Sat, 9:30–4:45. Memorial Day to Labor Day: Mon–Fri, 9:30–4:45

Featuring American decorative arts from the Neoclassical through the Arts and Crafts Period, this shop contains the highest quality 18th, 19th, and 20th century American and European paintings, drawings, and sculpture in addition to 18th, 19th, and 20th century American prints. PR: $$$$$. CC: No.

Hubert des Forges, Inc.

1193 Lexington Avenue (10028)
(212) 744-1857
Hours: Mon–Thur, 10–6; Fri, 10–5; closed Sat & Sun

This shop offers a fine selection of 19th and 20th century decorative accessories, both quirky and eclectic. Crystal, tole, porcelain, brass, wood, floral, figural and architectural style lamps, paisley throws, majolica, and door stops are always on display. In addition, an extensive collection of Italian (circa 1930-1940) gilded metal rope and tassel motif tables, chairs, planters, etagères, and sconces are available—plus, Black Forest Teddy Bears. CC: MC, V, AMEX, D.

Imperial Fine Books, Inc.

790 Madison Avenue, Suite 200 (10021)
(212) 861-6620
(212) 249-0333 fax
Hours: Mon–Fri, 10–5:30; Sat, 10–5

Imperial Fine Books offers a magnificent selection of fine leather bindings, beautiful sets, vintage children's books, fore-edge paintings, first editions, and unique single volumes—many with highly decorated and gold tooled bindings. Appraisals, a book search service, and a complete restoration service are available. PR: $50+. CC: MC, V.

J. Dixon Prentice, Antiques

1036 Lexington Avenue (10021)
(212) 249-0458
Hours: Mon–Fri, 11–5; Sat, 11–2

This dealer specializes in chandeliers, sconces, mirrors, lamps, and picture frames—mostly 19th century decorative. CC: AMEX.

Jules Cheret: Palais de Glace, 1896. *(Courtesy of La Belle Epoque Vintage Posters, Inc.,New York City)*

Japan Gallery
1210 Lexington Avenue (10028)
(212) 288-2241
(212) 794-9497 fax
Hours: Tues–Sat, 11–6

This dealer specializes in Japanese woodblock prints of the 18th, 19th, and 20th century. PR: $$$$$. CC: MC, V, AMEX.

Jean Hoffman & Jana Starr Antiques
236 East 80th Street (10021)
(212) 535-6930, 861-8256
Hours: Daily 12–6 or by appointment

In addition to an extensive collection of vintage clothing for weddings, evening wear, and display, these dealers also offer antique textiles, lace, linens for the bed and table, jewelry, accessories, and silver. CC: MC, V, AMEX.

Jeffrey Myers. Ltd.
12 East 86th Street, Suite 239 (10028)
(212) 472-0115
(212) 650-0118 fax
Hours: 10–7, by appointment only

With an emphasis on figural objects and items of museum quality, this dealer carries an inventory of antique Eskimo art from 250 B.C. through the 19th century and art of the Northwest Coast Indians. PR: $$$$$. CC: No.

John Rosselli Ltd.
255 East 72nd Street (10021)
(212) 737-2252
(212) 737-9919 fax
Hours: Mon–Fri, 9–6

This dealer offers lighting, furniture, decorations, and various other antiques. CC: No.

Joseph G. Gerena Fine Art
12 East 86th Street, #1409 (10028)
(212) 650-0117
(212) 650-0118 fax
Hours: By appointment only

This private gallery offers Oriental and Tribal art and antiquities. PR: $500+.

Judith and James Milne, Inc.—American Country Antiques
506 East 74th Street (10021)
(212) 472-0107
Hours: Mon–Fri, 9:30–5:30 and by appointment

This shop contains the highest quality American country furniture, paintings, and folk art as well as garden furniture, architecturals, and accessories. More than 300 antique quilts, pieced and appliqued, are carried. Appraisals, prop rentals, research, and quilt repair and restoration are available. CC: MC, V.

Karen Warshaw Ltd.
167 East 74th Street (10021)
(212) 439-7870
(212) 439-7871 fax
Hours: Mon–Fri, 11–5

A 19th century townhouse is the setting for English and French decorative antiques: furniture, paintings, accessories, mirrors, lamps, porcelain, and sconces. An antique locating service is offered. PR: $$$. CC: AMEX.

Kenneth W. Rendell Gallery, Inc.
989 Madison Avenue (10021)
(212) 717-1776
(212) 717-1492 fax
Hours: Mon–Sat, 10–6

This dealer offers historical letters and documents of human endeavor—military, political, science, the arts, music, literature, and the like from Renaissance times to the present, and all Western languages. CC: MC, V, AMEX.

Lands Beyond, The
1218 Lexington Avenue (10028)
(212) 249-6275
Hours: Tues–Sat, 11:30–6

In the same location for twenty-six years, these dealers are specialists in Pre-Columbian art. One will find all cultures and price ranges represented. Each item is guaranteed authentic. PR: $$$$$. CC: No.

L'Art de Vivre
978 Lexington Avenue (10021)
(212) 734-3510
Hours: Variable, but usually 11–6; call for summer hours

This shop contains French Art

Deco and French furniture, lighting, and decorative arts from the 1920s, 1930s and 1940s.

Leigh Keno American Antiques
19 East 74th Street (10021)
(212) 734-2381
(212) 879-1601 fax
Hours: Mon–Sat, 9:30–5:30

Specializing in 18th and early 19th century American furniture, this dealer offers formal and rural furniture in the William and Mary, Queen Anne, Chippendale, and Federal styles.

Lenox Court Antiques
980 Lexington Avenue (10021)
(212) 772-2460
(212) 861-6273 fax
Hours: Mon–Fri, 11–6; Sat, call for hours; summer, Mon–Thur, 11–6

Early through mid 19th century English, Continental, and French furniture in a variety of woods as well as painted surfaces are offered. While mirrors and both floral and architectural engravings enhance the furniture, lighting fixtures, porcelain, ceramics, majolica, and glass also complement the store's appeal. CC: All.

Leo Kaplan Ltd.
967 Madison Avenue (10021)
(212) 249-6766
(212) 861-2674 fax
Hours: Mon–Sat, 10–5:30 (Mon–Fri during June, July, & August

Leo Kaplan Ltd. specializes in antique and contemporary French and American paperweights, 18th century English pottery and porcelain, English and French cameo glass, and Russian enamel and porcelain. PR: $$$$$. CC: MC, V, AMEX.

Leo Kaplan Modern
965A Madison Avenue (10021)
(212) 535-2407
(212) 535-2495 fax
Hours: Mon–Sat, 10–6 (Mon–Fri during June, July, & August)

This business offers contemporary studio furniture and contemporary glass. PR: $$$$$. CC: MC, V, AMEX.

Linda Horn Antiques
1015 Madison Avenue (10021)
(212) 772-1122
(212) 288-0449 fax
Hours: Mon–Sat, 10–6

A vast array of unusual, whimsical, and out of the ordinary English and Continental antiques, collectibles, and objects d'art fill this shop. CC: MC, V, AMEX.

Linda Morgan Antiques
152 East 70th Street (10021)
(212) 628-4330
Hours: Tues–Fri, 10:30–6; Sat 11–5

Estate jewelry, Art Nouveau, decorative smalls, and English furniture will be found in this shop. PR: $$$. CC: MC, V, AMEX.

Macklowe Gallery

667 Madison Avenue (10021)
(212) 644-6400
(212) 755-6143 fax
Hours: Mon–Fri, 10:30–6; Sat, 10:30–5 except closed Sat during the summer

On two floors occupying 6,000 square feet, one will discover an elegant display of the finest European and American objets d'art and furniture from 1890 to 1935 including a superb collection of jewelry, ancient to the 1960s. Repair, restoration, and appraisals are done on pieces purchased at the gallery. PR: $$$$$. CC: MC, V, AMEX, DC.

Madison Avenue Antique Center (MD)

760 Madison Avenue (10021)
(212) 717-6500
(212) 717-1486 fax
Hours: Mon–Sat, 10–6

Located between 65th and 66th Street, this antique center contains seventeen independently owned galleries featuring everything from antique clothing, furniture, lighting, and paintings to toys and folk art. CC: MC, V, AMEX.

Malcolm Franklin, Inc.

762 Madison Avenue, 2nd floor (10021)
(212) 288-9054
(212) 288-0560 fax
Hours: Mon–Fri, 10–5; Sat 10–4 except closed on Sat from Memorial Day to Labor Day

Specializing in fine English furniture and accessories, mostly from the 17th through early 19th century with a particular emphasis on Queen Anne and other early walnut pieces, this business, established in 1947, also offers brass, ceramics, and related decorations plus English genre, marine, and landscape paintings of the same periods. An appraisal service is available. Malcolm Franklin, Inc. is also located at 56 East Walton Street, Chicago, IL 60611. PR: $$$$$. CC: No.

Malvina Solomon, Inc.

1122 Madison Avenue (10028)
(212) 535-5200
Hours: Mon–Fri, 11–5:30; Sat, 11–5

American and European Art Pottery from 1900 through 1950 including large collections of Roseville, Fulper, Weller, and Rookwood plus sterling silver and costume jewelry from the same period are offered by this dealer. PR: $$. CC: V, AMEX, DC.

Margot Johnson, Inc.

18 East 68th Street, Apt. 1A (10021)
(212) 794-2225
Hours: By appointment

This dealer offers top quality American Victorian furniture, Aesthetic, Renaissance Revival, Egyptian Revival, Art Nouveau, and similar styles with an emphasis on furniture by Tiffany, Horner, Pottier & Stgmus, Henter Brothers, etc. PR: $$$$$. CC: No.

A small Ohio poplar stepback cupboard in original condition including red paint and glass, ca. 1840. *(Courtesy of Webb and Brennan, Pittsford)*

Marie E. Betteley
1131 Madison Avenue (10028)
(212) 517-2300, 684-3608
Hours: Mon–Fri, 10–6; Sat, 11–5

Marie E. Betteley offers an excellent collection of Russian prerevolutionary works of art including Fabergé, objects vertu, and Imperial porcelain. In addition to antique and estate jewelry from Europe and America, a line of unique Fabergé inspired contemporary jewelry including cuff links and miniature egg pendants is offered. PR: $$$$$. CC: MC, V, AMEX.

Marvin Alexander, Inc.
315 East 62nd Street (10021)
(212) 838-2320
(212) 754-0173 fax
Hours: Mon–Fri, 9–5 (Trade shop through decorators and architects)

In addition to an extensive collection of antique chandeliers and lighting from the 18th century through Art Deco period, there is an impressive offering of antique decorative accessories—candlesticks, lamp material, and mirrors. There is a separate showroom for fine reproduction sconces and flush mounted fixtures. This business was established in 1954. PR: Expensive. CC: No.

Newman's Collectibles
242 East 71st Street (10021)
(212) 717-5910
Hours: Mon–Sat, 11–6:30

In this interesting men's toy store, you will find all kinds of vintage militaria, political items, antique toys, comics, prints, and sports memorabilia. PR: $. CC: MC, V.

North Star Galleries
1120 Lexington Avenue (10021)
(212) 794-4277
(212) 794-5264 fax
Hours: Mon–Sat, 10–6

In addition to museum quality ship models and collectible trains, airplanes, and other means of transportation, rare photographs as well as prints of historic ships and ocean liners are offered by this dealer. PR:$$$$$. CC: MC, V, AMEX, D.

Oak Smith & Jones
1321 Second Avenue (10021)
(212) 535-1451
(212) 535-1451 fax
Hours: Daily 10–8

This antique and collectibles home furnishings specialty store is noted for its international selection of one of a kind antiques and reproductions. An eclectic resource, it is a favorite of designers for conversation pieces and finishing touches in a wide range of styles and wood finishes. PR: $$$. CC: MC, V, AMEX.

Objets Plus Inc.
315 East 62nd Street (10021)
(212) 832-3386
Hours: Mon–Fri, 10–5

Fine antique French, Continental, and English furniture, paintings, and decorative accessories are carried. CC: No.

Old Versailles, Inc.
315 East 62nd Street, 3rd floor (10021)
(212) 421-3663
Hours: Mon–Fri, 12–5

In addition to French and Continental furniture carved in solid woods and lacquered or painted, Old Versailles offers faience, porcelain, old master paintings, and decorations—all from the 17th to 19th century. PR: Medium—High. CC: No.

Oldies, Goldies, & Moldies
1609 2nd Avenue (10028)
(212) 737-3935
Hours: Tues–Fri, 12–7; Sat, 11–6; Sun, 11–5

Located in a town house with multilevel showrooms and workshops, one will find Art Deco and Moderne, and 1940s through 1960s furnishings, lighting, neon clocks, radios, Bakelite, chrome, jewelry, vintage clothing for women, and much more. Furniture, metal, clock, and lighting repair and restoration, caning, home restoration, jewelry repair, plating, a silver matching service, and prop rentals are offered. Custom made furniture is also available. PR: $$$$. CC: No.

Paul Steinhacker—Primitive & Asiatic Art

151 East 71st Street (10021)
(212) 879-1245
Hours: Tues–Sat, 12–6 or by appointment

This dealer specializes in antique Eskimo and American Indian art, early African and Oceanic art, and antique Tibetan arts. The gallery is on the second floor of a townhouse. No appointment is needed but a call is suggested. Appraisal and consulting services are available. CC: No.

Pimlico Way/Amdier Antiques

1028 Lexington Avenue (10021)
(212) 439-7855
Hours: Mon–Sat, 10:30–5:30

This shop is filled with antique furniture, decorations, lamps, sconces, and fireplace accessories such as andirons, tool sets, and screens. Ironstone, porcelain, and collectibles are also stocked.

Renate Halpern Galleries, Inc.

325 East 79th Street (10021)
(212) 988-9316
(212) 985-2954 fax

Hours: By appointment only

Established in 1970, this private gallery specializes in the purchase, sale, and appraisal of antique textiles, tapestries, weavings, embroideries, Oriental and European carpets, American Indian and hooked rugs, paisley and kashmir shawls, and needlework from the Coptic and pre-Columbian Period to Art Deco. CC: No.

Rita Ford Music Boxes Inc.

19 East 65th Street (10021)
(212) 535-6717
Hours: Mon–Sat, 9–5

This dealer offers both antique and contemporary music boxes of all types. Music collectibles, jewel boxes, and hand crafted artist pieces are also available. A complete, on premises repair and restoration service is offered. PR: $$$. CC: MC, V.

Robert Altman

1148 Second Avenue (10021)
(212) 832-3490
Hours: Mon–Fri, 11–5

This shop which sells to the trade contains French and American antiques and decorations with a special emphasis on lamps, mirrors, elegant rustica, and early industrial. PR: $$$$$. CC: No.

Robert M. Peters/Arctic Fine Arts

12 East 86th Street, Suite 639 (10028)
(212) 628-3174
(212) 535-9269 fax
Hours: By appointment

This dealer offers a quality selection of American Indian, Eskimo, and Pre-Columbian art, antiquities, and Latin American religious paintings. PR: $$$$$. CC: No.

S. Wyler Inc.

941 Lexington Avenue (10021)
(212) 879-9848
(212) 472-8018 fax
Hours: Mon–Sat, 9:30–5:45; Summer Hours: Mon–Fri, 9:30–5

Established in 1890, this is the oldest store of its kind in continued existence. In addition to offering 18th and 19th century English and Chinese porcelain, this business specializes in antique English silver, antique Sheffield plate, and antique Victorian English plate. The late Seymour B. Wyler wrote the authoritative book on English Silver entitled **The Book of Old Silver**. CC: AMEX.

Shepard Gallery

21 East 84th Street (10028)
(212) 861-4050
(212) 772-1314 fax
Hours: Tues–Sat, 10–6

This gallery specializes in 19th and early 20th century paintings, drawings, and sculpture. PR: $$$$$. CC: No.

Smith Gallery

1045 Madison Avenue (10021)
(212) 744-6171
Hours: Mon–Sat, 11–5

In addition to specializing in 19th century American marine paintings by artists such as Buttersworth, Bard, Jacobsen, and Salmon, this gallery represents the contemporary work of Frank Wagner, Keith Miller, Scott Cameron, and Mark Whitcombe. American bronzes of Harry Jackson and Gerson Frank, western paintings, salt glazed pottery of Eileen Murphy, and some fine folk art and furniture are also offered. PR: $$$$$. CC: No.

Stair & Company, Inc.

942 Madison Avenue (10021)
(212) 517-4400
(212) 737-4751 fax
Hours: Mon–Fri, 9:30–5:30; Sat 11–5; During the summer, Mon–Fri, 9:30–5

Considered to be one of the finest English antique galleries in America, this shop is designed to simulate period rooms where 18th and 19th century furniture, English sporting paintings, and porcelain are displayed in appropriate settings. CC: No.

Sylvia Pines-Uniques

1102 Lexington Avenue (10021)
(212) 744-5141
Hours: Daily 10–5

In addition to presenting the largest collection of spectacular purses in the States which includes beaded, jeweled, and tapestry of the Victorian, Edwardian, Art Deco, and Art Nouveau eras, this dealer also carries estate jewelry of the same periods and signed costume jewelry. Bag repairs can be done. PR: $$. CC: MC, V, AMEX.

Thos. K. Woodard American Antiques & Quilts
799 Madison Avenue (10021)
(212) 988-2906
(212) 734-9665 fax
Hours: Mon–Sat, 11–6 except closed Sat in July & August

Antique quilts, painted country furniture, garden embellishments, accessories, hooked and woven rugs, folk art, and Americana—all of the finest quality—are offered. This is also the home of Woodard Weave classical American woven rugs. PR: Quilts, $750+.

Throckmorton Fine Art, Inc.
153 East 61st Street (10021)
(212) 223-1059
(212) 223-1937 fax
Hours: By Appointment Only

Throckmorton Fine Art not only specializes in Pre-Columbian art and jewelry but also focuses on Modern and Contemporary art, works on paper, and photography from Latin America.

Treillage, Ltd.
418 East 75th Street (10021)
(212) 535-2288
(212) 517-6589 fax
Hours: Mon–Fri, 10–6; Sat 11–5 except during the summer

This unique garden specialty shop, owned by Bunny Williams and John Rosselli, offers a hybrid array of antiques, garden furniture, ornaments, and special accessories—many are one of a kind pieces. Exclusive reproductions are also stocked. PR: $$$$. CC: All major ones.

20th Century Antiques Ltd.
878 Madison Avenue (10021)
(212) 988-5181
(212) 861-8119 fax
Hours: Mon–Sat, 11–5:30

Specializing in Art Nouveau and Art Deco, this shop not only contains a fine selection of lamps and glass by Tiffany, Galle, and Daum but also etchings by Icart and posters by Mucha, Lautrec, Cassandre, Colin, and others. CC: AMEX.

Yale R. Burge Antiques, Inc.
305 East 63rd Street (10021)
(212) 838-4005
(212) 838-4390 fax
Hours: Mon–Fri, 9–5 *Open to the trade*

A wide selection of 18th and 19th century English and French antiques and accessories will be found in this shop. The inventory combines a variety of classic and unusual furniture that is decorative and affordable. PR: $$$$$. CC: AMEX.

Yew Tree House Antiques
450B East 78th Street (10021)
(212) 249-6612
Hours: Mon–Fri, 11–5:30; Sat and other times by appointment

Specializing in period mirrors, leather upholstered furniture, ele-

Exceptional pair of Continental carved wood, painted, and parcel-gilt torcheres in the Neo-Classical Manner, ca. 1790.
(Courtesy of Georgian Manor Antiques, Inc., New York City)

gant pairs of lamps, as well as whimsical one-of-a-kind decorative objects, these dealers offer country and formal furniture form England and the Continent plus American and European garden antiques. A finders service is available. PR: $$$. CC: No.

Zane Moss Antiques
10 East End Avenue (10021)
(212) 628-7130
Hours: By appointment only

This dealer stocks formal American and English furniture, porcelain, paintings, and appropriate accessories. CC: No.

60th Street to 42nd Street, East Side

A La Vieille Russie, Inc.
781 Madison Avenue (10022)
(212) 752-1727
Hours: Mon–Fri, 10–5; Sat, 10:30–4; closed Saturday during the summer

This shop specializes in Russian Imperial treasures, most notably works of art by Carl Fabergé, silver, enamels, jewelry, porcelains, icons, paintings, furniture, and lacquer. Also offered are gold snuffboxes, antique jewelry, fine furniture, decoration, and European porcelains from various countries, in addition to Russia. PR: $$$$$. CC: MC, V, AMEX.

A. Smith Antiques, Ltd.
235 East 60th Street (10022)
(212) 888-6337
(212) 754-5674 fax
Hours: Mon–Fri, 10–5

Established in 1988, this dealer specializes in 18th and 19th century English, Continental, and Oriental furniture, art, and decoration. PR: $$$$$. CC: No.

Aaron's Antiques
576 Fifth Avenue (10036)
(212) 447-5868
(212) 764-7931 fax
Hours: Mon–Fri, 11–6

This shop is widely known for its ability to provide sterling flatware replacements. A large inventory of active, obsolete, and inactive patterns guarantees that individual pieces, sets, and many serving pieces are always on hand. All pieces are at discount prices. A sterling flatware matching service is available. CC: MC, V.

Charles P. Rogers Brass & Iron Bed Co.
899 First Avenue (10022)
(212) 935-6900
(212) 935-4214 fax
Hours: Mon–Fri, 10–7; Sat, 10–6; Sun, 12–5

Founded in 1855, this is America's oldest manufacturer of iron and brass beds. The factory showroom, which is open to the public, contains a tremendous selection of original and restored beds. PR: $$. CC: MC, V, AMEX, D.

Dalva Brothers, Inc.
44 East 57th Street (10022)
(212) 758-2297
(212) 758-2607 fax
Hours: Mon–Sat, 9–5:30 (closed Sat during the summer)

On five floors, one will find the highest quality French 18th century decorative arts and sculpture, furniture by the great ebenistes and menuisiers, and fine Italian 18th century furniture and decorations. CC: No.

Earle D. Vandekar of Knightsbridge, Inc.
209 East 60th Street (10022)
(212) 308-2022
(212) 308-2105 fax
Hours: Mon–Fri, 10–5:30; Sat, 10–4:30

Established in 1916, this business specializes in English and Continental ceramics and Chinese Export porcelain. In addition to English and Continental furniture, the largest collection of portrait miniatures in America can be found in this shop. PR: $$$$$. CC: AMEX.

Federico Carrera
238 East 60th Street, 2nd floor (10022)
(212) 750-2870
Hours: Mon–Sat, 10:30–5:30

This dealer specializes in European and American Decorative Arts, silver, porcelain, and objets de vertu of the 18th and 19th century. A fine selection of French First Empire and Charles X bronze doré is also offered. PR: $$$$$. CC: MC, V.

Flying Cranes Antiques Ltd.
1050 Second Avenue (10022)
(212) 223-4600
(212) 223-4601 fax
Hours: Mon–Sat, 10:30–6

Flying Cranes Antiques Ltd specializes in Japanese and Chinese antiques of the 18th and 19th century. Extensive collections of Imari and Chinese porcelains, Satsuma, Japanese cloisonné, bronzes, silver, Oriental furniture, and Samuri weaponry and armor are offered. CC: All major ones.

Fossner Timepieces, Inc.
1057 Second Avenue (10022)
(212) 980-1099
(212) 935-0339 fax
Hours: Mon–Fri, 10–6; Sat, 11–5

This shop offers fine modern, vintage, and antique pocketwatches, wristwatches, and clocks. These fourth-generation, European-trained watchmakers offer a full repair and restoration service for watches and clocks. PR: $$$$$. CC: AMEX.

Garden Antiquary, The
724 Fifth Avenue (10019)
(212) 757-3008
(212) 757-3904 fax
Hours: By appointment

Antique garden ornaments from Europe, America, and Asia made in the 17th, 18th, and 19th centuries are stocked. CC: No.

Gardner & Barr, Inc.
213 East 60th Street (10022)
(212) 752-0555
(212) 355-6031 fax
Hours: Mon–Sat, 10:30–6:30

This shop contains America's largest collection of vintage Venetian glass. Venetian goblets given in pairs are the ideal wedding or anniversary gift. PR: $$$$. CC: MC, V, AMEX.

I. Freeman & Son, Inc.
60 East 56th Street (10022)
(212) 759-6900
(212) 759-6905 fax

Established in London in 1900 and the United States in 1929, I. Freeman & Son, Inc. specializes in a wide variety of antique and modern English, American, and Continental silver and old Sheffield and Victorian plate. Reproduction silver and silver-plated gift items are available in all price ranges. CC: MC, V.

J. J. Lally & Co.
41 East 57th Street (10022)
(212) 371-3380
Hours: Mon–Fri, 9–5; Sat, 10–4

Archaic Chinese bronzes, sculpture, and jade plus early ceramics, porcelains, and works of art from China, Korea, and Japan are carried by this business CC: No.

J & P Timepieces, Inc.
1057 Second Avenue (10022)
(212) 980-1099
(212) 935-0339 fax
Hours: Mon–Fri, 10–6; Sat, 11–5

With an emphasis of the very expensive and rare, this business buys, sells, and repairs vintage and modern wristwatches, pocketwatches, and clocks.
CC: AMEX.

James Robinson Inc.
480 Park Avenue (10022)
(212) 752-6166
Hours: 10–5

Exceptional antique jewelry, silver of outstanding quality, and antique porcelain are offered by this business. Handmade sterling silver reproductions are also available. PR: $$$$$. CC: MC, V, AMEX.

James II Galleries, Ltd.
11 East 57th Street, 4th Floor (10022)
(212) 355-7040
(212) 593-0341 fax
Hours: Mon–Fri, 10–5:30; Sat, 10:30–5 (closed Sat in the summer)

Established in 1966, this gallery specializes in the finest quality 19th century English furniture, decorative arts, and jewelry. CC: MC, V, AMEX.

Jean Karajian Gallery
250 East 60th Street (10022)
(212) 751-6728
(212) 751-4707 fax
Hours: Mon–Fri, 10–5

This gallery offers French Art Deco furniture, lighting by Lalique and Daum, and accessories. CC: No.

Laura Fischer/Antique Quilts & Americana
1050 Second Avenue, Gallery 84 (10022)
(212) 838-2596
(212) 355-4403 fax
Hours: Mon–Sat, 10–6 and by appointment

This gallery contains New York City's largest, most in-depth selection of quilts, hooked rugs, paisley shawls, woven coverlets, Southwest blankets, antique home furnishings, accessories, and American folk art. Pieces are available for the collector, corporation, or simply the lover of Americana. Appraisals are done. A restoration and cleaning service for quilts and hooked rugs is available. PR: $$$$$. CC: AMEX.

Manhattan Art & Antiques Center (MD)
1050 Second Avenue (10022)
(212) 355-4400
(212) 355-4404 fax
Hours: Mon–Sat, 10:30–6; Sun 12–6

Established in 1974, this multi-dealer complex is considered one of the largest and finest in the United States. One hundred and four shops and galleries offer period furniture, Japanese art, jewelry, quilts, Chinese art, silver, porcelain, china, bronzes, tapestries, clocks, Americana, and African art from every time period. There is something for everyone at this complex. PR: $$$$$. CC: Most dealers accept credit cards.

Newel Art Galleries, Inc.
425 East 53rd Street (10022)
(212) 758-1970
(212) 371-0166 fax
Hours: Mon–Fri, 9–5

This gallery is comprised of six floors of antiques and decorations ranging from Renaissance to Art Deco. Individual floors exhibit English and French, 20th century, and country furniture. PR: $$$$$. CC: No.

Nicholas Antiques
979 Third Avenue (10022)
(212) 688-3312
(212) 688-3802 fax
Hours: Mon–Fri, 9–5

Selling to the trade, decorators, and architects only, this shop contains antique and reproduction lighting (chandeliers, sconces, and lamps). Paintings, mirrors, furniture, and accessories are also available. CC: No.

Norman Crider Antiques
725 Fifth Avenue (10022)
(212) 832-6958
Hours: Mon–Sat, 10–6

Located in Trump Tower, this shop contains costume jewelry from the 1940s and 1950s, Russian art (nesting dolls and lacquered boxes), and Russian porcelain. CC: MC, V, AMEX, D.

Casting of a 59 1/2 inch diameter skeletonized dial from an English tower clock, circa 1890. *(Courtesy of Fanelli Antique Timepieces, Ltd., New York City)*

Paris to Province
210 East 60th Street (10022)
(212) 750-0037
Hours: Mon–Fri, 10–6; Sat, 11–5; Sun, 1–5

Since 1980, this shop has been noted for its distinguished collection of 18th and 19th century European furniture, accessories, and fine art.

Proctor Galleries
247 East 60th Street (10022)
(212) 421-7310
(212) 421-4609 fax
Hours: Mon–Fri, 10–6; Sat, 11–5

This gallery features Continental and Oriental objects of art, fine European and American paintings and sculptures, and a choice selection of interesting period furniture, rugs, and tapestries. PR: $$$$$. CC: MC, V, AMEX.

Ralph M. Chait Galleries, Inc.
12 East 56th Street (10022)
(212) 758-0937
(212) 319-0471 fax
Hours: Mon–Sat, 10–5:30, closed Saturday during June, July, and August

This business deals in fine works of Chinese art dating from the Neolithic Period through the 18th century—porcelain, pottery, bronzes, hardstones, and sculpture. Chinese Export silver of the 18th and 19th century is also available. PR: $$$$$. CC: MC, V, AMEX.

Robert Altman
See listing under "61ST AND ABOVE"

Roger Gross Ltd.
225 East 57th Street (10022)
(212) 759-2892
(212) 838-5425 fax
Hours: By appointment

This dealer specializes in autographs, antiquarian books, ephemera, and manuscripts related to opera and classical music. Signed photos; musical quotes; autographs; letters of conductors, composers, instrumentalists, and singers; and manuscripts are only some of the items that are available for purchase. Want lists are welcomed. A catalog will be sent upon request. This dealer is also available for international auction representation. CC: No.

S.J. Shrubsole, Corp.
104 East 57th Street (10022)
(212) 753-8920
(212) 754-5192 fax
Hours: Winter: Mon–Fri, 10–5:30; Sat, 10–5; Summer: Mon–Fri, 10–5

Established in London in 1910 and in the United States in 1936, this gallery offers fine authentic English and American silver from the 16th through 19th century, antique jewelry, antique gold and silver boxes, and antique glass. CC: MC, V, AMEX.

Schmul Meier, Inc.
328 East 59th Street (10022)
(212) 644-8590
Hours: Tues–Fri, 11–5

This dealer offers antique textiles and fabrics from the entire world, 17th to the mid-20th century. PR: $$$$$. CC: All major cards.

Suchow & Siegel Antiques
207 East 60th Street (10022)
(212) 888-3489
(212) 355-6031 fax
Hours: Mon–Sat, 10:30–6:30

Established in 1968, this business offers 18th and early 19th century English and Chinese Export porcelain, pottery, glass, and objects of Vertu. PR: $$. CC: MC, V, AMEX.

Suttonbridge
328 East 59th Street (10022)
(212) 355-3584
Hours: Mon–Fri, 11–6

Suttonbridge is a showroom specializing in the decorative arts. Exceptional and unusual furniture, lighting, and decorations are available for the well-appointed home. CC: No.

Vernay & Jussel
625 Madison Avenue, 2nd floor (10022)
(212) 308-1906
(212) 308-1944 fax
Hours: Mon–Fri, 9:30–5:30; Saturday by appointment

In addition to a fine selection of 17th, 18th, and 19th century English furniture and related works of art, this business also offers a large selection of decorative items, especially with animal motifs.

Zeron Ayvazian Inc.

1137 2nd Avenue (10022)
(212) 319-6252
(212) 980-7563 fax
Hours: Mon–Fri, 9:30–6; Sat, 11–5

This dealer specializes in antique tapestries from the 16th to the 19th century and antique kilims. Tapestry and rug conservation, repair, and cleaning services are offered. CC: AMEX.

41st Street to Houston, East Side

Abe's Antiques
815 Broadway (10003)
(212) 260-6424
(212) 529-9085 fax
Hours: Mon–Fri, 9:30–5:30

Nineteenth century antiques and accessories that include mirrors, fireplaces, chandeliers, statuary, bronzes, lighting, pottery and porcelain plus a smattering of Art Deco fill this shop. PR: $$$$$. CC: No.

Agostino Antiques, Ltd.
808 Broadway (10003)
(212) 533-3355
(212) 477-4128 fax
Hours: Mon–Fri, 9–5

One will find excellent examples of fine 18th and 19th century English, French, and Continental furniture in this shop. PR: $$$$$. CC: No.

Antiques by Patrick
64 East 13th Street (10003)
(212) 254-8336
Hours: Mon–Fri, 10–6; Sat, 12–5

This old fashioned, general antique store is filled with medium price items and the hidden bargain. American, European, and Asian furniture; paintings; porcelain; pottery; bronzes; and antiquities can be found. Most of the items are from the 18th, 19th, and 20th century but there are some ancient pieces. Retail, decorators, and dealers are welcome. CC: No.

Bruce Gimelson
305 East 24th Street (10010)
(212) 889-4273
(212) 683-8305 fax
Hours: Private

Bruce Gimelson is a private dealer and consultant for autographs, ephemera, manuscripts, and oil paintings.

City East Antiques Center (MD)
201 East 31st Street (10016)
(212) 779-0979
Hours: Daily 12–6

A multi-dealer shop where the unusual is commonplace. Thirteen dealers feature decorative items, porcelain, glass, furniture, toys, collectibles, and paintings. PR: $$$. CC: MC, V.

David Seidenberg Inc.
836 Broadway (10003)
(212) 260-2810
Hours: Mon–Sat, 10–5

This shop carries works of art and sculpture, decorative accessories, silver, and both European and Oriental porcelain. CC: No.

Dullsville, Inc.
143 East 13th Street (10003)
(212) 505-2505
Hours: Mon–Sat, 11:30–7

Established in 1988, this shop contains a funky, eclectic mix of Bakelite jewelry, folk art, lodge items, and cowboy kitch. Furniture and unusual smalls from the 1900s to the 1960s, rustic furniture and smalls, and lamps and paintings in exquisitely bad taste fill the shop. PR: $$. CC: MC, V, AMEX.

Eastside Antiques
55 East 11th Street (10003)
(212) 677-8820
Hours: Mon–Fri, 9–4:30

This shop carries a wide variety of English, Continental, and Oriental Furniture and accessories. CC: No.

Far Eastern Antiques & Art, Inc.
799 Broadway (10003)
(212) 460-5030
Hours: Mon–Fri, 10–5:30; Sat,11–6

Occupying 5,000 square feet, this trade showroom is filled with directly imported Oriental and European colonial furniture and decorative accessories—sculpture, screens, porcelain, architectural carvings, lacquer, bronzes, early Chinese ceramics, all from 2000 B.C. to the 20th century. PR: $$$. CC: AMEX.

Florence Sack Ltd.
813 Broadway (10003)
(212) 777-2967
Hours: Mon–Fri, 10–5

Conducting business since 1978, this shop is known for having 17th through early 20th century American, English, French, Italian, and Continental furniture, mirrors, lamps, and decorative accessories in both bronze and wood. PR: $$$$$. CC: No.

Flores & Iva Antiques
799 Broadway (10003)
(212) 673-1866
(212) 673-1866 fax
Hours: Mon–Sat, 10–5:30

Operating three stores in the same area, this business carries ancient ceramics and Russian arts and antiques which are offered to the trade and to the public. CC: No.

H. M. Luther
61 East 11th Street (10003)
(212) 505-1485
(212) 505-0401 fax
Hours: Mon–Sat, 9–5

Russian, English, Italian, French, and Scandinavian furniture from the 18th and 19th century fill this shop. CC: No.

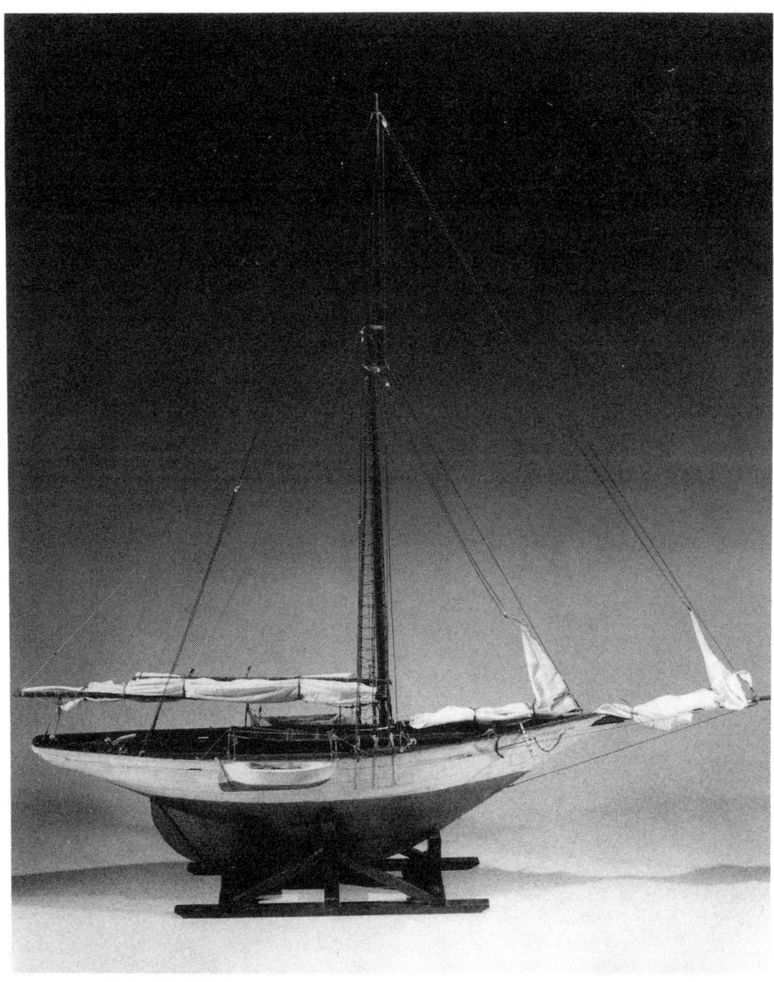

A model of the gaff rigged cutter, "Ruth E. McMahon," built in the United States in 1870. This model was probably built in the 1880s by one of her crew. *(Courtesy North Star Galleries, New York City)*

Howard Kaplan Antiques
827-831 Broadway (10003)
(212) 674-1000
(212) 228-7204 fax
Hours: Mon–Fri, 9–5

This shop contains rare and unusual antique furniture for daily use. Many feel it is the largest source of large dining tables, queen size beds, billiard chandeliers, bistro/bar furniture, iron and polished steel tables, brass and wood floor lamps, 19th century French paintings, and leather upholstery. Custom iron furniture, lampshades, and leather upholstery are available. PR: Expensive. CC: MC, V, AMEX.

Howard Kaplan Bath Shop

47 East 12th Street (10003)
(212) 674-1000
(212) 228-7204 fax
Hours: Mon–Fri, 10–5

In addition to offering fantastic and unique bath fixtures from England and France such as copper tubs, showers, brass mirrors, standing towel racks, floral sinks, cabinet and pedestal sinks, bidets, and toilets, the highest quality reproductions are offered. Custom brass castings, faux finishes, and marble tops for vanities are available. CC: MC, V, AMEX.

Hyde Park Antiques

836 Broadway (10003)
(212) 477-0033
(212) 477-1781 fax
Hours: Mon–Fri, 9–5:30; please call for Saturday hours

In addition to an exception collection of 17th, 18th, and early 19th century English furniture (William & Mary through Regency) which includes lacquered and painted pieces, one will find accessories such as Chinese Export porcelain; mirrors; ceramics; English porcelains; and 18th and 19th century seascapes, portraits, landscapes, and sporting art. CC: No.

Irreplaceable Artifacts N.A.

14 2nd Avenue (10003)
(212) 780-9700, 777-2900
(212) 780-0642 fax
Hours: Mon–Fri, 10–6;
Sat–Sun, 11–5

Irreplaceable Artifacts is dedicated to saving any and all architectural ornamentation and art work from buildings. A large stock of fireplaces, interior and exterior doors, bath fixtures, paneled rooms, lighting fixtures, exterior stone and terra cotta architectural facade work, and stained glass from single pieces to entire churches and synagogues is available. The dismantling and reassembling of entire facades or buildings and other related interior services are available. PR: $$$$$. CC: MC, V.

J. Garvin Mecking, Inc.

72 East 11th Street (10003)
(212) 677-4316
Hours: Mon–Fri, 10–5, To The Trade Only

This business is known for an eclectic collection of English Regency, Victorian furniture, and decorative accessories. PR: $300+. CC: No.

Karl Kemp and Assoc. Ltd. Antiques

29 East 10th Street (10003)
(212) 254-1877
(212) 228-1236 fax
Hours: Mon–Fri, 10–5:30; Sat, 12–5

In addition to fine French Art Deco, this dealer specializes in German and Austrian Biedermeier furniture with selected pieces of French Empire and Neo-Classical antiques. PR: $1,500+. CC: No.

Kensington Place Antiques
80 East 11th Street (10003)
(212) 533-6378
Hours: Mon–Sat. 9:30–5

Established in 1984, this shop contains 18th and 19th century English, French, and Continental antique and decorative furniture as well as original prints. CC: No.

Kentshire Galleries, Ltd.
37 East 12th Street (10003)
(212) 673-6644
(212) 979-0923 fax
Hours: Mon–Fri, 9–5; Sat, 10–3 during the winter

English 18th and 19th century furniture and accessories and jewelry are shown in period room settings. CC: V, AMEX.

L'Epoque Antiques
30 East 10th Street (10003)
(212) 353-0973
(212) 353-0957 fax
Hours: Mon–Fri, 10–5; Sat, 11–4

This shop specializes in fine quality provincial and elegant French furniture of the 18th and 19th century. PR: $$$$$. CC: No.

Maison Gerard
36 East 10th Street (10003)
(212) 674-7611
(212) 475-6314 fax
Hours: Mon–Fri, 11–6 or by appointment

Maison Gerard has specialized in fine Art Deco, furniture, carpets, lighting, and objects d' art since 1974. In addition to being a wholesale and retail business, rentals are also available. PR: $100+. CC: AMEX.

Martell Antiques
53 East 10th Street (10003)
(212) 777-4360
Hours: Mon–Fri, 10–5:30; Sat, 11–5

Martell Antiques offers a varied selection of French provincial antiques of the 18th and 19th century. The inventory includes armoires, buffets, tables, chairs, and chandeliers. PR: $$$$. CC: No.

Midtown Antiques, Inc.
814 Broadway (10003)
(212) 529-1880, 529-1881; 1-800-626-7726 out of town
Hours: Mon–Fri, 12–6 or by appointment

This family business, established in 1940, specializes in quality 17th through 19th century English and Continental furniture and objects of art at affordable prices. PR: $$$$$. CC: AMEX.

Old Print Shop, Inc., The
150 Lexington Avenue (10016)
(212) 683-3950
(212) 779-8040 fax
Hours: Tues–Sat, 9–5; Memorial Day to Labor Day, M–F, 9–5

Established in 1898 and in its present location since 1927, this

Tramp Art miniature dresser, 36" h x 24" w x 12' d, from the late 19th century incorporating period ceramic tile in its construction. *(Courtesy Paper Moons, New York City)*

shop encourages customers to browse through its stock of 18th, 19th, and early 20th century fine prints. Whether one is searching for quality prints, early maps, or custom framing, this shop is definitely worth a visit. PR: $50+. CC: MC, V.

Pantry & Hearth

121 East 35th Street (10016)
(212) 532-0535, 889-0026
Hours: Daily by appointment or chance

In an 1856 townhouse, three floors are filled with quality 18th and 19th century American painted country and high country furniture, early lighting, wrought iron, folk art, treen, and other rare and decorative domestic objects for hearth and home. Consignments are accepted. A finders service and prop rentals are available. PR: $$$$$. CC: No.

Paramount Antiques

58 East 11th Street (10003)
(212) 777-9131
(212) 777-9414 fax
Hours: Mon–Fri, 9–6

One will find English and French furniture, bronzes, and antique reproductions such as chandeliers in this shop. PR: $$. CC: MC, V, AMEX.

Phillip Colleck

830 Broadway (10003)
(212) 505-2500
(212) 529-1836 fax
Hours: Mon–Fri, 10–5:30

This shop offers a fine selection of English furniture made from 1690 to 1830 (William & Mary, Queen Anne, and Chippendale) plus appropriate accessories such as mirrors, chandeliers, lamps, candelabra, porcelain, screens, and paintings. CC: No.

Renee Antiques Inc.

8 East 12th Street (10003)
(212) 929-6870
Hours: Mon–Fri, 9–6; Sat, 9–3

This shop specializes in 1850 to 1960 accessories, lighting, and furniture. Art Glass; porcelain; bronzes; paintings; posters; and

American, Austrian, and German pottery are always available. Art Deco and Art Nouveau pieces by Lalique, Tiffany, Galle, and Daum are also offered.

Repeat Performance, A

156 1st Avenue (10009)
(212) 529-0832
Hours: Mon–Sat, 12–7; Sun, 2–7 (open later during the summer)

One will find a little bit of everything in this shop—1920s to 1960s telephones, furniture, lamps, hundreds of unusual shades, instruments, English accessories, vintage fabric, old photos, jewelry, and pottery. PR: $. CC: MC, V, AMEX.

Reymer-Jourdan Antiques

43 East 10th Street (10003)
(212) 674-4470
(212) 228-9471 fax
Hours: Mon–Fri, 10–4:30; Sat, 12–5

Known as one of New York's first specialists in Neoclassical furniture—a tradition that still continues—this business also offers a large selection of furniture, lighting, and objects from the 1920s, 1930s, and 1940s which complements the very pure and sober classical pieces. PR: $$$$$. CC: No.

Roger Appleyard, Ltd.

67 East 11th Street (10003)
(212) 529-9505
(212) 260-2778 fax
Hours: Mon–Fri, 9:30–5:30 (often earlier and later, but call)

Although specializing in raw (unfinished) mahogany reproduction pieces, this shop carries a wide variety of English and Continental reproductions, both furniture and accessories, which are available to both the trade and the collector. Refinishing and gilding services are available at cost. PR: $$$. CC: No.

Roland's Antiques

67 East 11th Street (10008)
(212) 260-2000
(212) 260-2007 fax
Hours: Mon–Fri, 9–5:30

In addition to architectural and musical items, one will find 18th, 19th, and 20th century furniture, paintings, Oriental rugs, and bric-a-brac in this shop. PR: $$$. CC: No.

Treasures from the Past

201 East 37th Street, Suite 14H (10016)
(212) 243-0522
(212) 243-0061 fax
Hours: By Appointment only

In addition to specializing in perfume bottles, this business offers vintage jewelry and table top items for dressers and desks wholesale to fine stores and by appointment to the general public. PR: $. CC: V.

Tudor Rose Antiques

28 East 10th Street (10003)
(212) 677-5239
(212) 677-5239 fax
Hours: Mon–Sat, 10:30–6

This shop is filled with sterling

silver candlesticks, sterling and crystal vanity items, unique sterling frames, plus holloware and decorative silver items. CC: MC, V, AMEX, DC.

Turbulence
812 Broadway (10003)
(212) 598-9030
(212) 260-2301 fax
Hours: Mon–Fri, 10–6 and evenings by appointment

Occupying more than 10,000 square feet, Turbulence which specializes in Continental antique furniture and decorations from the 17th to early 20th century also features an eclectic mixture juxtaposing rare and unusual antiques with contemporary paintings, photographs, and artist designed furniture. PR: $$$$$.

Universe Antiques
833 Broadway (10003)
(212) 260-9292
(212) 533-0114 fax
Hours: Mon–Fri, 10–4; To The Trade Only

This shop contains reproduction Tiffany lamps, cameo glass, and bronze and marble statuary. CC: No.

Victor Carl Antiques
55 East 13th Street (10003)
(212) 673-8740
(212) 673-8741 fax
Hours: Mon–Fri, 9–5; Sat, 12–4

This dealer specializes in antique lighting and accessories such as chandeliers, wall sconces, and lamps. PR: $$$$$. CC: No.

Waves
32 East 13th Street (10003)
(212) 989-9284
(201) 461-7121 fax
Hours: Tues–Fri, 12–6; Sat, 12–5

Established in 1976, Waves is known for having the largest and best selection of vintage radios, phonographs, televisions, telephones, and related material in New York City. A radio and phonograph repair service is available. CC: MC, V, AMEX.

61st Street and Above, West Side

Alice Underground
380 Columbus Avenue (10024)
(212) 724-6682
Hours: Sun–Fri, 11–7; Sat, 11–8

This large vintage clothing shop stocks a wide variety of men's and women's styles from the 1920s to the present. Lace, linen, fabrics, and draperies are specialty areas. Glassware and pottery from the 1930s to 1950s is also for sale. PR: $. CC: MC, V, AMEX.

Alice's Antiques
505 Columbus Avenue (10024)
(212) 874-3400
(212) 874-3421 fax
Hours: Tues–Sat, 12–8; Sun, 12–5

In addition to a collection of antique furnishings, collectors and decorators will find an extremely large selection of French, English, and American antique beds including iron, iron and brass, and wood in all sizes. CC: MC, V, AMEX.

Allan Daniel
230 Central Park West at 83rd Street (10024)
(212) 799-0825
Hours: By advance appointment

American folk art including weathervanes, primitive paintings, carvings, and cast iron is offered. Appraisals are available.

Better Times Antiques, Inc.
500 Amsterdam Avenue (10024)
(212) 496-9001
Hours: Thurs–Tues, 12–6:30

Two floors occupying more that 2,900 square feet are stocked with English and American furniture from the 19th century. PR: $$$$$. CC: MC, V.

Diane Gerardi's Vintage Jewelry
565 West End Avenue (10024)
(212) 580-9187
Hours: Mon–Sat, 9–7

This showroom is filled with vintage costume jewelry from the 1820s through the 1960s. Many pieces are by designers such as Chanel, Schiaperelli and Haskell. Special requests are taken for estate jewelry. A costume jewelry repair service is available. PR: $. CC: No.

Emporium, Ltd., The
20 West 64th Street (10023)
(212) 724-9521
Hours: Daily 1–7

A hidden source for designers and collectors, The Emporium, Ltd. carries porcelains, antique jewelry, collectibles, and decorative items from antiquity to the present. It is located one block east of Lincoln Center. PR: $$$. CC: MC, V, AMEX, D, DC.

A selection of fine English silver and brass from the first half of the 18th century. *(Courtesy of Mark & Marjorie Allen, Putman Valley)*

Gallery II Collections
2244 Broadway (10024)
(212) 877-9780
Hours: Mon–Sat, 11–7:30; Sun, 12–5

Gallery II Collections offers a selection of fine jewelry with an emphasis on Victorian and Art Deco. There is a wide selection of wedding bands from the 1800s to the 1950s and platinum Deco diamond engagement rings. This business which was established in 1980 has another shop at 175 Bleecker Street. PR: $$. CC: MC, V, AMEX.

Golden Treasury, The
550 Columbus Avenue (10024)
(212) 787-1411
Hours: Mon–Fri, 12:30–6:30; Sat–Sun, 1:30–6:30

Known for offering the unique and unusual, this shop is filled with Art Deco and Nouveau items. Estate jewelry, vintage watches, clocks, silver, Black Americana, decorative smalls, artwork, cookie jars, dolls, and lighting devices and fixtures are only some of the items that one will uncover. PR: $$. CC: MC, V, AMEX, D.

Kendra Krienke
230 Central Park West at 83rd Street (10024)
(212) 580-6516
Hours: By advance appointment

This dealer specializes in original watercolors, drawings, and oils created for children and fantasy primarily between 1880 and 1950. The works of many prominent artists including Arthur

Rackham and Jessie Willcox Smith are available. A catalog at the cost of $7.00 is available. PR: $$$$$. CC: No.

La Belle Epoque Vintage Posters Inc.

282 Columbus Avenue (10023)
(212) 362-1770
(212) 362-1843 fax
Hours: Mon–Sat, 12–8; Sun, 12–6

La Belle Epoque carries one of the largest collections of Art Nouveau and Art Deco original lithographic advertising posters covering many subjects (bicycles, travel, theater, sports products, wine & spirits, etc.) by leading artists of the period including Cheret, Mucha, Lautrec, Cappiello, Cassandre, and many others. Consultations to build private and corporate collections as well as design services to create decorative environments for commercial and residential spaces can be arranged. Creative custom conservation framing can be done. PR: $$$$$. CC: MC, V, AMEX.

Welcome Home Antiques

556 Columbus Avenue (10024)
(212) 362-4293
Hours: Mon–Fri, 12–8; Sat–Sun, 12–6

This shop carries 19th and 20th century furniture, lamps, and accessories. Rentals can be arranged. Consignments are accepted. Furniture repair and restoration services are available. CC: MC, V, AMEX, D.

60th Street to 42nd Street, West Side

Sacks Fine Art Inc.
50 West 57th Street (10019)
(212) 333-7755
(212) 541-6065 fax
Hours: Tues–Sat, 12–5 or by appointment

This gallery specializes in American paintings from the first half of the 20th century: African-American, women, regionalists, nonobjective, surrealist, social realism, magic realism, impressionist, and in discovering works of forgotten masters of American art. CC: AMEX.

Tic-Toc Clock Shop, Inc.
763 Ninth Avenue (10019)
(212) 247-1470
Hours: Tues–Fri, 10–5:30; Sat, 12–4

Since 1970, this business has specialized in antique clocks and watches. A restoration service for the five boroughs including service calls only for grandmother and grandfather clocks is offered. PR:$$$$$. CC: MC, V, AMEX.

41st Street to Houston, West Side

A. Goldstein for Wrought in America, Inc.
111 West 24th Street, 2nd floor (10011)
(212) 229-0991
(212) 229-0991 fax
Hours: By appointment only

In the private studio/showroom of this award winning artist, one will find not only custom accessories and hardware in silver, bronze, and pewter but also an antique tool and artifact display. Custom wall designs composed of authentic hand forged tools and artifacts can be commissioned. PR: $25+. CC: No.

Acanthus Books
54 West 21st Street, Room 908 (10010)
(212) 463-0750
(212) 463-0752 fax
Hours: By appointment

Acanthus Books specializes in rare and out of print reference books

Gustav Stickley drop-arm spindle Morris chair, Gustav Stickley lamp table, and Dirk Van Erp lamp. *(Courtesy of Peter-Roberts Antiques, New York City)*

on antiques, the decorative arts, and architecture. New imported titles on the decorative arts and decorative prints are also available. Catalogs are issued. Appraisals can be arranged.CC: MC, V.

Chelsea Antiques Building
110 West 25th Street (10001)
(212) 929-0929
(212) 924-8535 fax
Hours: Daily 10–6, open later in the summer

This twelve story building houses 75 dealers who offer a wide variety of antiques and collectibles suitable for all types of decor. Oriental art, 20th century toys, Art Deco furniture, Retro furnishings, vintage clothing, Venetian glass, jewelry, Art Pottery, advertising, bronzes, and decorative accessories are only some of the items that collectors, decorators, and dealers will encounter. For example, Lubin Galleries occupies the 10th floor, the Chris Ellis Collection is found on the 12th floor, the Bohemian Bookworm and the Antiquarian Book Arcade occupy the ninth floor. And, in addition to antiques and collectibles, Café Mozart Express occupies the 11th floor. PR: $$$$$. CC: MC, V.

Constantine Kollitus
440 West 34th Street (10001)
(212) 736-0947
Mail order only

This dealer specializes in 18th,

19th, and 20th century American silver. Some English and Continental silver is also stocked. Consignments are accepted. A finders service and a silver matching service are offered. PR: $$$$$. CC: No.

John Charles & Co.

344 West 15th Street (10011)
(212) 255-9174
Hours: Tues–Sat, 1–5

In a charming and appropriate setting, one will find a varied selection of fine period furniture, paintings, and rare accessories with an emphasis on the 17th through 19th century. A collection of copper, brass, and iron antiquities is also offered. CC: No.

John Koch Antiques

514 West 24th Street (10011)
(212) 243-8625
Hours: Sat–Sun, 11–6; Mon–Fri by appointment

This 4,000 square foot warehouse is filled with vintage and antique furniture from area estates. CC: MC, V, AMEX.

Metropolis Collection

7 West 18th Street (10011)
(212) 627-9691
(212) 627-5947 fax
Hours: Daily 10–6

This shop deals in vintage comic books, movie posters, and baseball memorabilia. A mail order service is available. Authentication and appraisals are done. CC: Yes.

Vintage Restoration

41 Union Square West, Studio 325 (10003)
(212) 645-8344
Hours: Mon–Fri, 9–5

These restorers of antique and fine furniture use old-world craftsmanship and methods including hand French polishing, water gilding, marquetry, and carving. They believe the care and maintenance of fine furniture is essential to its beauty and value. CC: No.

Wendover's Ltd of England

6 West 20th Street (10011)
(212) 924-6066
(212) 463-7092 fax
Hours: Mon–Fri, 9–6; Sat, 10–6; Sun, 11–6

Displaying more than 500 pieces, Wendover's carries one of the largest selections of authentic antique English pine furniture in the United States. Customizing and restoration to customers' specifications can be done. CC: MC, V, AMEX.

BROOKLYN

ANTIQUE STREET GUIDE

Atlantic Avenue

352	Town & Country Antiques
357	In Days of Old, Ltd.
362	City Barn Antiques
368	Time Trader
377A	Repeat Performances Antiques
377	Circa Antiques Ltd.
378-300	Silhouette Antiques/Mahogany Classics

Coney Island Avenue

593	Kramer's Antiques
624	Scotties Gallery
785-787	Times & Again Inc.
822	Sciarrino Antiques
1054	Roy Electric Co. Inc.
1061	Abbey Galleries
1131	Charlotte's Antiques

Court Street

213	A Matter of Time

Fifth Avenue

6742	Jukebox Classics & Vintage Slot Machines, Inc.

Fulton Street

753	South Portland Antiques

Greene Avenue

15	From The Past, Ltd.

Montgomery Place

24	Robin A. Stafford

President Street

823	Gaslight Time

Smith Street

99	Mel's Antiques

Third Avenue

8407	Discoveries

Warren Street

247	Frank Galdi Antiques

BROOKLYN

Abby Galleries
1061 Coney Island Avenue (11230)
(718) 377-1171
Hours: Mon–Sat, 11–5

This shop carries antique paintings, mahogany furniture, French inlaid furniture, fine porcelain pieces, silver, rugs, and chandeliers. Appraisals and free estimates are given. PR: $$$$$. CC: No.

Antiques and Decorations
4319 Fourteenth Avenue (11229)
(718) 633-6393
Hours: Sun–Fri, 12–6

Featuring 20th century decorative arts, especially French and English, this shop also offers furniture, porcelain, silver, chandeliers, paintings, curio cabinets, lamps, mirrors, and all types of collectibles. CC: No.

Charlotte's Antiques
1131 Coney Island Avenue (11230)
(718) 252-0088
Hours: Mon–Sat, 11–5

Among this shop's decorative items and collectibles, one will find watches, fountain pens, rugs, costume jewelry, and the like. PR: $$. CC: No.

Circa Antiques
377 Atlantic Avenue (11217)
(718) 596-1866
Hours: Tues–Fri, 11:30–5:30; Sat, 11–6; Sun 12–6

This shop offers quality 19th century furniture in walnut, mahogany, cherry, and rosewood from period American Empire through late Victorian. Paintings, lighting, and accessories from the same period are also available. Continental furniture and paintings from the 19th century are also offered. PR: $$$. CC: AMEX.

City Barn Antiques
362 Atlantic Avenue (11217)
(718) 855-8566
Hours: Tues–Fri, 1–6; Sat, 11–6; Sun, 12–6

This shop specializes in 20th century American modern design—Fifties, Moderne, Art Deco, and Arts & Crafts. Furniture, lighting, and accessories such as bedroom, dining room. and living room sets by Heywood Wakefield, Conant Ball, Herman Miller, and other makers are featured. CC: No.

Discoveries
8407 Third Avenue (11209)
(718) 836-0583
Hours: Tues–Sat, 11:30–5

Emphasizing furniture, this shop offers home furnishings and accessories from the Victorian era through the Art Deco period. In addition to furniture, one will find lamps, mirrors, silver, porcelain, and ceramics. PR: $$. CC: D.

Frank Galdi Antiques

247 Warren Street (11201)
(718) 875-9293
Hours: Tues–Fri, 2–7; Sat, 10–6; Sun, 12–6; Mon closed

Established in 1982 and located in historic Cobble Hill, this dealer specializes in 19th and 20th century decorative arts. The shop is filled with Mission oak, Arts & Crafts furniture, and English and American Arts & Crafts decorative smalls and Art pottery. CC: No.

From the Past, Ltd.

15 Greene Avenue (11217)
(718) 852-8065
Hours: Wed–Sat, 12–6:30; Sun, 12–4:30

Antique furniture and quality collectibles such as crystal, china, silver, and jewelry are in this shop. PR: $$. CC: No.

Gaslight Time

823 President Street (11215)
(718) 789-7185
(718) 768-2501 fax
Hours: Saturday

Victorian and period lighting from the 1850s to the 1930s such as chandeliers, wall sconces, table and floor lamps, and some original gas burning fixtures will be found in this shop. In addition, there is a wide selection of antique clocks and vintage fountain pens. Original gas and electric shades are available as is a complete wiring and restoration service for all types of lighting. PR: $$$$$. CC: No.

In Days of Old, Ltd.

357 Atlantic Avenue (11217)
(718) 858-4233
Hours: Wed–Sat, 11–5; Sun, 1–5

Quality furniture with an emphasis on oak, walnut, and mahogany and architectural details from the 1860s to the 1920s are the specialty areas of this dealer. All items are in either fine original condition or professionally restored. CC: MC, V, AMEX.

Jukebox Classics & Vintage Slot Machines, Inc.

6742 Fifth Avenue (11220)
(718) 833-8455
(718) 833-0560 fax
Hours: Sat, 11–5 (call before coming) and by appointment

A very large selection of jukeboxes, slot machines, neons, nickelodeons, telephones, old arcade machines, barber shop items, pinball machines, Coca Cola memorabilia and machines and mutoscopes can be found in this shop. In addition to gumball and nut machines, trade stimulators, and panchinko games, there are hundreds of cookie jars and salt & pepper shakers. A repair service for jukeboxes and slot machines is available. PR: $$$$$. CC: MC, V, AMEX.

Kramer's Antiques

593 Coney Island Avenue (11218)
(718) 284-7218
Hours: Mon–Fri, 11–4:30

This general line shop emphasizes 19th and early 20th century paintings, bronzes, and furniture from private homes. No collectibles are offered. And, most of the transactions are with the trade. PR: $$. CC: No.

Matter of Time, A

213 Court Street (11201)
(718) 624-7867
Hours: Wed–Sat, 11–6; Sun, 1–6

Established in 1977, this shop carries a general line of antiques with an emphasis on lighting, Art Pottery, Oriental rugs, furniture, and prints—a good source for both dealers and collectors. PR: $$. CC: MC, V, AMEX.

Mel's Antiques

99 Smith Street (11226)
(718) 834-8700
Hours: Mon–Sat, 9–7; Sun, 12–5

Furniture including Art Deco and English and American oak, pine, and mahogany and accessories such as fireplace equipment, brass chandeliers, and mirrors are offered. A furniture repair, refinishing, and restoration service is available. CC: No.

Repeat Performance Antiques

377A Atlantic Avenue (11217)
(718) 875-9555
Hours: Sat–Sun, 1–5; Mon, closed; Tues–Fri, by chance or appointment

Established in 1979, this business specializes in high quality and unusual Victorian and turn of the century furnishings and accessories in excellent original condition or painstakingly and properly restored. There is always a selection of hard to find, interesting pieces as well as the most sought after living, dining, and bedroom pieces. In addition to furnishing several brownstones, this business has provided furnishings for several Broadway shows and Hollywood movies. All pieces are guaranteed authentic and original. PR: $$$$$. CC: No.

Robin A. Stafford

24 Montgomery Street (11215)
(718) 399-0294
Hours: By appointment only

This private dealer offers furniture and pottery with an emphasis on Mission, Deco, Modern, and Fifties furniture; Art Pottery from Rookwood to McCoy; and 20th century accessories. PR: $$. CC: No.

Roy Electric Co., Inc.

1054 Coney Island Avenue (11230)
(718) 434-7002
(718) 421-4678 fax
Hours: Mon–Sat, 10–5

In addition to manufacturing brass lighting fixtures—Victorian, turn of the century, Art Deco, and Mission—since 1969, this business carries a large selection of reproduction and antique lighting and glass shades. Both a custom design service and a complete restoration and repair service are available. CC: MC, V, AMEX.

Sciarrino Antiques
822 Coney Island Avenue (11218)
(718) 462-8134
Hours: Mon–Sat, 10–6

Although specializing in 19th and 20th century art from still lifes to landscapes, this shop also carries fine furniture. A restoration service for both paintings and furniture is available.
PR: $$$. CC: No.

Scotties Gallery
623 Coney Island Avenue (11218)
(718) 851-8325
1217)
(718) 522-3114
(718) 965-3815 fax
Hours: Tues–Fri, 12–5; Sat, 11–6; Sun, 1–5

Specializing in furniture from 1800 to 1930, this shop features dining room and bedroom furniture, especially turn of the century mahogany. PR: $$$. CC: No.

Silhouette Antiques/ Mahogany Classics
378-380 Atlantic Avenue (11217)
(718) 522-3114
(718)965-3815 fax
Hours: Tues-Fri, 12-5,; Sat, 11-6; Sun, 1-5

Offering a large sele tion of turn of the century mahogany and furniture from 1800 to 1930, this shop offers a fine selection of pieces for dining rooms and bedrooms. PR:$$$. CC: No.

South Portland Antiques
753 Fulton Street (11217)
(718) 596-1156
Hours: Daily 10–7:30

This shop offers dining room and bedroom furniture, mainly mahogany, from the Victorian period to the 1940s. Complementing these offerings are a fine selection of oil paintings and decorative lighting accessories.
PR: $$. CC: MC, V, AMEX.

Time & Again, Inc.
785-787 Coney Island Avenue
(718) 856-2135
(718) 856-2135 fax
Hours: Mon–Sat, 10–6

This shop offers furniture, Oriental rugs, paintings, and bric-a-brac. CC: No.

Time Trader
368 Atlantic Avenue (11217)
(718) 852-3301
Mon–Fri, 11–7; Sat–Sun, 11–6

Specializing in refinished furniture from the mid 19th to the 20th century, this shop features amoires, tables, chairs, and chests of drawers in all types of wood. Lighting, paintings, prints, and some architectural details are also featured. In addition, there is a 3,000 square foot annex which offers various types of furniture. A full staff restoration service is available. PR: $$$. CC: MC, V, AMEX.

Town & Country Antiques

352 Atlantic Avenue (11217)
(718) 875-7253
Hours: Tues–Sun, 12:30–6

This shop offers all types of collectibles from the 1880s to the 1950s, furniture from the Victorian period to the 1950s, decorative smalls, and architectural items. Clock and lamp repair and restoration services are offered. And, prop rental service is also available. PR: $$. CC: MC, V, AMEX.

QUEENS

FLUSHING

Feelings Antique Boutique
42-17 162 Street (11358)
(718) 321-1939
Hours: Mon–Sat, 1–6

In addition to furniture, lamps, and accessories from 1900 to 1950, this shop also carries hand painted furniture, Victorian flowers, and fabric pieces the owner creates. CC: No.

Golden Oldies Ltd.
132-29 33rd Avenue (11354)
(718) 445-4400
(718) 445-4986 fax
Hours: Mon–Thur & Sat, 9–5:L30; Fri, 9–8; Sun, 11–5

Established in 1971, this business specializes in antique, vintage, and replica furnishings and accessories from around the world. The warehouse, which comprises more than 62,000 square feet, has more armoires under one roof than any other business. Caning, furniture stripping, and prop rentals are available. PR: Moderate. CC: MC, V.

Peter Setzer Antiques
43-62 162nd Street (11358)
(718) 461-6999
(212) 353-3947 fax
Hours: Daily, 12–5

Located in the heart of the antique section in old Flushing, this dealer specializes in estate and costume jewelry, American furniture, lighting, and collectibles. CC: MC, V.

Rae's Antiques & Clocks
43-66 162 Street (11358)
(718) 353-5577
Hours: Daily 12:30–5

In addition to clocks, this dealer also offers crystal, Hummels, and bric-a-brac. An antique clock repair and restoration service is available. CC: No.

FOREST HILLS

Metropolitan Gardens Antique Center (MD)
105-20-22 Metropolis Avenue (11375)
(718) 575-9100
Hours: Tues–Sun, 11–8

In more than 3,000 square feet plus a basement and yard, 38 dealers offer a wide range of antiques and collectibles from period to the 1950s. Among the items displayed in booths and cases are lawn and garden furniture, statuary, pottery, lighting fixtures, advertising, emphemera, estate jewelry, and period pieces. CC: MC, V, AMEX, D.

KEW GARDENS

Sad Iron Anitiques

82-02 Lefferts Boulevard (11415)
(718) 849-1648
Hours: Tues–Fri, 11–7; Sat, 11–5

Established in 1978, this shop carries 18th and 19th century furniture, decorative accessories, prints, etchings, and paintings. CC: AMEX

REGO PARK

T&G Antiques

62-47 Woodhaven Boulevard (11374)
(718) 507-2492
(718) 507-2492 fax
Hours: Wed–Sat, 11–7

T&G Antiques offers quality art, watches, jewelry, furniture, porcelain, glass, and many unique objects. PR: $$. CC: MC, V, AMEX.

WOODHAVEN

Oldies

96-18 Jamaica Avenue (11421)
(718) 441-0874
Hours: Mon–Sat, 10–5

Oldies offers "items that make a house a home." Decorative objects, 19th and 20th century furniture, lace, linens, mirrors, and lamps are some of the items for sale. CC: No.

STATEN ISLAND

Elly Oops Old Postcards and Real Photographs
7426 Amboy Road (10307)
(718) 356-9548
Hours: Mon, Wed–Sat, 10–5

In addition to collectibles, Depression glass, old books, toys, dolls, and miniatures, this shop offers early post cards (60,000+) and real photographs from Dexter Press (10,000+). PR: $. CC: No.

THE BRONX

Mooncurser Antiques
229 City Island Avenue (10464)
(718) 885-0302
Hours: Mon–Sat, 9–6; Sun, 1–6

This shop offers 78 records from 1900 to 1950, 45s and LPs in all fields, sheet music, musical instruments, and some phonographs. PR: $. CC: No.

Specialty Areas—New York City

To conserve space in the Specialty Areas and Services listings, the boroughs in which the dealers are located are abbreviated as follows: M, for Manhattan; Q, for Queens; SI, for Staten Island; B, for Brooklyn; Bx, for the Bronx.

Advertising
Home Town, M, p. 16
Lost City Arts, M, p. 17
Metropolitan Gardens Antiques Center, Q, p. 74

African Art
Beyond the Bosphorus, M, p. 12
280 Modern, M, p. 20

American Indian
America Hurrah Antiques, M, p. 28
Jeffrey Myers Ltd., M, p. 36
Kelter Malcé, M, p. 24
Paul Steinhacker, M, p. 42
Robert M. Peters/Arctic Fine Arts, M, p. 42
Susan Parrish, M, p. 27

Americana
Alan M.Goffman, M, p. 28
American Folk Art Gallery, M, p. 22
American Primitive Gallery, M, p. 12
Brian Windsor Art, Antiques, M, p. 13
Coming to America, M, p. 14
David A. Schorsch Inc., M, p. 32
Frank J. Miele Gallery, M, p. 34
Godel & Co. Fine Art, M, p. 34
Home Town, M, p. 16
Leigh Keno American Antiques, M, p. 38
Lost City Arts, M, p. 17
Pantry & Hearth, M, p. 58
Ricco/Maresca Gallery, M, p. 19
Susan Parrish, M, p. 27
Thos. K. Woodard American Antiques & Quilts, M, p. 44

Antiquities

Antiquarium Fine Ancient Arts Gallery Ltd., M, p. 28
Far Eastern Antiques & Arts Inc., M, p. 54
Jeffrey Myers Ltd., M, p. 36
Joseph G. Gerena Fine Art, M, p. 37
Lands Beyond, The, M, p. 37
North Star Galleries, M, p. 41
Palace Galleries Inc, M, p. 26
Paul Steinhacker, M, p. 42

Architectural Antiques

c.i.t.e., M, p. 13
Chameleon, M, p. 13
E. Buk, M, p. 14
Garden Antiquary, The, M, p. 47
Howard Kaplan Bath Shop, M, p. 56
In Days of Old Ltd., B, p. 70
Irreplaceable Artifacts N.A., M, p. 56
Lost City Arts, M, p. 17
Repeat Performance Antiques, B, p. 71
Roland's Antiques, M, p. 59
Rooms & Gardens, M, p. 19
Time Trader, B, p. 72
Treillage Ltd., M, p. 44
Urban Archaeology, M, p. 20

Art Deco

Artisan Antiques, M, p 22
Bizarre Bazaar Ltd., M, p. 30
Chameleon, M, p. 13
City Barn Antiques, B, p. 69
D. T. L. Trading, M, p. 31
Discoveries, M, p. 69
Dullsville, Inc., M, p. 54
Eileen Lane Antiques, M, p. 15
El Ombu, M, p. 24
Elan Antiques, M, p. 15
Fred Silberman Co., M, p. 15
Golden Treasury The, M, p. 62
Jean Karajian Gallery, M, p. 48
Karl Kemp and Assoc. Ltd. Antiques, M, p. 56
L'Art De Vivre, M, p. 37

La Belle Epoque Vintage Posters Inc., M, p. 63
Lost City Arts, M, p. 17
Macklowe Gallery, M, p. 39
Maison Gerard, M, p. 57
Marvin Alexander Inc., M, p. 40
Newel Art Galleries Inc., M, p. 49
Norman Crider Antiques, M, p. 49
Oldies, Goldies and Moldies, M, p. 41
Rene Kerne Antiques, M, p. 26
Renee Antiques Inc., M, p. 57
Reymer-Jourdan Antiques, M, p. 59
Robin A. Stafford, B, p. 71
Roy Electric Co Inc., B, p. 71
Sacks Fine Art Inc., M, p. 64
Sad Iron Antiques, Q, p. 75
Town & Country Antiques, B, p. 73
20th Century Antiques Ltd., M, p. 44
Welcome Home Antiques, M, p. 63
Wooster Gallery, M, p. 21

Art Nouveau

Chelsea Antiques Building, M, p. 65
D. T. L Trading, M, p. 31
Fichera & Perkins Antiques, M, p. 24
Golden Treasury, The, M, p. 62
La Belle Epoque Vintage Posters Inc., M, p. 63
Leo Kaplan Ltd., M, p. 38
Linda Morgan Antiques, M, p. 38
Macklowe Gallery, M, p. 39
Margot Johnson Inc., M, p. 39
Newel Art Galleries Inc., M, p. 49
Renee Antiques Inc., M, p. 57
Roy Electric Co Inc., B, p. 71
Sacks Fine Art Inc., M, p. 64
20th Century Antiques Ltd., M, p. 44
Welcome Home Antiques, M, p. 63

Art Pottery

Flores & Iva Antiques, M, p. 54
Frank Galdi Antiques, B, p. 70
Gallery 532 Soho, M, p. 15
Gem Antiques, M, p. 34

Malvina L. Solomon Inc., M, p. 39
Matter of Time, A, B, p. 71
Michael Carey, M, p. 17
Peter-Roberts Antiques Inc., M, p. 18
Robin A. Stafford, B, p. 71

Arts & Crafts

Arlene Berman Fine Arts, M, p. 28
Chameleon, M, p. 13
City Barn Antiques, B, p. 69
Elan Antiques, M, p. 15
Forthright Furniture, M, p. 15
Frank Galdi Antiques, B, p. 70
Gallery 532 Soho, M, p. 15
Michael Carey, M, p. 17
Peter-Roberts Antiques, Inc., M, p. 18

Autographs

Bruce Gimelson, M, p. 53
Kenneth W. Rendell Gallery Inc., M, p. 37
Roger Gross Ltd., M, p. 51

Automobilia

Bizarre Bazaar Ltd., M, p. 30

Barber Shop Collectibles

Jukebox Classics & Vintage Slot Machines, Inc., B, p. 70

Black Americana

Golden Treasury, The, M, p. 62

Books/Antiquarium

Acanthus Books, M, p. 64
Charlotte F. Safir, M, p. 30
Imperial Fine Book, Inc., M, p. 35
Metropolis Collectibles, M, p. 66
Roger Gross Ltd., M, p. 51

Books on Antiques

Acanthus Books, M, p. 64
Art Trading, M, p. 29
Classic Toys, M, p. 13

Brass
Charles P. Rogers Brass & Iron BedCo., M, p. 46
John Charles & Co., M, p. 66
Malcolm Franklin Inc., M, p. 39
Mel's Antiques, B, p. 71
Roy Electric Co Inc., B, p. 71

Bronzes
Abe's Antiques, M, p. 53
Antiques by Patrick, M, p. 53
Florence Sack Ltd., M, p. 54
Flying Cranes Antiques Ltd., M, p. 47
Jane Werner-Aye Asian Fine Arts & Appraisals, M, p. 24
Palace Galleries Inc., M, p. 26
Paramount Antiques Inc, M, p. 58
Renee Antiques Inc., M, p. 57
Sad Iron Antiques, Q, p. 75
Smith Gallery, M, p. 43
Universe Antiques, M, p. 60

Cartoon Art
Darrow's Fun Antiques & Collectibles, M, p. 31
Metropolis Collectibles, M, p. 66

Cast Iron
A. Goldstein for Wrought in America Inc., M, p. 64
Allan Daniel, M, p. 61
Charles P. Rogers Brass & Iron Bed, Co., M, p. 46
E. Buk, M, p. 14
John Charles & Co., M, p. 66
Metropolitan Gardens Antiques Center, Q, p. 74
T & K French Antiques Inc., M, p. 19
Treillage Ltd., M, p. 44

China
Mood Indigo, M, p. 17

Chinese Export Porcelain
Art Trading, M, p. 29
Chinese Porcelain Company, The, M, p. 31
E & J Frankel Ltd., M, p. 32
Earle D. Vandekar of Knightsbridge, M, p. 47
Guild Antiques II, M, p. 35

Clocks/Watches

Coin Operated Machines

Coins

Collectibles

Town & Country Antiques, B, p. 73

Cookie Jars

Jukebox Classics & Vintage Slot Machines Inc., B, p. 70
Mood Indigo, M, p. 17

Country Antiques

American Folk Art Gallery, M, p. 22
Cobweb, M, p. 13
Coming to America, M, p. 14
El Ombu, M, p. 24
Golden Oldies Ltd., Q, p. 74
L'Epoque Antiques, M, p. 57
Martell Antiques, M, p. 57

Decorative Smalls

Agostino Antiques Ltd., M, p. 53
C. M. Leonard Antiques, M, p. 30
Distinctive Furnishings, M, p. 23
Ellen Berenson Antiques, M, p. 32
Elly Oops Old Postcards, SI, p. 76
Hubert des Forges Inc., M, p. 35
James II Galleries Ltd., M, p. 48
Karen Warshaw Ltd., M, p. 37
Linda Morgan Antiques, M, p. 38
Lyme Regis Ltd., M, p. 17
Marvin Alexander Inc., M, p. 40
Midtown Antiques, Inc., M, p. 57
Objects & Images, M, p. 17
Oldies, Q, p. 75
Paper Moons, M, p. 26
Schmul Meier Inc., M, p. 51
Suchow & Seigel Antiques, M, p. 51
Suttonbridge, M, p. 51
Sylvia Pines-Uniquities, M, p. 43
Twin Fires, M, p. 19
280 Modern, M, p. 20
Wooster Gallery, M, p. 21
Yale R. Burge Antiques Inc, M, p. 44

Depression Glass

Elly Oops Old Postcards, SI, p. 76

Frog Alley Antiques, M, p. 34
From the Past Ltd., B, p. 70

Dolls

Lucy Anna Folk Art & Antique Quilts, M, p. 25
Norman Crider Antiques, M, p. 49
Old Japan Inc., M, p. 26

Ephermera

Bruce Gimelson, M, p. 53
La Belle Epoque Vintage Posters Inc., M, p. 63
Newman's Collectibles, M, p. 41
Roger Gross Ltd., M, p. 51

Fireplace Equipment

Mel's Antiques, B, p. 71
Pimlico Way/Amdier Antiques, M, p. 42
Thomas, M, p. 27

Folk Art

Alan M. Goffman, M, p. 28
Allan Daniel, M, p. 61
American Folk Art Gallery, M, p. 22
American Hurrah Antiques, M, p. 28
American Primitive Gallery, M, p. 12
Art Asia Inc., M, p. 29
Bertha Black Antiques, M, p. 12
Brian Windsor Art, Antiques, M, p. 13
Coming to America, M, p. 14
David A. Schorsch Inc., M, p. 32
Dullsville, Inc., M, p. 54
E. Buk, M, p. 14
Frank J. Miele Gallery, M, p. 34
Gemini Antiques Ltd., M, p. 34
Home Town, M, p. 16
Kelter Malcé, M, p. 24
Laura Fisher/Antique Quilts & Americana, M, p. 49
Leigh Keno American Antiques, M, p. 38
Madison Avenue Antique Center, M, p. 39
Old Japan Inc., M, p. 26
Pantry & Hearth, M, p. 58
Paper Moons, M, p. 26

Ricco/Maresca Gallery, M, p. 19
Rooms & Gardens, M, p. 19
Smith Gallery, M, p. 43
Susan Parrish, M, p. 27
Thos. K. Woodard American Antiques & Quilts, M, p. 44

Frames

Eli Wilner & Company, M, p. 32
Godel & Co. Fine Art, M, p. 34
J. Dixon Prentice Antiques, M, p. 35
Old Print Shop, Inc, The, M, p. 57
Sciarrino Antiqies, B, p. 72

French Antiques

Agostino Antiques, Ltd., M, p. 53
Chrystian Aubusson Inc., M, p. 31
Dalva Brothers Inc., M, p. 46
Federico Carrera, M, p. 47
Howard Kaplan Antiques, M, p. 55
Howard Kaplan Bath Shop, M, p. 56
John Charles & Co., M, p. 66
L'Art De Vivre, M, p. 37
L'Epoque Antiques, M, p. 57
Les 2 Iles, M, p. 16
Martell Antiques, M, p. 57
Midtown Antiques Inc., M, p. 57
Newel Art Galleries Inc., M, p. 49
Objets Plus Inc., M, p. 41
Proctor Galleries, M, p. 50
Robert Altman, M, p. 42
Rooms & Gardens, M, p. 19
T & K French Antiques Inc., M, p. 19
Yale R. Burge Antiques Inc., M, p. 44

Furniture/American

Abbey Galleries, B, p. 69
Alice's Antiques, M, p. 61
American Folk Art Gallery, M, p. 22
Atelier, M, p. 12
Bernard & S. Dean Levy Inc., M, p. 30
Better Times Antiques Inc., M, p. 61
c.i.t.e., M, p. 13
CIRCA Antiques Ltd., B, p. 69

David A. Schorsch Inc., M, p. 32
Distinctive Furnishings, M, p. 23
Elan Antiques, M, p. 15
Frank Galdi Antiques, B, p. 70
Hamilton-Hyre Ltd., M, p. 24
Hirschl & Adler Galleries Inc., M, p. 35
In Days of Old Ltd., B, p. 70
Leigh Keno American Antiques, M, p. 38
Margot Johnson Inc., M, p. 39
Matter of Time, A, B, p. 71
Mel's Antiques, B, p. 71
Oldies, Q, p. 75
Peter Setzer Antiques, Q, p. 74
Sad Iron Antiques, Q, p. 75
Schmul Meier Inc., M, p. 51
Secondhand Rose, M, p. 19
Silhouette Antiques Inc., B, p. 72
South Portland Antiques, B, p. 72
Thos. K. Woodard American Antiques & Quilts, M, p. 44
Town & Country Antiques, B, p. 73
Zane Moss Antiques, M, p. 45

Furniture/Continental

A. Smith Antiques Ltd., M, p. 46
Abbey Galleries, B. p. 69
Abe's Antiques, M, p. 53
Antiquarius Ltd., M, p. 22
Antiques & Decorations, B, p. 69
Atelier, M, p. 12
Cobweb, M, p. 13
Dalva Brothers Inc., M, p. 46
Eastside Antiques, M, p. 54
Eileen Lane Antiques, M, p. 15
El Ombu, M, p. 24
Ellen Berenson Antiques, M, p. 32
Emporium, The, M, p. 61
Evergreen Antiques, M, p. 33
Florian Papp, Inc., M, p. 34
Fred Silberman Co., M, p. 15
Georgian Manor Antiques Inc., M, p. 34
H. M. Luther Inc., M, p. 54
Hamilton-Hyre Ltd., M, p. 24
Howard Kaplan Antiques, M, p. 55

Furniture/English

J. Garvin Mecking Inc, M, p. 56
Kensington Place Antiques, M, p. 57
Kentshire Galleries Ltd., M, p. 57
Lenox Court Antiques, M, p. 38
Linda Horn Antiques, M, p. 38
Linda Morgan Antiques, M, p. 38
Madison Avenue Antique Center, M, p. 39
Malcolm Franklin Inc., M, p. 39
Mel's Antiques, B, p. 71
Midtown Antiques Inc, M, p. 57
Newel Art Galleries Inc., M, p. 49
Niall Smith Antiques, M, p. 26
Oak Smith & Jones, M, p. 41
Paramount Antiques Inc., M, p. 58
Phillip Colleck, M, p. 58
Reymer-Jourdan Antiques, M, p. 59
Roger Appleyard Ltd., M, p. 59
Stair & Company, M, p. 43
Turbulence, M, p. 60
Vernay & Jussel, M, p. 51
Yale R. Burge Antiques Inc., M, p. 44
Yew Tree House Antiques, M, p. 44
Zane Moss Antiques, M, p. 45

Furniture/French

Abbey Galleries, B, p. 69
Agostino Antiques Ltd., M, p. 53
Alice's Antiques, M, p. 61
C. M. Leonard Antiques, M, p. 30
Chelsea Antiques Building, M, p. 65
Emporium, The, M, p. 61
H. M. Luther, Inc., M, p. 54
Karl Kemp and Assoc. Ltd. Antiques, M, p. 56
Kensington Place Antiques, M, p. 57
Lenox Court Antiques, M, p. 38
Old Versailles Inc., M, p. 41
Paramount Antiques Inc., M, p. 58

Furniture/Fruitwood

Les 2 Iles, M, p. 16

Furniture/General

Antiques by Patrick, M, p. 53

Furniture/Mahogany

Furniture/Oak

Silhouette Antiques Inc., B, p. 72

Furniture/Painted
Bertha Black Antiques, M, p. 12
Coming to America, M, p. 14
Home Town, M, p. 16
Judith & James Milne Inc., M, p. 37
Kelter Malcé, M, p. 24
Nicholas Antiques, M, p. 49
Pantry & Hearth, M, p. 58
Paper Moons, M, p. 26
Pine Country Antiques Inc., M, p. 19
Susan Parrish, M, p. 27
Wendover's Ltd of England, M p. 66

Furniture/Pine
Golden Oldies Ltd., Q, p. 74
Pine Country Antiques Inc., M, p. 19
Twin Fires, M, p. 19
Wendover's Ltd of England, M, p. 66

Furniture/Victorian
Discoveries, B, p. 69
Margot Johnson, Inc., M, p. 39
Scotties Gallery, B, p. 72

Furniture/Walnut
In Days of Old, B, p. 70
Repeat Performance Antiques, B, p. 71

Games & Puzzles
Burlington Antique Toys, M, p. 30
Darrow's Fun Antiques & Collectibles, M, p. 31

Garden Accessories
Brian Windsor Art, Antiques, M, p. 13
Cobweb, M, p. 13
Garden Antiquary, The, M, p. 47
Roland's Antiques, M, p. 59
Rooms & Gardens, M, p. 19
T & K French Antiques Inc., M, p. 19
Treillage Ltd., M, p. 44

Urban Archaeology, M, p. 20
Vernay & Jussel, M, p. 51

Glass

Alan M. Goffman, M, p. 28
Antiquarium Fine Ancient Arts Gallery Ltd., M, p. 28
Chrystian AuBusson Inc., M, p. 31
City East Antiques Center, M, p. 53
D. T. L. Trading, M, p. 31
Elan Antiques, M, p. 15
F. H. Coins & Collectibles Ltd., M, p. 33
Fichera & Perkins Antiques, M, p. 24
Gardner & Barr Inc., M, p. 47
Georgian Manor Antiques Inc., M, p. 34
James II Galleries Ltd., M, p. 48
James Robinson Inc., M, p. 48
Kramer's Antiques, B, p. 70
Leo Kaplan Ltd., M, p. 38
Rene Kerne Antiques, M, p. 26
Renee Antiques Inc., M, p. 57
Treasures From The Past, M, p. 59
Universe Antiques, M, p. 60

Holiday Collectibles

Kelter Malcé, M, p. 24

Hooked Rugs

American Hurrah Antiques, M, p. 28
Judith & James Milne Inc., M, p. 37
Laura Fisher/Antique Quilts & Americana, M, p. 49
Renate Halpern Galleries Inc., M, p. 42

Jewelry

Art of the Past, M, p. 29
Chelsea Antiques Building, M, p. 65
Dullsville, Inc., M, p. 54
Edith Weber & Assoc. Inc., M, p. 32
First Peoples Gallery, M, p. 15
Gallery II Collections, M, p. 24
Jacques Carcanagues Inc., M, p. 16
Lyme Regis Ltd., M, p. 17
Malvina L. Solomon Inc., M, p. 39

Jewelry/Costume

Jewelry/Estate

Tudor Rose Antiques, M, p. 59

Lace & Linen

Alice Underground, M, p. 61
Jean Hoffman & Jana Starr Antiques, M, p. 36

Lighting Devices & Fixtures

Antique Addiction, M, p. 12
Artisan Antiques, M, p. 22
Barry of Chelsea Antiques, M, p. 22
Brian Windsor Art, Antiques, M, p. 13
Chameleon, M, p. 13
Chrystian AuBusson Inc., M, p. 31
CIRCA Antiques Ltd., B, p. 69
David George Antiques, M, p. 31
Eastside Antiques, M, p. 54
El Ombu, M, p. 24
Ellen Berenson Antiques, M, p. 32
Fichera & Perkins Antiques, M, p. 24
Florence Sack Ltd., M, p. 54
Fred Silberman Co., M, p. 15
Gallery 532 Soho, M, p. 15
Gaslight Time, B, p. 70
Golden Treasury, The, M, p. 62
Guild Antiques II, M, p. 35
Hamilton-Hyre Ltd., M, p. 24
Howard Kaplan Antiques, M, p. 55
Howard Kaplan Bath Shop, M, p. 56
Hubert des Forges Inc., M, p. 35
Irreplaceable Artifacts N.A., M, p. 56
J. Dixon Prentice Antiques, M, p. 35
John Rosselli Ltd., M, p. 37
L'Art De Vivre, M, p. 37
Lenox Court Antiques, M, p. 38
Les 2 Iles, M, p. 16
Marvin Alexander Inc., M, p. 40
Matter of Time, A, B, p. 71
Michael Carey, M, p. 17
Nicholas Antiques, M, p. 49
Oldies,Goldies and Moldies, M, p. 41
Paramount Antiques Inc., M, p. 58
Peter Setzer Antiques, Q, p. 74
Peter-Roberts Antiques Inc., M, p. 18
Pimlico Way/Amdier Antiques, M, p. 42

Repeat Performance, A, M, p. 59
Robert Altman, M, p. 42
Roy Electric Co Inc., B, p. 71
Schmul Meier Inc., M, p. 51
Scotties Gallery, B, p. 72
South Portland Antiques, B, p. 72
Suttonbridge, M, p. 51
Time Trader, B, p. 72
20th Century Antiques Ltd., M, p. 44
280 Modern, M, p. 20
Universe Antiques, M, p. 60
Urban Archaeology, M, p. 20
Victor Carl Antiques, M, p. 60
Wooster Gallery, M, p. 21
Yew Tree House Antiques, M, p. 44

Majolica
Hubert des Forges Inc., M, p. 35
Linda Horn Antiques, M, p. 38

Manuscripts
Bruce Gimelson, M, p. 53
Kenneth W. Rendell Gallery Inc., M, p. 37
Roger Gross Ltd., M, p. 51

Maps
Old Print Shop, The, Inc., M, p. 57

Militaria
Charlotte's Antiques, B, p. 69
Newman's Collectibles, M, p. 41

Miniatures
Earle D. Vandekar of Knightsbridge, M, p. 47
Newman's Collectibles, M, p. 41

Mirrors
Abe's Antiques, M, p. 53
Antiques & Decorations, B, p. 69
Florence Sack Ltd., M, p. 54
Guild Antiques II, M, p. 35
Hamilton-Hyre Ltd., M, p. 24
Hyde Park Antiques, M, p. 56
J. Dixon Prentice Antiques, M, p. 35

Movie Memorabilia

Musical Instruments

Nautical/Marine

Needlework

Oriental Arts

Oriental Carpets/Rugs

Paintings

Kendra Krienke, M, p. 62
Kramer's Antiques, B, p. 70
Objects & Images, M, p. 17
Old Versailles Inc., M, p. 41
Palace Galleries Inc., M, p. 26
Paris To Province, M, p. 50
Phillip Colleck, M, p. 58
Proctor Galleries, M, p. 50
Ricco/Maresca Gallery, M, p. 19
Robert M. Peters/Arctic Fine Arts, M, p. 42
Roland's Antiques, M, p. 59
Sacks Fine Art Inc., M, p. 64
Sciarrino Antiques, B, p. 72
Scotties Gallery, B, p. 72
Shepherd Gallery, M, p. 43
Smith Gallery, M, p. 43
South Portland Antiques, B, p. 72
Stair & Company, M, p. 43
Throckmorton Fine Art Inc., M, p. 44
Time & Again Inc., B, p. 72
Zane Moss Antiques, M, p. 45

Paperweights
Gem Antiques, M, p. 34
Leo Kaplan Ltd., M, p. 38

Pens & Pencils
Charlotte's Antiques, B, p. 69
Den of Antiquity, M, p. 23
Gaslight Time, B, p. 70

Phonographica
Waves, M, p. 60

Political Memorabilia
Newman's Collectibles, M, p. 41

Postcards
Elly Oops Old Postcards, SI, p. 76

Porcelain
A La Vieille Russie, Inc., M, p. 46
Abbey Galleries, B, p. 69

Pottery

Art Trading, M, p. 29
Chrystian Aubusson Inc., M, p. 31
Cobweb, M, p. 13
First Peoples Gallery, M, p. 15
Gem Antiques, M, p. 34
Leo Kaplan Ltd., M, p. 38
Metropolitan Gardens Antiques Center, Q, p. 74
Objects & Images, M, p. 17
Smith Gallery, M, p. 43
Suchow & Seigel Antiques, M, p. 51

Primitives

American Primitive Gallery, M, p. 12
Distinctive Furnishings, M, p. 23
Frank J. Miele Gallery, M, p. 34
Jeffrey Myers Ltd., M, p. 36
Pantry & Hearth, M, p. 58

Prints

Art Asia Inc., M, p. 29
David George Antiques, M, p. 31
Hirschl & Adler Galleries Inc., M, p. 35
Japan Gallery, M, p. 36
Kendra Krienke, M, p. 62
Kensington Place Antiques, M, p. 57
La Belle Epoque Vintage Posters Inc., M. p. 63
Metropolis Collectibles, M, p. 66
North Star Galleries, M, p. 41
Old Print Shop Inc., The, M, p. 57
Throckmorton Fine Art Inc., M, p. 44
20th Century Antiques Ltd., M, p. 44

Quilts

America Hurrah Antiques, M., p. 28
Cora Ginsburg Inc., M, p. 31
Judith & James Milne Inc., M, p. 37
Kelter Malcé, M, p. 24
Laura Fisher/Antique Quilts & Americana, M, p. 49
Lucy Anna Folk Art & Antique Quilts, M, p. 25
Panache Antique Clothing, M, p. 18
Susan Parrish, M, p. 27
Thos. K. Woodard American Antiques & Quilts, M, p. 44

Radios

Oldies, Goldies, & Moldies, M, p. 41
Waves, M, p. 60

Scientific Instruments

Den of Antiquity, M, p. 23
E. Buk, M, p. 14
Waves, M, p. 60

Sculpture

A. Smith Antiques Ltd., M, p. 46
Antiquarium Fine Ancient Arts & Gallery Ltd., M, p. 28
Art Asia Inc., M, p. 29
Art of the Past, M, p. 29
Bertha Black Antiques, M, p. 12
Chinese Porcelain Company, The, M, p. 31
Dalva Brothers Inc., M, p. 46
David Seidenberg Inc., M, p. 53
First Peoples Gallery, M, p. 15
Fred Silberman Co., M, p. 15
Hirschl & Adler Galleries Inc., M, p. 35
Irreplacable Artifacts N.A., M, p. 56
Kramer's Antiques, B, p. 70
Manhattan Art & Antiques Center, M, p. 49
Sacks Fine Art Inc., M, p. 64
Shepard Gallery, M, p. 43
Treillage Ltd., M, p. 44
Universe Antiques, M, p. 60

Shaker

David A. Schorsch, Inc., M, p. 32

Silver

Aaron's Antiques, M, p. 46
Abby Galleries, B, p. 69
Antiquarius Ltd., M, p. 22
Antique Buff, The, M, p. 22
Bernard & S. Dean Levy Inc., M, p. 30
C. M. Leonard Antiques, M, p. 30
Constantine Kollitus, M, p. 65
David Seidenberg Inc., M, p. 53
Federico Carrera, M, p. 47

Old Japan Inc., M, p. 26
Panache Antique Clothing, M, p. 18
Peter-Roberts Antiques, M, p. 18
Renate Halpern Galleries Inc., M, p. 42
Schmul Meier Inc., M, p. 51
Susan Parrish, M, p. 27

Tools
A. Goldstein for Wrought in America Inc., M, p. 64

Toys
Bizarre Bazaar Ltd., M, p. 30
Burlington Antique Toys, M, p. 30
City East Antiques Center, M, p. 53
Classic Toys, M, p. 13
Darrow's Fun Antiques & Collectibles, M, p. 31
Gemini Antiques Ltd., M, p. 34
Newman's Collectibles, M, p. 41
Second Childhood, M, p. 26

Tramp Art
Paper Moons, M, p. 26

Tribal Art
Jacques Carianagues Inc., M, p. 16
Jeffrey Myers Ltd., M, p. 36
Joseph G. Gerena Fine Arts, M, p. 37
Paul Steinhacker, M, p. 42

Victoriana
In Days of Old Ltd., B, p. 70
Repeat Performances Antiques, B, p. 71
Time Trader, B, p. 72
Welcome Home Antiques, M, p. 63

Vintage Clothing
Alice Underground, M, p. 61
Antique Addiction, M, p. 12
Cora Ginsburg Inc., M, p. 31
Dorothy's Closet, M, p. 23
Jean Hoffman & Jana Starr Antiques, M, p. 36
Oldies, Goldies and Moldies, M, p. 41
Panache Antique Clothing, M, p. 18

Rene Kerne Antiques, M, p. 26
Star Struck Ltd., M, p. 26

Weathervanes
Allan Daniel, M, p. 61
Judith & James Milne Inc., M, p. 37

ANTIQUE DEALERS AND CO-OP MANAGERS, PLEASE SEE PAGE 342

Services - New York City

Note: Some of the categories below have no shops listed under them; the categories have, however, been included for completeness's sake and to indicate that at present no shops in this region provide these services.

Appraisals

Abby Galleries, B, p. 69
Acanthus Books, M, p. 64
American Hurrah Antiques, M, p. 28
American Illustrators Gallery, M, p. 28
Antiquarius, Ltd., M, p. 28
Antique Buff, The, M, p. 22
Art Trading (U.S.) Ltd., M, p. 29
Better Times Antiques Inc., M, p. 61
Brian Windsor Art, Antiques, & Garden Furniture, M, p. 13
Cora Ginsburg, Inc., M, p. 31
D.T.L. Trading, M, p. 31
Darrow's Fun Antiques & Collectibles, M, p. 31
David A. Schorch Inc., M, p. 32
E&J Frankel, LTD, M, p. 32
Edith Weber & Assoc., Inc., M, p. 32
Eli Wilner & Company, M, p. 32
F.H. Coins & Collectibles, M, p. 33
Federico Carrera, M, p. 47
Flying Cranes Antiques Ltd., M, p. 47
Frank J. Miele Gallery, M, p. 34
Gem Antiques, M, p. 34
Hirschl & Adler Galleries, Inc., M, p. 35
Home Town, M, p. 16
Imperial Fine Books, Inc., M, p. 35
Jane Werner-Aye Asian Fine Art & Appraisals, M, p. 24
Jean Hoffman & Jana Starr Antiques, M, p. 36
Jeffrey Myers LTD, M, p. 36
Judith & James Milne Inc-Am. Country Antiques, M, p. 37
Kendra Krienke, M, p. 62
Lands Beyond, The, M, p. 37
Laura Fisher/Antiques Quilts & Americana, M, p. 49
Le Monde Des Kilims/Martman, Inc., M, p. 16
Macklowe Gallery, M, p. 39
Malcolm Franklin, Inc., M, p. 39
Manhattan Art & Antiques Center, M, p. 49

Authentication

Book Binding & Restoration

Cabinetry

China & Pottery Restoration

China Matching Service

Clock Repair & Restoration

Fossner Timepieces, Inc., M, p. 47
Manhattan Art & Antiques Center, M, p. 49
Rae's Antiques & Clocks, Q, p. 74
Sad Iron Antiques, Q, p. 75
Tic-Toc Clock Co., Inc, M, p. 64

Crystal & Glass Restoration

Consignments
American Folk Art Gallery, M, p. 22
American Illustrators Gallery, M, p. 28
Antiquarius, Ltd., M, p. 22
Art Trading (U.S.) Ltd, M, p. 29
Constantine Kollitus, M, p. 65
Darrow's Fun Antiques & Collectibles, M, p. 31
David A. Schorch Inc., M, p. 32
Edith Weber & Assoc., Inc., M, p. 32
Elan Antiques, M, p. 15
Fanelli Antique Timepieces, Ltd., M, p. 33
Federico Carrera, M, p. 47
Frank J. Miele Gallery, M, p. 34
Godel & Co. Fine Art, M, p. 34
Hirschl & Adler Galleries, Inc., M, p. 35
Old Japan Inc., M, p. 26
Pantry & Hearth, M, p. 58
Roland's Antiques, M, p. 59
Schmul Meier, Inc., M, p. 51
Smith Gallery, M, p. 43
Suchow & Siegel Antiques, M, p. 51

Display Material
American Primitive Gallery, M, p. 12
c.i.t.e, M, p. 13

Doll Repair

Electric Train Repair

Finders Service
A. Goldstein For Wrought in America, inc., M, p. 64
American Folk Art Gallery, M, p. 22
Bizaare Bazaar Ltd, M, p. 30
Charlotte F. Safir, M, p. 30

Constantine Kollitus, M, p. 65
Golden Treasury, The, M, p. 62
Home Town, M, p. 16
Imperial Fine Books, Inc., M, p. 35
Karen Warshaw Ltd., M, p. 37
Midtown Antiques, Inc., M, p. 57
Pantry & Hearth, M, p. 58
Peter-Roberts Antiques, Inc., M, p. 18
Yew Tree House Antiques, M, p. 44

Fixtures
Howard Kaplan Bath Shop, M, p. 56
Roland's Antiques, M, p. 59

Frame Restoration
Eli Wilner & Company, M, p. 32

Furniture Refinishing
El Ombu, M, p. 24
Golden Oldies, Ltd., Q, p. 74
Howard Kaplan Antiques, M, p. 55
Midtown Antiques, Inc., M, p. 57
Oldies, Goldies, & Moldies, M, p. 41
Roger Appleyard, M, p. 59
Vintage Restoration, M, p. 66

Furniture Reproduction
Eileen Lane Antiques, M, p. 15
Twin Fires, M. p. 19
Wendover's Ltd. of England, M, p. 66

Furniture Repair & Restoration
Howard Kaplan Antiques, M, p. 55
Irreplaceable Artifacts, N.A., M, p. 56
Michael Carey, M, p. 17
Midtown Antiques, Inc., M, p. 57
Oldies, Goldies, & Moldies, M, p. 41
Pine Country Antiques, Inc., M, p. 19
Sad Iron Antiques, Q, p. 75
Vernay & Jussel, M, p. 51
Vintage Restoration, M, p. 66
Welcome Home Antiques, M, p. 63
Wendover's Ltd. of England, M, p. 66

Glass Matching Service

Hooked Rug Repair & Restoration
Laura Fisher/Antique Quilts & Americana, M, p. 49

Home Restoration
Irreplaceable Artifacts, N.A., M, p. 56

Hardware
A. Goldstein For Wrought in America Inc., M, p. 64
Golden Treasury, The, M., p. 62
Howard Kaplan Bath Shop, M, p. 56

Jewelry Repair
Antique Buff, The, M, p. 22
Diane Gerardi's Vintage Jewelry, M, p. 61
Edith Weber & Assoc., Inc., M, p. 32
Gallery II Collections, M, p. 24, 62
Malvina L.Solomon, Inc., M, p. 39

Lamp Repair & Restoration
Urban Archaeology, M, p. 20

Leather Restoration
Les 2 Iles, M, p. 16

Marble Repair & Restoration

Metal Repair & Restoration

Mirror Resilvering
Oldies, Goldies, & Moldies, M, p. 41

Oriental Rug Repair & Restoration
Le Monde Des Kilims/Martman, Inc., M, p. 16
Zeron Ayvazian Inc., M, p. 52

Painting Restoration

Pewter Repair & Restoration

Phonograph Repair
Waves, M, p. 60

Piano & Organ Repair

Prop Rentals

American Folk Art Gallery, M, p. 22
American Primitive Gallery, M, p. 12
Antique Addiction, M, p. 12
c.i.t.e, M, p. 13
Darrow's Fun Antiques & Collectibles, M, p. 31
Eileen Lane Antiques, M, p. 15
Elan Antiques, M, p. 15
Fanelli Antique Timepieces, Ltd., M, p. 33
Far Eastern Antiques & Art, Inc., M, p. 54
Florence Sack Ltd., M, p. 54
Golden Oldies Ltd., Q, p. 74
Golden Treasury,The, M, p. 62
Home Town, M, p. 16
Jean Hoffman & Jana Starr Antiques, M, p. 36
Judith & James Milne, M, p. 37
Lyme Regis, Ltd, M, p. 17
Midtown Antiques, Inc., M, p. 57
Mood Indigo, M, p. 17
Old Japan Inc., M, p. 26
Oldies, Goldies, & Moldies, M, p. 41
Pantry & Hearth, M, p. 58
Peter-Roberts Antiques, Inc. M, p. 18
Renee Antiques Inc., M, p. 58
Repeat Performance, A, M, p. 59
Roland's Antiques, M, p. 59
Rooms & Gardens, M, p. 19
Schmul Meier, Inc., M, p. 51
Secondhand Rose, M, p. 19
T & K French Antiques, Inc., M, p. 19
Urban Archaeology, M, p. 20
Waves, M, p. 60

Quilt Repair & Restoration

American Hurrah Antiques, M, p. 28
Judith & James Milne, Inc., M, p. 37
Laura Fisher/Antique Quilts & Americana, M, p. 49
Susan Parrish, M, p. 27

Radio Repair & Restoration

Waves, M, p. 60

Research
A. Goldstein For Wrought in America, Inc., M, p. 64
American Folk Art Gallery, M, p. 22
Art Trading (U.S.) Ltd., M, p. 29
Darrow's Fun Antiques & Collectibles, M, p. 31
Illustration House, M, p. 16
Judith & James Milne, Inc., M, p. 37
Paul Steinhacker-Primitive & Asiatic Art, M, p. 42
Smith Gallery, M, p. 43

Restoration (General)
Jane Werner-Aye Asian Fine Art & Appraisals, M, p. 24
North Star Galleries, M, p. 41
Rita Ford Music Boxes Inc., M, p. 42
Susan Parrish, M, p. 27
Vintage Restoration, M, p. 66

Silver Matching Service
Aaron's Antiques, M, p. 46
Constantine Kollitus, M, p. 65

Toy Repair & Restoration

Wicker/Caning Repair & Restoration
Golden Oldies Ltd., Q, p. 74
Oldies, Goldies, & Moldies, M, p. 41

ANTIQUE DEALERS AND CO-OP MANAGERS, PLEASE SEE PAGE 342

Long Island

AMAGANSETT

Balasses House Antiques
2 Main Street, corner of Hedges Lane (11930)
(516) 267-3032
(516) 267-1048 fax
Hours: Daily 10:30-5 except closed Tues & Wed during the winter

English and French country furniture such as tables and armoires fill this shop; one will also find lighting fixtures which include chandeliers and table lamps. These dealers have been in business for thirty-three years. PR: $$. CC: No.

Nellies of Amagansett
303 Main Street (11930)
(516) 267-1000
Hours: Fri, 2–5; Sat & Sun, 10–5

This dealer specializes in Pennsylvania antiques, quilts, decorative smalls, and toys. CC: MC, V, AMEX.

BABYLON

Babylon Antiques Shoppe
206 East Main Street (11702)
(516) 321-6848
Hours: Mon–Sat, 10–6; Sun, 12–6

This shop carries a rapidly changing general line of antiques, furniture, and collectibles such as costume and antique jewelry, mahogany furniture, and porcelain. PR: $. CC: No.

Tempus Fugit Antiques - Bay Gallery
134 West Main Street (11702)
(516) 661-2487
(516) 661-2715 fax
Hours: Appointment suggested or by chance

Since this dealer's stock comes from the liquidation of estates, it is always changing, always full of surprises, and is never dull. One will find all sorts of antiques and collectibles that are fresh to the market. CC: No.

BALDWIN

Yankee Trader Antiques Inc.
1649 Grand Avenue (11510)
(516) 623-7192
Hours: Tues–Thur, 11–5; Sat & Sun 11–5

Antique clocks, especially American and European wall and shelf types, are complemented by American oak, walnut, and mahogany furniture. CC: V, MC.

BAYPORT

Antiques at Bayport
273 Snedecor Avenue, corner of Montauk Highway (11705)
(516) 472-8279
Hours: Mon–Sat, 11–5; Sun, 9–3

This shop carries a full line of antiques and collectibles from the 18th through the 20th century. Along with Mission, Art Deco, Art Glass, paintings, pottery, and porcelain, one will also find toys, crystal, Depression glass, autographica, fine books, advertising, and new antique books. PR: $$. CC: MC, V.

Country Junque Shop
597 Middle Road (11705)
(516) 472-2650
Hours: Daily 10:30–5:30

A mixture of old and new items that includes furniture, jugs, quilts, and holiday collectibles can be found at this shop. PR: $. CC: V, AMEX.

BAY SHORE

End Shop, The
153 East Main Street (11706)
(516) 665-3380
Hours: Mon–Sat, 11:30–4

Depression glass, silver, and jewelry are only some of the items at this fun shop which also features nostalgia, unusual memorabilia, and decorative smalls. PR: $. CC: No.

Harry's Antiques
137 East Main Street (11706)
(516) 666-4311
Hours: Mon–Sat, 11–4

This eclectic store is filled with, among other things, furniture including chairs of all description, picture frames, and brass beds. A repair service for furniture is offered. CC: No.

Joanne's Antiques
133 East Main Street (11706)
(516) 968-6576
Hours: Mon, 12–4 and by chance

Glass, china, pottery, lamps, furniture, costume jewelry, old toys, Oriental rugs, chandeliers, and pictures can be found in this shop. CC: No.

Legacy Antiques, Inc.
156 East Main Street (11706)
(516) 666-3815
Hours: Daily 11–4 except closed Sun; Wed by chance or appointment

In addition to a large selection of early American pattern and pressed glass, this shop also contains a unique selection of American Art Pottery, European and American Art Glass, American brilliant crystal, American and European porcelain, lamps,

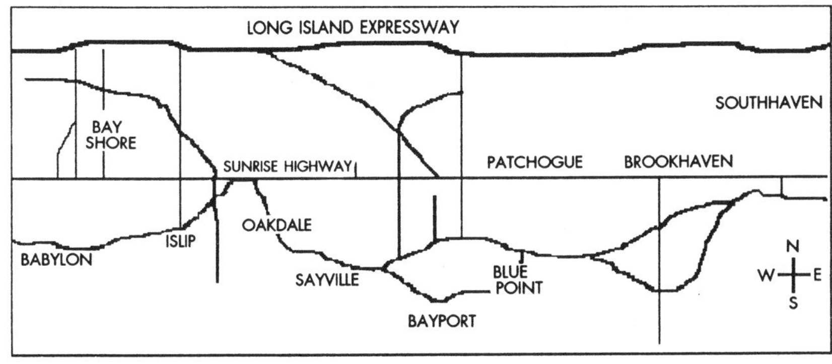

Bayport & Babylon area

prints, quilts, collectibles, and other fine smalls. CC: No.

BELLMORE

Antique Parlor, The
2970 Merrick Road, The Antique Pavilion (11710)
(516) 783-1959
Hours: Tues–Sun, 12–5

This shop contains Victorian furnishings of all types - a large assortment of unusual jewelry, beautifully refinished furniture, and many great lamps. The shop is also packed with loads of decorative accessories. CC: MC, V, D.

Antique Pavilion, The (MD)
2970 Merrick Road (11710)
(516) 783-3183
Hours: Tues–Sat, 12–5

Eight individually owned air conditioned shops contain a vast array of antiques and collectibles certain to please the tastes of collectors, dealers, and decorators. Merchandise includes Victoriana, silver, Art Pottery, clocks, Art Glass, Americana, furniture, lighting, and porcelain. CC: MC, V, D.

Antiques by Addie
2970 Merrick Road (11710)
(516) 221-5600
Hours: Tues–Sun, 12–5 or by appointment

This shop contains a mix of fine antiques and decorative items for the collector, decorator, and anyone who appreciates the finer things. Estate jewelry, prints, paintings, Oriental and European porcelain, bronzes, clocks, and lamps are only some of the items for sale. CC: MC, V.

Austern's
2970 Merrick Road, The Antique Pavilion (11710)
(516) 221-0098
Hours: Tues–Sun, 12–5

In addition to specializing in ladies' items such as beaded bags, perfume bottles, jewelry, and dolls, this business has been dealing in Roseville for more than fifteen years. All items are in excellent condition, authentic, and reasonably priced. Dealers are welcome. PR: Moderate. CC: MC, V, D.

Bernard's Antiques
2928 Merrick Road (11710)
(516) 221-5260
(516) 671-4603 fax
Hours: Mon–Fri, 11:30–4:30; Sat–Sun, 12–5

In addition to being the largest importer of French furniture and accessories on Long Island, this business also offers stained glass and etched glass windows and doors, lighting devices, and clocks. PR: $$$. CC: MC.

Gem Quest Jewelry and Antiques, Inc.
2970 Merrick Road, The Antique Pavilion (11710)
(516) 783-8030
(516) 783-4308 fax
Hours: Tues–Sat, 12–5 and by appointment

This shop contains fine authentic estate jewelry including a large display of engagement and wedding bands. Furniture and ceramics such as Flow Blue and Royal Dalton are also offered. Excellent repair services and custom made jewelry are also available. PR: $$$. CC: MC, V.

Hide 'n Seek Antiques
2970 Merrick Road, The Antique Pavilion (11710)
(516) 783-3183
Hours: Tues–Sun, 12–5 and by appointment

This hectic, eclectic shop is stocked with a little of everything—dolls, jewelry, furniture, porcelain, silver, and the like. Browsers, dealers, and decorators are always welcome. PR: Affordable CC: No.

L. Calderon, Pink Wagon Antiques
2918 Merrick Road (11710)
(516) 221-8805
Hours: Daily 11–5

This dealer carries a general line of antiques that includes jewelry, bronzes, porcelain, Art Glass, furniture, Hummels, Oriental items, and Royal Dalton. PR: $$. CC: MC, V.

Ray's Antiques
2974 Merrick Road (11710)
(516) 826-7129
Hours: Tues–Sat, 11–5

In addition to specializing in militaria (firearms, swords, uniforms, medals, etc.) and nautical and aviation items, this dealer also offers clocks, pocketwatches, jewelry, scientific instruments, taxidermy, and the unusual. PR: $$. CC: MC, V, AMEX, D.

BRIDGEHAMPTON

Antiques at East Marion
Main Street, Sandford Building (11932)
(516) 537-7115 (shop), 324-2084 (home)
Hours: Mon–Sat, 10–5; Sun 12–5

This shop features country furni-

"The Road,—Winter." Large folio lithograph by N. Currier, 1853. *(Courtesy of The Old Print Shop Inc., Kenneth M. Newman, New York City)*

ture, decorative smalls, estate and costume jewelry, pottery, and porcelain. CC: AMEX.

Barbara Trujillo
Main Street (11932)
(516) 537-3838
Hours: Fri–Mon, 11–5

American Indian jewelry, country furniture and accessories, paintings, toys, and holiday collectibles fill this shop. PR: $$. CC: No.

Beach Plum Antiques
Main Street, near monument (11932)
(516) 537-7403
Hours: call

This shop specializes in Arts & Crafts, Mission furniture and accessories, American hand painted furniture, unique lamps, and hand tinted photographs by Nutting, Davidson, and Thompson.

English Country Antiques
Snakehollow Road (11932)
(516) 537-0606
(516) 537-2657 fax
Hours: Mon–Sat, 10–5; Sun, 10:30–5; closed Tues during the winter

Pine and dark antique furniture plus reproductions made to order in England are complemented by a large selection of rugs, coffee and dining tables, beds, armoires, indoor and outdoor lighting, and upholstered furniture. New shipments, which contain both furniture and accessories, arrive quarterly from England. PR: $$$$. CC: MC, V, AMEX.

John Salibello Antiques
Montauk Highway (11932)
(516) 537-1484
Hours: Daily 11–5 during the summer; Fri–Mon, 11–5 during the winter

Located in a lovely turn of the century farmhouse, each room setting, which contains decorative furniture and accessories such as gilded mirrors, lamps, painted furniture, and sconces, is carefully assembled for the discerning decorator and collector. Located in the Americana Room is a vast collection of cookie jars, banks, doorstops, and black memorabilia. A unique selection of vintage costume jewelry is also available. CC: MC, V, AMEX.

Mill Pond Antiques
Main Street, Sandford House (11932)
(516) 537-4242
Hours: Summer, Daily 11–5; winter closed Tues & Wed

This shop contains a nicely presented mixture of American country pine furniture with an emphasis on harvest tables, primitive furniture in old paint, Roseville pottery, and decorative objects. Consignments are accepted. PR: $$. CC: MC, V.

Robert E. Kinnamen & Brian A. Ramaekers, Inc.
Main Street (11932)
(516) 537-0779, 537-3838
(516) 537-0779 fax
Hours: Spring & summer, Mon–Fri, 11–5; winter, Fri–Sun, 11–5

Established in 1969, this business offers the finest quality American antique furniture, paintings, folk art, and Native American art. CC: AMEX.

Ruby Beets
Corner of Poxabogue Road and Montauk Highway (11932)
(516) 537-2802
Hours: Fri–Mon, 11–5

In an 1850s shingled farmhouse, eight rooms are filled to the rafters with iron beds, wainscoted cupboards, painted furniture, mirrors, folk art, paintings, American pottery, kitchenware plus slipcovered chairs, vintage fabric pillows, and lamps. PR: $$. CC: MC, V.

Sterling & Hunt
Butter Lane, Box 300 (11932)
(516) 537-1096
Hours: Daily 1–5 or by appointment

Established in 1972, this business specializes in fine quality Americana from the late 19th century to the early 20th century. Weathervanes, sculpture, paintings, folk art, and decorative art fill this shop. PR: $$$. CC: No.

Urban Archaeology
2231 Montauk Highway
(516) 537-0124
(516) 537-7123 fax
Hours: Daily 10–5:30

Being dedicated to architectural salvage and restoration, this shop, which also has a branch in New York City, is filled with all types of elements that can be used for both indoor and outdoor decoration. High quality reproductions of antique lighting fixtures and bathroom accessories are also featured. A complete restoration service is available for most antique and architectural pieces. PR: $$$$$. CC: MC, V, AMEX.

CEDARHURST

Carl's Antiques, Ltd.
445 Central Avenue, The Atrium Mall (11516)
(516) 569-0545
Hours: Mon–Sat, 10–4:30

The dealer carries Oriental art and estate jewelry. PR: $. CC: All.

Carriage Trade, The
477 Chestnut Street (11516)
(516) 569-2299
Hours: Mon–Sat, 10–5

Established in 1956, The Carriage Trade which is a well known and highly regarded shop takes pride in the quality of its merchandise and personal service. American and European silver, English accessories, majolica, and European enameled glass are but a few of the antiques and collectibles that are constantly in stock. CC: The Carriage Trade charge accounts.

Cugino Antiques
454 Central Avenue (11516)
(516) 374-3511
Hours: Mon–Fri, 11–5; Sun, 12–4

This small shop specializes in fixtures, mirrors, and bric-a-brac. Unique and off-beat objects and some furniture such as consoles, chairs, and settees are also stocked. PR: $$. CC: No.

COLD SPRING HARBOR

Lyman Thorne Enterprises, Ltd.
169 Main Street & 135 Main Street (11724)
(516) 692-2834
Hours: Tues–Sat, 12–5; Sun by chance

The store at 169 Main Street specializes in 18th and 19th century American and English furniture, art, and accessories. The 135 Main Street shop features art and antiques as well as decorative pieces and consignments. Furniture repair and restoration and clock repair are available. Estate appraisals are given. Consignments are accepted. CC: V, MC.

Valdemar F. Jacobsen Antiques
5 Main Street, Route 25A (11724)
(516) 692-7775
Hours: Tues–Sat, 9–5

Having been in the antique and appraising business for more than forty years and exhibiting at the best antique shows in the country such as the New York City Winter East Side Show for 25 years, this dealer offers only period pieces with no major repairs, restorations, alterations, or embellishments. Chinese export porcelain and lamps, American paintings and folk art, and early brass and fireplace equipment are also offered. PR: Medium to Upper. CC: MC, V.

CORAM

Coram Shop & Swap

325A Route 25 (11727)
(516) 732-2204
Hours: Daily 10–5

Since these dealers buy the complete contents of homes, their shop contains a mixture of antiques, bric-a-brac, collectibles, and good used furniture. CC: MC, V.

CUTCHOGUE

Antiques & Old Lace

31935 Main Road, Route 25 (11935)
(516) 734-6462
Hours: Daily 11–5

Upon entering this 5,000 square foot establishment, you can expect the unexpected. An unusual and eclectic grouping of antiques and collectibles, which includes baskets, cupboards, armoires, thimbles, and sleighs. PR: $$$. CC: MC, V.

EAST HAMPTON

Abbott & Jackson, Inc.

50 Newtown Lane (11937)
(516) 324-1499
Hours: In season, Daily 10–5; out of season, Sat–Mon, 10–5

This shop offers a fine selection of American and English furniture from the 18th through early 20th century with appropriate accessories. American pottery, doorstops, and unusual collectibles are also available. PR: $$$. CC: MC, V, AMEX.

Antiques Center of East Hampton (MD)

251 Pantigo Road, Montauk Highway (11937)
(516) 329-2831
Hours: In season, Thurs–Mon; November–March, Fri–Mon; call for hours

Opened since 1992, this multi-dealer shop offers collectors and dealers a constantly changing stock of vintage fabrics, country and painted furniture, 1930s and 1940s kitchenware, Nippon, decorative accessories, pottery, ironwork, and antique frames. In addition to featuring McCoy, Roseville, and Weller pottery, American dinnerware by Russell Wright, Stangl, Blue Ridge, Jadeite, and others is offered. Pottery repair and frame restoration are available. CC: AMEX, D.

Architrove

74 Montauk Highway #3 (11937)
(516) 329-2229
(516) 329-1155 fax
Hours: Mon–Fri, 10–6; Sat–Sun, 9–6

High-quality European and American furniture, garden furniture and appointments, antique lighting, and architectural elements fill this shop. PR: $$$$. CC: No.

Christina Borg Inc.
41 Main Street (11937)
(516) 324-6997
(516) 324-7084 fax
Hours: In season, Daily 10–7; November–May, Thur–Mon 10–6

Featuring fine antiques and interior decoration, this shop is considered by many to be one of the most exclusive on eastern Long Island. The diverse offerings include rare and unusual decorative European furniture including painted Italian, French, and English from the 18th through the 20th century, unique Art Deco and Art Nouveau pieces, dramatic decorative accessories such as majolica, Venetian glass, objets d'art, lighting, and Oriental porcelains. Shipping and gift wrapping are available. PR: $$$$$. CC: MC, V, AMEX.

Elaine's Room Antiques
251 Pantigo Road (11937)
(516) 324-4734
Hours: Call

This shop carries both English and American Art Pottery, crystal, silver, and estate jewelry.

Faces Antiques at the Antique Center of East Hampton (MD)
251 Pantigo Road (11937)
(516) 324-9510
Hours: Daily 11–6 during the summer; Fri–Mon, 11–6 during the winter

Faces, which is one of five shops in this center, carries a diverse line of quality antiques and jewelry. Tiffany lamps, decorative accessories, lighting, silver, and Art Pottery are always offered. CC: MC, V, AMEX.

Grand Acquisitor, The
110 North Main Street (11937)
(516) 324-7272
Hours: Daily 11–5 from Memorial Day through Labor Day; Sat & Sun, 11–5 during the spring & fall

Established in 1980, this shop has an outstanding selection of textiles from the 19th and 20th century, domestic linens, lace, children's clothing, silver, and porcelain. PR: $$$$. CC: No.

Hamptique Antiques
10 Main Street, 2nd floor (11937)
(516) 329-3916
Hours: Fri–Mon, 1–5

Specializing in decorative country antiques and collectibles, this shop offers select pieces of painted and stripped furniture and wicker. One is also likely to find Art Pottery, bronzes, original art, and architectural elements. CC: MC, V.

Lars Bolander Ltd.
5 Toilsome Lane (11937)
(516) 329-3400
(516) 329-3172 fax
Hours: Thur–Mon, 10–5 except Sun, 11–5

This retail shop features European antiques and reproductions as well as new decorating items for the interior. The owner, Lars Bolander, also runs an international decorating business. CC: MC, V.

Renés Antiques
21 Main Street (11937)
(516) 324-3282
Hours: Wed–Mon, 10–5

Established in 1978, this shop features a fine selection of French country, English, and Continental furniture. A large selection of Oriental art, antiques, accessories, and Dutch colonial furniture is available. PR: $$$. CC: MC, V, AMEX.

Victory Garden Ltd.
63 Main Street (11937)
(516) 324-7800
(516) 324-2849 fax
Hours: May–September, Daily 10–6; October–April, Thurs–Mon, 10–6

This shop offers a fine selection of country French antiques for both indoor and outdoor living. Fruitwood and wrought iron furniture, faience pottery, tabletop accessories, architectural fragments, and garden urns—all tastefully displayed in period style settings—represent only some of the items available. CC: MC, V, AMEX.

EAST MORICHES

Affordable Antiques
533 Montauk Highway, P.O. Box 596 (11940)
(516) 878-5990
Hours: Fri–Tues, 11–5

This shop offers an eclectic selection of items that range from period furniture and accessories to 20th century collectibles such as iron, wicker, pottery, oak, American Indian, and whatever. In addition furniture stripping, refinishing, and restoration; painting cleaning and restoration; and the copying of old master paintings can be done. PR: Below retail. CC: No.

Almost Anything Shop
112 Montauk Highway (11940)
(516) 874-4600
Hours: Thurs–Mon, 9–4

As implied by its name, this shop carries a little bit of everything—furniture, bric-a-brac, tools, glass, smalls, gold and silver. PR: $$. CC: AMEX.

Hodge Podge Antique Emporium
242 Montauk Highway (11940)
(516) 281-9059 (before 10 and after 6)
Hours: Thur–Mon, 10–4

This shop contains an eclectic mix of antiques and collectibles from the 1800s to the 1950s. Furniture, brass, bric-a-brac, pottery, cast iron, and novelties are only some of the items available. PR: $. CC: No.

EAST QUOGUE

Respectable Collectibles
Montauk Highway (11942)
(516) 653-4372
Hours: Daily 11–6

This shop contains a varied selec-

A cast iron horse weathervane figure by the Rochester Iron Works of New Hampshire, late 19th century. *(Courtesy of Robert E. Kinnamen & Brian A. Ramaekers, Inc., Bridgehampton)*

tion of 19th and 20th century antiques that ranges from furniture to smalls. CC: AMEX.

EASTPORT

Arro Antiques

510 Main Street (11941)
(516) 325-2251
Hours: Daily, 10–5 or by appointment

Offering fine 18th through 20th century antiques, this shop contains a nice assortment of formal painted furniture, lighting devices and fixtures, country and formal French furniture, decorative smalls, and the unusual. CC: Coming.

Ragamuffins, The

486 Montauk Highway (11941)
(516) 325-1280
Hours: Wed–Mon, 11–5

In this shop's eclectic environment, examples of 18th century furniture and country furniture are found intermingled with Art Deco items. Decorative accessories include clocks, pottery, crystal, silver, and jewelry. PR: $$. CC: No.

FREEPORT

Orleans Lamps

68 West Merrick Road (11520)
(516) 623-8600
(516) 623-8601 fax
Hours: Mon–Fri, 10–6; Sat, 10–5

This business offers antique

chandeliers, lamps, globes, lampshades, and bases. Both a repair service and a full decorating service are available. CC: No.

GARDEN CITY

Prilik Galleries
753 Franklin Avenue (11530)
(516) 873-8888
Hours: Mon–Sat, 10–5

This dealer specializes in American and European timepieces, fine period furniture, fine art from the 17th through the 20th century, and decorative accessories. Restoration and conservation services for antique clocks, watches, fine art, and furniture including French polishing and gilding are offered. PR: $$$$$. CC: MC, V.

William Roberts Company
99 Seventh Street (11530)
(516) 741-0781
(516) 741-0781 fax
Hours: By appointment only

Horologic books, Sandwich glass from 1800 to 1850, and both early and rare clocks and maps are offered by this dealer. Mail and phone orders accepted. PR: $$$. CC: No.

GLEN COVE

Let Bygones Be Antiques
59 Sea Cliff Avenue (11542)
(516) 671-0404
Hours: Mon–Fri, 10:30–4 and by appointment

In a showroom and warehouse, one will find original restored Victorian-Deco wicker (painted and natural) complemented by quilts, hooked rugs, samplers, all types of American folk art, table lamps (signed and unsigned), porcelain, glass, and Art Glass. Appraisals can be done. A complete wicker restoration service is available. This shop is listed in **Living with Wicker**. CC: MC, V.

GREAT NECK

Kings Point Antique Shop Inc.
113 Middle Neck Road (11021)
(516) 487-2204
Hours: Tues–Sat, 10–5:30

This shop is filled with decorative accessories such as mirrors, clocks, lamps, small furniture, silver, and collectibles. PR: $$. CC: MC, V, AMEX.

Lawrence Levine Antiques Inc.
117 Middle Neck Road (11021)
(516) 487-4881
(516) 487-4813 fax
Hours: Mon–Sat, 9:30–5

In addition to dramatic decorative accessories, both large and small from various periods, this dealer offers custom work in wood, metal, stone, and glass done to specification from original designs to custom sizes and finishes. PR: Varied. CC: V, AMEX.

Sabi Antiques

112 Middle Neck Road (11021)
(516) 829-1330
Hours: Mon–Fri, 10–7; Sun, 12–7

This shop contains china, pottery, and various types of lighting fixtures from chandeliers to lamps. Repair and restoration services for china, pottery, and lighting devices are offered. CC: No.

Showcase Antiques

113 Middle Neck Road (11021)
(516) 487-7815
Hours: Tues–Sat, 10–5:30

This is the oldest and largest antique shop in Great Neck. In it, one will find decorative accessories, lighting fixtures, silver, furniture, clocks, and mirrors. PR: $$. CC: MC, V, AMEX.

Team Antiques

P.O. Box 1052 (11023)
(516) 487-1826
Hours: Mail order only, complimentary catalog by request

In business for 28 years, this dealer specializes in Tiffany, dealing in original items made by Louis C. Tiffany and Tiffany Studios such as glass, lamps, desk items, bronzes, and pottery. In addition, Art Glass of the period by Lalique, Galle, and Daum plus European pottery is also offered. Each item is guaranteed authentic. **Team Tiffany Treasures**, a catalog, is published by this dealer; a complimentary copy is available. PR: $100+. CC: No.

GREENPORT

Friendly Spirit Antiques

419 Main Street (11944)
(516) 477-8680
Hours: Tues–Sun, 11–5; Mon by chance

In addition to a large collection of working vintage radios, speakers, and horns, one will also discover sports memorabilia, postcards, and glass here. In addition to a repair service for vintage radios, tubes and other radio supplies can be purchased. PR: Moderate. CC: MC, V, AMEX, D.

Furniture Store Antiques

214 Front Street (11944)
(516) 477-2980
Hours: Daily 11–5

This dealer has had 15 years of experience specializing in pristine antique linens and lace, quality furniture, and unique vintage clothing from the turn of the century. A vast selection of costume jewelry, antique tools, and various collectibles is also offered. CC: MC, V, AMEX.

Kapell's Antiques

400 Front Street, P.O. Box 463 (11944)
(516) 477-0100
(516) 477-2488 fax
Hours: Daily 9–5

Ship models, paintings, country antiques, pottery, early tools and implements, folk art, fishing tackle, books, signs, advertising, cast iron, and grand pianos fill this shop. PR: $$$. CC: No.

Old School House Antiques
68320 Main Road, Route 25 (11944)
(516) 477-8122, 765-1053
Hours: Summer, Daily 11–6; winter, Thur–Mon, 12:30–4:30

In a country setting antiques, old furniture, Christmas and holiday items, old quilts, toys, clocks, and oil lamps are offered for sale. PR: $. CC: No.

HAMPTON BAYS

Dee's Caning & Wicker, Inc.
200 West Montauk Highway (11946)
(516) 728-4997
Hours: Fri–Sat & Mon–Tues, 10–12 & 1–5

Established in 1971, this shop has three floors of wicker, furniture, and collectibles. A repair and restoration service which includes stripping, weaving, rush, splint, spray painting, and refinishing is offered. In addition to giving appraisals, prop rental and consignment services are available. CC: Yes.

HUNTINGTON

Antique & Design Center of Cold Spring Hills, Ltd.
830 West Jericho Turnpike (11743)
(516) 673-4079
(516) 673-4079 fax
Hours: Mon–Sat, 10–6, Sun 12–5

English, French, Continental, and American furniture complemented by appropriate accessories and collectibles such as Oriental rugs are displayed in more than 8,000 square feet of space. A design service is available. CC: Yes.

Baycrest Antiques & Design (MD)
302 New York Avenue (11743)
(516) 427-7113
(516) 427-7123 fax
Hours: Mon–Sat, 11–6; Sun, 12–5

In addition to offering a full design service, these three antique dealers specialize in English and American furniture, decorative smalls, cut glass, porcelain, silver, and lighting. CC: MC, V.

Country-Tique, Inc.
229 Main Street (11743)
(516) 547-7000
(516) 547-7001 fax
Hours: Mon–Sat, 10–5:30

This shop specializes in pine English country antiques imported directly from Europe. In addition to unique accessories, other antiques and fine reproductions are available. PR: $$. CC: MC, V, AMEX, D.

Cracker Barrel Gallery, Inc.
17 Green Street (11743)
(516) 421-1400
Hours: Tues–Sun, 9–5

Occupying more than 6,000 square feet, this gallery which has been doing business since 1950 specializes in antique and fine used furniture, Oriental rugs, glass, porcelain, mirrors, and silver. Antique lighting fixtures, decorative smalls, and collectibles are also offered. Consignments are accepted. Furniture and lamp repair and restoration services are offered. CC: No.

Huntington Antique Center (MD)
231 Wall Street (11743)
(516) 549-0105
Hours: Tues–Sat, 10:30–5:30; Sun, 12–5

This is a group shop of fifteen dealers on three floors who feature 18th and 19th century furniture and a choice selection of accessories such as pottery, porcelain, country items, tea caddies, boxes, and silver in room settings. Chair caning and lamp rewiring are done. CC: MC, V.

Just Kids Nostalgia
310 New York Avenue (11743)
(516) 423-8449
(516) 423-4326 fax
Hours: Mon–Sat, 11–5

Catering to the kid in all of us, this shop offers a large selection of vintage toys, memorabilia, sports collectibles, records, movie posters, magazines, comics, and other items from the past. CC: MC, V.

Wall Street Antiques
27 Wall Street (11748)
(516) 351-6902
(516) 671-4603 fax
Hours: Open daily except Sun & Mon during the summer

In addition to offering directly imported French furniture and accessories, this shop also carries American furniture and textiles. PR: $$. CC: Visa

HUNTINGTON STATION

Browsery, The (MD)
449 East Jericho Turnpike (11746)
(516) 351-8893
Hours: Daily 11–5

In this huge co-op with 25 dealers in individual shops, one can find anything from trinkets to Tiffany. All periods of furniture and appropriate accessories and collectibles fill the various shops. PR: $$. CC: AMEX.

JAMESPORT

Long Island Heritage
Main Road, Box 326 (11947)
(516) 722-4905
Hours: Daily 1–5

This shop contains a general line of antiques and collectibles which includes fine china, pottery, glass, bird cages, dolls, doll carriages, lamps, paintings, chests and many interesting "one of a kind" items.

A unique astronomical regulator timepiece signed Howard & Davis Makers, Boston, ca. 1851. (*Courtesy Fanelli Antique Timepieces, Ltd., New York City*)

LOCUST VALLEY

Birch Hill Antiques
173 Birch Hill Road (11560)
(516) 676-9052
Hours: Tues–Sat, 11–5

The shop emphasizes furniture, mainly mahogany and mostly country. Hutches, dumbwaiters, serving tables, wash stands, drum tables, and bureaus are always in stock. In addition, one will always find mirrors and paintings of either shore scenes, portraits, or Hudson Valley scenes in stock. PR: $$$. CC: No.

Early & Co., Inc. Antiques
53 Birch Hill Road (11560)
(516) 676-4800
Hours: Tues–Sat, 11–4

Directly imported 18th and 19th

century French furniture and accessories, painted armoires, beautiful mirrors, cages, pottery, and paintings can be purchased in this shop. PR: $$. CC: No.

Epel & Company Inc.
108 Forest Avenue (11560)
(516) 676-7695
(516) 759-4653 fax
Hours: Tues–Sat, 11–5

Established in 1986, this shop specializes in 18th and 19th century English furniture in exemplary condition. Decorative smalls, mirrors, and paintings which complement the warmth of this atypical collection of fine furniture are also offered. CC: No.

Heisig Antiques Ltd.
Plaza 5 (11560)
(516) 674-4090
Hours: Mon–Sat, 11–5

In addition to offering garden fountains, statues, and urns, this shop also features country French, English, and American furniture. CC: No.

Little Acorn, The
294 Forest Avenue (11560)
(212) 676-7488, 759-1325
Hours: 10:30–5:30, almost every day

Established in 1979, this shop contains furniture in old paint and in as found condition, old and new rugs, costume jewelry, and smalls. Cobalt blue gift glass and doorstops are also stocked. Consignments are accepted. PR: $. CC: No.

Oster-Jensen Antiques, Ltd.
86 Birch Hill Road (11560)
(516) 676-5454
Hours: Wed–Sat, 12–5 or by appointment

This shop contains an interesting and large selection of fine furniture from the 1780s to the 1880s from Europe and America that is either formal or country in design. PR: $$. CC: No.

Raymond B. Knight Corp.
121 Birch Hill Road (11560)
(516) 671-7046
(516) 759-0059 fax
Hours: Mon–Sat, 9–6

This shop offers quality furniture including 18th and 19th century walnut and mahogany English furniture and 18th and 19th century Chinese Export porcelain. The owners have been providing furniture repair and restoration services for more than thirty years. CC: No.

MINEOLA

Wendan Clock Workshop, Inc.
321 Willis Avenue (11501)
(516) 741-4410
Hours: Tues–Sat, 10–5 and by appointment

In addition to offering a wide selection of antique clocks for sale, this dealer specializes in the repair and restoration of tall case, mantel, and wall clocks. PR: Moderate. CC: No. LOC: L.I.

Expressway Exit 37 South for two and four tenth miles.

MONTAUK

Montauk Antiques and Art Gallery

649 Montauk Highway, 2nd floor (11954)
(516) 668-3839
Hours: Summer, Thur–Tues, 11–5; winter, Sat–Sun, 11–5

In more than 1,400 square feet, one will find American furniture and paintings, blue decorated stoneware, and various antique accessories. PR:$$$. CC: No.

NORTHPORT

Antique Freaks, The

146 Main Street (11768)
(516) 262-3347
Hours: Mon–Sat, 11–5; Sun, 12–5; call for summer hours

This fun place to browse and shop offers an eclectic selection of antiques and collectibles, predominantly from 1890-1930, and features refinished oak furniture, old hand-made quilts, early dolls and toys, china, glass, and decorative smalls. CC: MC, V, AMEX.

Glass Slipper Antiques

245 Main Street (11768)
(516) 757-8538
Hours: Daily 11–4:30 except closed Wed & Sun

Quilts, crocheted items, porcelain, cut glass, pottery, baskets, jewelry, silver, small furniture, and oil lamps fill this shop. CC: No.

Harbor Lights Antiques

110 Main Street (11768)
(516) 757-4572
Hours: Mon–Fri, 10:30–5:30; Sat, 10–6; Sun, 11:30–5:30

In addition to a fabulous selection of antique and collectible jewelry, laces, linens, and curios, one will also find mirrors, prints, small furniture, and vintage apparel and accessories. PR: Very Reasonable. CC: MC, V.

Scarlett's

166 Main Street (11768)
(516) 754-0004
Hours: Mon–Sat, 11–5 except closed Wed; Sun 12–5

Upon entering this shop, one will find all types of Victorian antiques—parlor furniture, love seats, sofas, chairs, desks, armoires, side boards, beds, and more. Decorative accessories including lamps, glassware, silver, oils, mirrors, and framed prints are also available. CC: MC, V, AMEX.

Somewhere In Time Antiques (MD)

162 Main Street (11768)
(516) 757-4148
Hours: Mon–Sat, 11–5; Sun, 12–8

This multidealer shop offers a wide variety of antiques, collectibles, jewelry, and decorator items. A complete line of plate and cup & saucer stands, watch and collectible domes, and doll stands is available. PR: Every. CC: MC, V, AMEX.

OLD BETHPAGE

Filmart Galleries

P.O. Box 128 (11804)
(516) 935-8493
(516) 822-5323 fax
Hours: 10–6:30

This business offers a wide variety of vintage, contemporary, and limited edition animated art. Original clay models and sets actually used on the classic Gumby film and television productions are also available. This gallery is the exclusive representative for Gumby, The Lockhorns, and Krazy Kat. All types of cartoon art are sold, bought, and consigned. Dealer inquires are invited. CC: MC, V, D.

PORT JEFFERSON

Antiques at Trader's Cove

230 Trader's Cove (11774)
(516) 331-2261
Hours: Tues–Sat, 12–5

This shop specializes in the rental and sale of antique and vintage costumes and props from the medieval to the modern era. Although the accent is on weddings, items are available for commercials, film, theater, book covers, and theme parties. CC: No.

Discover Yesterday Antiques

31C East Broadway (11777)
(516) 473-1149
Hours: Daily 12–5

Featured in **Victoria Magazine,** this shop specializes in Victoriana with an accent on feminine accoutrements such as pre-1950s clothing, museum quality lace and linens, and quality costume jewelry. Also featured is an extensive collection of decorative smalls: prints, porcelain, and the like. CC: MC, V, AMEX.

PORT WASHINGTON

Cat Lady Antiques, The

164 Main Street (11050)
(516) 883-4334
Hours: Tues–Sat, 12–5

Victorian furniture and accessories, estate jewelry, Victorian through Art Deco wicker and garden furnishings, fine silver, and a nice selection of chandeliers fill this shop. And, of course, there are cat collectibles for sale. PR: $$$$. CC: MC, V.

Giles Antiques

287 Main Street (11050)
(516) 883-1104
Hours: Tues–Sat, 12–6; Sun, 1–6

This dealer offers country furniture and appropriate accessories. PR: $$. CC: No.

Mickey Mikiter
287 Main Street (11050)
(516) 944-8767
Hours: Tues–Sat, 12–6; Sun, 1–6

In addition to carrying a general line of antiques, this dealer specializes in Art Glass, old glass, and silver. PR: $$. CC: No.

ROCKVILLE CENTRE

Treasures in the Attic
528 Merrick Road (11570)
(516) 764-2580
Hours: Tues–Sat, 11–5

This shop is filled with fine oak furniture, painted pieces, primitives, and Victoriana to enhance the home. It presents a nice mixed look from formal to country complemented by beautiful small decorative accent pieces. CC: AMEX, D.

ROSLYN

Homestead House
1515 Old Northern Boulevard (11576)
(516) 621-4140
Hours: Mon–Sat, 10–5

Established in 1970, this is one of Long Island's largest antique and consignment shops. Although decorative smalls, English and American furniture, lighting fixtures, and porcelain are always in stock, many items range from the sublime to the ridiculous. PR: $$$. CC: No.

Joan Bogart
1392 Old Northern Boulevard (11576)
(516) 621-2454
Hours: By chance or appointment

This dealer specializes in high style 19th century American furniture: Empire, Rococo, Gothic, and Renaissance. A large selection of chandeliers and Argand and Astral lamps is complemented by an equally impressive selection of majolica, parian, American silverplate, and 19th century porcelain. CC: No.

SAG HARBOR

Fisher's
Main & Spring (11963)
(516) 725-0006
(516) 725-0516 fax
Hours: Daily 10–5

On display in five showrooms and a large warehouse, which together occupy more than 20,000 square feet, is Long Island's largest source of fine European pine furniture and accessories. Realistically priced, these pieces can be shipped anywhere. PR: Mid. CC: All Major.

Sag Harbor Antique Shop
Madison Street, P.O. Box 1500 (11963)
(516) 725-1732
Hours: Fri–Mon, 10–5

Established in 1964, this business specializes in period furniture, folk art, decorative smalls, and architectural antiques. PR: $$$. CC: No.

Sage Street Antiques
Corner of Route 114 & Sage Street (11963)
(516) 725-4036
Hours: Sat, 11–5; Sun 1–5

In four rooms of an 1850s house, one will find American country furniture, appropriate accessories, kitchenware, lamps, fireplace equipment, and rugs. A separate building is overflowing with inexpensive do-it-yourself furniture and yard sale finds. PR: $$. CC: No.

Time Machine, The
Main Street, in the Shopping Cove (11963)
(516) 725-5632
Hours: Summer, Fri–Sun, 12–5 or by appointment; winter, Sat–Sun, 12–5

Since 1988, this shop has been selling anything interesting at the right price. Affordable small furniture, rugs, old leather bound books, and china are only some of the items that one will find displayed. PR: $. CC: AMEX.

Victorian Heart, The
150 Main Street, Box 1446 (11963)
(516) 725-4102
Hours: Daily 11–5 except closed Tues & Wed after Labor Day

This brick floored browserie offers a dainty collection of jewelry, linens, and vintage items. PR: $. CC: MC, V.

Young America
Main Street, opposite the American Hotel (11963)
(516) 725-4377
Hours: Daily 9–6 except closed January or call

This shop is known for its fine offerings of folk art, decorative smalls, and furniture. Antique marine ship models, ice fishing decoys, stoneware, figural cast and wrought iron, vintage jewelry, and duck decoys are only some of the items that are available. PR: $$$. CC: MC, V.

SAYVILLE

Sayville Antique Center
111-113 Railroad Avenue (11782)
(516) 589-2405
Hours: Daily 11–6

This 3,000 square foot shop contains a general line of antiques and collectibles with an emphasis on Victorian furniture. Pottery, kitchen items, cast iron, linen, quilts, advertising, toys, military items, glass, and ephemera are also on hand. CC: MC, V.

SHELTER ISLAND

Home Port Antiques

9 South Midway Road (11964)
(516) 749-2373
Hours: Mon–Sat, 10–5; Sun, 12–5; Jan–May by chance or appointment

In addition to specializing in early American pressed and pattern glass, this shop also contains a unique selection of furniture, pottery, nauticals, linen, and kitchenware. PR: $$. CC: MC, V, AMEX.

SHIRLEY

Antique Center at Shirley (MD)

648 Montauk Highway (11967)
(516) 281-1801
Hours: Daily 11–5

Eighteen dealers offer a large variety of antiques and collectibles at affordable prices. This interesting shop has everything from dolls, toys, and games to jewelry, sterling silver, and paintings. PR: $$. CC: No.

SHOREHAM

Chinalai Tribal Antiques and Interiors Ltd.

P.O. Box 815 (11786)
(516) 821-4272
(516) 821-4272 fax
Hours: By appointment only or call to be placed on mailing list for shows

These dealers offer fine quality ethnographic antiques from mainland Southeast Asia: Thailand, Burma (Myanmar), Laos (Laos PDR), and Cambodia (Kampuchea). Textiles, costumes, silver jewelry and objects, furniture, sculpture, religious and spiritual artifacts, and architectural and interior ornaments and elements are always in stock. PR: $$$. CC: MC, V, AMEX.

SOUTHAMPTON

Another Time Antiques

765 Hill Street, Old Montauk Highway (11968)
(516) 283-6542
(516) 283-8456 fax
Hours: Thur–Tues, 10–5; Sun, 11–6 or by appointment

This eclectic shop, which is noted for carrying 19th and 20th century furniture, country antiques, kitchen collectibles, wicker and wrought iron, also contains a large selection of collectibles, Depression glass, pottery, china, glassware, paintings, and prints. A separate 190 square foot section of the shop is set aside for toys and trains, and an adjacent barn is full of furniture and architectural items in as found condition. PR: $$. CC: MC,V.

Arthur T. Kalaher, Inc.

24 Jobs Lane (11968)
(516) 283-6578
Hours: Daily 10–6 except Sun, 12–5

Fine 19th century American and

European oil painting, many by well-listed artists, are the specialty of this dealer. Antique European mahogany furniture, silver, and bronzes can also be purchased. PR: $$$. CC: V, MC, AMEX, D.

Bob Petrillo's Browserie
30 Main Street (11968)
(516) 283-6560
Hours: Mon–Sat, 11–5:30; Sun 12–6

On two floors, one will find English, French, and American furniture such as tables and chests of drawers from the 18th and 19th century. Appropriate accessories, Orientals, lamps, and collectibles can also be found. CC: No.

Croft Antiques
11 South Main Street (11968)
(516) 283-6445
Hours: June–August, Daily 11–5; Fri–Mon, 11–5 for the remainder of the year

In addition to a large selection of period and decorative accessories, this shop, which was established in 1978, carries a fine selection of English period furniture, mainly hardwoods in both country and formal styles, which is ideal for all types of decor. PR: $$$. CC: No.

Dower House Antiques
68 Main Street (11968)
(516) 283-5665
(516) 287-0037 fax
Hours: Oct 1 through April 30; Fri–Mon, 10–5; May 1 through Sept 30; Daily 10-5:30

English and Continental furniture of the 19th century along with decorative smalls such as porcelain, glass, textiles, silver, and garden ornaments can always be found in this shop. In addition, there is a large selection of lamps and lamp shades.
PR: $$$$. CC: MC, V, AMEX.

Elaine's Antiques & Decorative Accessories
9 Main Street (11968)
(516) 287-3276
Hours: Mon–Sat, 10–6; Sun, 12–5

A unique blend of French country furniture and hand carved teak window mirrors and cabinets from Indonesia will be found in this shop. In addition, needlepoint pillows, placemats, beeswax candles, and other accessories are offered. PR: $$. CC: MC, V, AMEX, D.

Hampton Antiques and Jerry's Caning & Wicker Repair
116 North Sea Road (11968-2004)
(516) 283-3436
Hours: Daily 12–5

Occupying two floors of a 19th century Bowden barn, this business features finely restored museum quality wicker. Chair caning and rush, splint, and wicker repairs are done at reasonable prices. PR: Reasonable. CC: No.

Morgan MacWhinnie Antiques
520 North Sea Road (11968)
(516) 283-3366
Hours: Call ahead

This shop carries a large stock of 18th century American furniture with appropriate accessories such as andirons and mirrors. Some 19th century Federal furniture is also in stock. PR: $$$$. CC: No.

Pine Street Antiques
89 Pine Street (11968)
(516) 283-6339
Hours: Thur–Sat, 10–5; Sun, 1–5; Mon, 10–5

This shop is noted for its English, French, and Scandinavian furniture and 19th century paintings. PR: Upper. CC: No.

Prints Charming, Inc.
70 Main Street (11968)
(516) 287-1919
Hours: Mon–Fri, 10–5:30; Sat, 10–6; Sun, 12–5

This business specializes in 19th century engravings, lithographs, and chromo lithographs on a wide range of topics—botanicals, dogs, hunting, New York State views, local views, marine, sporting, and maps. Custom framing with French matting can be done. And, a wide range of frame samples is available. PR: $$. CC: V, MC, AMEX.

Second Chance
45 Main Street (11968)
(516) 283-2988
(516) 283-2988 fax
Hours: Mon–Fri, 10–5; Sat, 10–5:30; Sun, 12–5

Conducting business since 1980, this dealer specializes in china, glassware, silver, linen, decorative accessories, toys, and collectibles. Consignments are accepted. Tag sales and appraisals can be done. PR: $$. CC: V, MC, AMEX.

Things I Love, The
51A Jobs Lane (11968)
(516) 287-2756
(516) 324-1374 fax
Hours: Daily 11–5:30 except closed Wednesday

This shop contains a unique and eclectic selection of 19th century antiques and art plus 20th century collectibles. One will always find painted furniture, Art Glass, paintings, prints, jewelry, lamps, and ornamental objects ready to take home. PR: $$$$. CC: AMEX.

Tom's Quilts
3 White Oak Lane (11968)
(516) 726-6881
Hours: By appointment only

At any given time, this dealer has more than 200 antique quilts and tops for sale. Some are as old as the 1860s; many are from the 1930s. The selection, which includes Amish and Mennonite quilts, runs from full to crib size. Prices for quilts start at about $150 and for tops at $40. CC: No.

SOUTHOLD

Long Island Doll Hospital & Jan Davis Antiques
45395 Main Road (11971)
(516) 765-2379
Hours: Daily 11–5 except closed Wed

In a restored 1856 country store,

Grouping of figural folk art from carved dolls to articulated dancing figures, 19th century. *(Courtesy American Primitive Gallery, New York City)*

one will find quality merchandise at affordable prices. Furniture, glassware, and dolls are only some of the items for sale. And this is the place to come for expert doll repairs and appraisals. CC: MC, V, AMEX.

Nostalgia Collectibles
Main Road at Ackerly Pond (11971)
(516) 765-5117
Hours: Fri–Sun, 11–4 and by chance

This shop offers an interesting and diverse assortment of sports memorabilia, Art Deco, Art Nouveau, Disney, country collectibles, Depression glass, World's Fair collectibles, and memorabilia from the 1950s and 1960s.

Pickwick Shop, The
45475 Main Road (11971)
(516) 765-3158
Hours: Thur–Mon, 11:30–5:30

Besides specializing in cut glass, crystal, china, and pottery, this shop also contains jewelry, sterling silver, paintings, postcards, books, and collectibles. PR: $. CC: MC, V.

Willow Hill Antiques
48405 Main Road, P.O. Box 1048 (11971-0931)
(516) 765-4124
Hours: Thur–Mon, 11–5

A unique selection of antiques, furniture, armoires, pottery, glassware, porcelain, collectibles, and architectural items will be found in this shop. PR: $$$. CC: No.

ST. JAMES

Gail's Treasures & Trifles

408 North Country Road
(516) 862-6526
Hours: Sat–Sun, 10–5; weekdays by chance or appointment

In five rooms, this general line shop offers mahogany and oak furniture, glass, pottery, dolls, and advertising; all at reasonable prices. CC: MC, V.

WAINSCOTT

Georgica Creek Antiques

Montauk Highway, P.O. Box 877 (11975)
(516) 537-0333
Hours: June 1st–Oct 1st, Daily 11–5; Oct 2nd–May 31st, Thur–Mon, 12–5

The owner of this very large shop has filled it with larger overscale pieces of furniture, decorative lamps and fixtures, ancestral portraits, quilts, and Oriental rugs. Architectural elements, garden furniture, weathervanes, ship models, and bird houses also fill this shop, which always carries both eclectic and classical pieces. PR: $$$$. CC: AMEX.

Richard Camp Antiques

Montauk Highway, Box 250 (11975)
(516) 537-0330
Hours: Daily 10–5

This shop carries English pine furniture. CC: MC, V.

WATERMILL

Collectibles Antiques

978 Montauk Highway (11976)
(516) 726-4885
Hours: Daily 10–5:30

Located in a 200 year old house, this shop presents English and American 19th and 20th century furniture and accessories, china, crystal, paintings, etchings, brass, Victoriana, wicker, lamps, chandeliers, fireplace equipment, and gift items in room settings. CC: MC, V, AMEX.

Succotash Oddments

Montauk Highway (11976)
(516) 726-6411
Hours: Thur–Tues, 10–5

This shop specializes in "fun" antiques and collectibles. One can expect to find carnival, amusement park, circus, theatrical, and window display collectibles as well as folk art, jewelry, advertising clocks and signs, and 1950s furniture and accessories. PR: $$. CC: No.

WESTHAMPTON

Ambiance Antiques, Ltd.

Montauk Highway and Jaegger Lane (11977)
(516) 288-6930
Hours: Daily, 11–5

This shop carries a large collection of different styles of furni-

ture such as French country and English pine in addition to fine bronze sconces, chandeliers, lamps, and other accessory pieces. Unusual pieces of wrought iron furniture are also a specialty.
PR: $$. CC: All.

WESTHAMPTON BEACH

Joyce Settel Ltd.
90 Main Street (11978)
(516) 288-0436
Hours: April–Sept, Daily 11–5; after Sept by chance or appointment

Decorated to make you feel as if you are walking into a home, this charming shop has room settings where you can buy anything in sight. English and American decorative smalls, chintz-ware, beaded and needlepoint pillows, paper-maché boxes, tole trays, carltonware, and candlesticks are offered. In a backroom, one will find American cookie jars, kitchenware, and English novelty teapots from the 1930s.
PR: Moderate to High. CC: All.

Specialty Areas—Long Island

Advertising
Antiques at Bayport, Bayport, p. 114
Gail's Treasures & Trifles, St. James, p. 138
Somewhere In Time Antiques, Northport, p. 130
Succotash Oddments, Watermill, p. 138

American Indian
Affordable Antiques, East Moriches, p. 122
Barbara Trujillo, Bridgehampton, p. 117
R. E. Kinnaman & B.A. Ramaekers Inc., Bridgehampton, p. 118

Americana
Long Island Heritage, Jamesport, p. 127
Sage Street Antiques, Sag Harbor, p. 133
Sterling & Hunt, Bridgehampton, p. 118
Urban Archaeology, Bridgehampton, p. 118
Young America, Sag Harbor, p. 133

Antiquities
Nostalgia Collectibles, Southold, p. 137
Tempus Fugit Antiques-Bay Gallery, Babylon, p. 113

Architectural Antiques
Architrove, East Hampton, p. 120
Georgia Creek Antiques, Wainscott, p. 138
Sag Harbor Antique Shop, Sag Harbor, p. 133
Urban Archaeology, Bridgehampton, p. 118
Willow Hill Antiques, Southold, p. 137

Art Deco
Christina Borg, Inc., East Hampton, p. 121
John Salibello Antiques, Bridgehampton, p. 118
L. Calderon Pink Wagon Antiques, Bellmore, p. 116
Lawrence Levine Antiques Inc., Great Neck, p. 124

Art Glass
Mickey Mikiter, Port Washington, p. 132
Team Antiques, Great Neck, p. 125

Cartoon Art
Filmart Galleries, Old Bethpage, p. 131

Cast Iron
Abbott & Jackson Inc., East Hampton, p. 120
Affordable Antiques, East Moriches, p. 122
Georgia Creek Antiques, Wainscott, p. 138
Hodge Podge Antique Emporium, East Moriches, p. 122
Kapell's Antiques, Greenport, p. 125
Sayville Antique Center, Sayville, p. 133

China
Second Chance, Southampton, p. 136

Chinese Export Porcelain
Raymond B. Knight Corp., Locust Valley, p. 129
Valdemar F. Jacobsen Antiques, Cold Spring Harbor, p. 119

Circus & Amusement Park Collectibles
Succotash Oddments, Watermill, p. 138

Clocks/Watches
Antiques & Old Lace, Cutchogue, p. 120
Antiques by Addie, Bellmore, p. 115
Bernard's Antiques, Bellmore, p. 116
Lyman Thorne Enterprises, Ltd., Cold Spring Harbor, p. 119
Old School House Antiques, Greenport, p. 126
Prilik Galleries, Garden City, p. 124
Ray's Antiques, Bellmore, p. 116
Wendan Clock Workshop, Inc., Mineola, p. 129
William Roberts Company, Garden City, p. 124
Yankee Trader Antiques Inc., Baldwin, p. 113

Coca Cola
Yankee Trader Antiques Inc., Baldwin, p. 113

Collectibles
Abbott & Jackson Inc., East Hampton, p. 120
A & D Ctr of Cold Spring Hills Ctr, Huntington, p. 126
Antique Pavilion, Bellmore, p. 115
Antiques & Old Lace, Cutchogue, p. 120
Bob Petnillo's Brouserie, Southampton, p. 135
Cracker Barrel Gallery Inc., Huntington, p. 126

Country Junque Shop, Bayport, p. 114
Dee's Caning & Wicker,Inc., Hampton Bays, p. 126
Filmart Galleries, Old Bethpage, p. 131
Friendly Spirits Antiques, Greenport, p. 125
Kings Point Antique Shop Inc, Great Neck, p. 124
Pickwick Shop, The, Southold, p. 137
Showcase Antiques, Great Neck, p. 125
Succotash Oddments, Watermill, p. 138
Victorian Heart, The, Sag Harbor, p. 133

Cookie Jars
John Salibello Antiques, Bridgehampton, p. 118
Joyce Settel Ltd., Westhampton, p. 139

Country Antiques
Country Tique Inc., Huntington, p. 126
English Country Antiques, Bridgehampton, p. 117
Fisher's, Sag Harbor, p. 132
Hamptique Antiques, East Hampton, p. 121
Huntington Antiques Center, Huntington, p. 127
LI Doll Hospital/Jan Davis Antiques, Southold, p. 136
Old School House Antiques, Greenport, p. 126
Ragamuffins, The, East Port, p. 123
Respectable Collectibles, East Quogue, p. 122
Victory Garden, Ltd., East Hampton, p. 122
Willow Hill Antiques, Southold, p. 137

Decorative Smalls
Almost Anything Shop, East Moriches, p. 122
Ambiance Antiques Ltd., Westhampton, p. 138
Antique Freaks, The, Northport, p. 130
Antique Parlor, Bellmore, p. 115
Arro Antiques, Eastport, p. 123
Baycrest Antiques & Design, Huntington, p. 126
Collectibles Antiques, Watermill, p. 138
Cracker Barrel Gallery Inc, Huntington, p. 126
Cugino Antiques, Cedarhurst, p. 119
Elaine's, Southampton, p. 135
End Shop, The, Bay Shore, p. 114
Epel & Company Inc, Locust Valley, p. 129
Home Port Antiques, Shelter Island, p. 134
Homestead House, Roslyn, p. 132
John Salibello Antiques, Bridgehampton, p. 118

Depression Glass

Dolls

Ephemera

Firearms

Fireplace Equipment

Folk Art

Sterling & Hunt, Bridgehampton, p. 118
Succotash Oddments, Watermill, p. 138
Valdemar F. Jacobsen Antiques, Cold Spring Harbor, p. 119
Young America, Sag Harbor, p. 133

Frames

Harry's Antiques, Bay Shore, p. 114

French Antiques

Arro Antiques, Eastport, p. 123
Bernard's Antiques, Bellmore, p. 116
Cugino Antiques, Cedarhurst, p. 119
Raymond B. Knight Corp, Locust Valley, p. 129
Rene's Antiques, East Hampton, p. 122
Victory Garden, Ltd., East Hampton, p. 122
Wall Street Antiques, Huntington, p. 127

Furniture/American

Abbott & Jackson Inc., East Hampton, p. 120
Affordable Antiques, East Moriches, p. 122
Antiques Center of East Hampton, East Hampton, p. 120
Architrove, East Hampton, p. 120
Baycrest Antiques & Design, Huntington, p. 126
Beach Plum Antiques, Bridgehampton, p. 117
Birch Hill Antiques, Locust Valley, p. 128
Bob Petnillo's Brouserie, Southampton, p. 135
Georgia Creek Antiques, Wainscott, p. 138
Giles Antiques, Port Washington, p. 131
Heisig Antiques Ltd., Locust Valley, p. 129
Homestead House, Roslyn, p. 132
Joan Bogart, Roslyn, p. 132
Lyman Thorne Enterprises, Ltd., Cold Spring Harbor, p. 119
Montauk Antiques & Art Gallery, Montauk, p. 130
Morgan Mac Whinnie Antiques, Southampton, p. 135
Oster-Jensen Antiques Ltd., Locust Valley, p. 129
Prilik Galleries, Garden City, p. 124
R. E. Kinnaman & B. A. Ramaekers, Inc., Bridgehampton, p. 118
Raymond B.Knight Corp, Locust Valley, p. 129
Sag Harbor Antique Shop, Sag Harbor, p. 133
Scarlett's, Northport, p. 130
Tempus Fugit Antiques-Bay Gallery, Babylon, p. 113
Time Machine The, Sag Harbor, p. 133

Valdemar F. Jacobsen Antiques, Cold Spring Harbor, p. 119
Wall St Antiques, Huntington, p. 127
Yankee Trader Antiques Inc., Baldwin, p. 113
Young America, Sag Harbor, p. 133

Furniture/Continental

Architrove, East Hampton, p. 120
Arthur T. Kalaher Inc., Southampton, p. 134
Birch Hills Antiques, Locust Valley, p. 128
Bob Petnillo's Brouserie, Southampton, p. 135
Christina Borg, Inc., East Hampton, p. 121
Dower House Antiques, Southampton, p. 135
John Salibello Antiques, Bridgehampton, p. 118
Lars Bolander Ltd., East Hampton, p. 121
Lawrence Levine Antiques Inc., Great Neck, p. 124
Oster-Jensen Antiques Ltd., Locust Valley, p. 129
Pine Street Antiques, Southampton, p. 136
Prilik Galleries, Garden City, p. 124
Rene's Antiques, East Hampton, p. 122

Furniture/English

Abbott & Jackson Inc., East Hampton, p. 120
Balasses House Antiques, Amagansett, p. 113
Baycrest Antiques & Design, Huntington, p. 126
Birch Hill Antiques, Locust Valley, p. 128
Bob Petnillo's Brouserie, Southampton, p. 135
Country Tique Inc., Huntington, p. 126
Croft Antiques, Southampton, p. 135
Dower House Antiques, Southampton, p. 135
English Country Antiques, Bridgehampton, p. 117
Epel & Company Inc., Locust Valley, p. 129
Georgica Creek Antiques, Wainscott, p. 138
Giles Antiques, Port Washington, p. 131
Heisig Antiques Ltd., Locust Valley, p. 129
Homestead House, Roslyn, p. 132
Lars Bolander, Ltd., East Hampton, p. 121
Lyman Thorne Enterprises, Ltd., Cold Spring Harbor, p. 119
Oster-Jensen Antiques Ltd., Locust Valley, p. 129
Pine Street Antiques, Southampton, p. 136
Raymond B. Knight Corp, Locust Valley, p. 129
Rene's Antiques, East Hampton, p. 122
Richard Camp Antiques, Wainscott, p. 138
Valdemar F. Jacobsen Antiques, Cold Spring Harbor, p. 119

Furniture/French

Furniture/General

Furniture/Mahogany

Furniture/Oak

Willow Hill Antiques, Southold, p. 137

Furniture/Painted

Antiques Center of East Hampton, East Hampton, p. 120
Arro Antiques, Eastport, p. 123
Beach Plum, Bridgehampton, p. 117
Hamptique Antiques, East Hampton, p. 121
Little Acorn, The, Locust Valley, p. 129
Montauk Antiques & Art Gallery, Montauk, p. 130
Nellies of Amagansett, Amagansett, p. 113
Ruby Beets, Bridgehampton, p. 118
Things I Love, Southampton, p. 136
Treasures in the Attic, Rockville Centre, p. 132

Furniture/Pine

Country Junque Shop, Bayport, p. 114
Country Tique Inc., Huntington, p. 126
English Country Antiques, Bridgehampton, p. 117
Fisher's, Sag Harbor, p. 132
Giles Antiques, Port Washington, p. 131
Mill Pond Antiques, Bridgehampton, p. 118
Richard Camp Antiques, Wainscott, p. 138

Furniture/Victorian

Antique Freaks, The, Northport, p. 130
Antique Parlor, Bellmore, p. 115
Austern's, Bellmore, p. 115
Cat Lady, The, Port Washington, p. 131
Respectable Collectibles, East Quogue, p. 122
Scarlett's, Northport, p. 130
Somewhere In Time Antiques, Northport, p. 130
Treasures in the Attic, Rockville Centre, p. 132

Furniture/Walnut

Croft Antiques, Southampton, p. 135
Raymond B. Knight Corp., Locust Valley, p. 129

Garden Accessories

Architrove, East Hampton, p. 120
Cat Lady Antiques, The, Port Washington, p. 131
Collectibles Antiques, Water Mill, p. 138
Heisig Antiques Ltd., Locust Valley, p. 129
Sage Street Antiques, Sag Harbor, p. 133

Urban Archaeology, Bridgehampton, p. 118
Victory Garden, Ltd., East Hampton, p. 122

Glass

Almost Anything Shop, East Moriches, p. 122
Another Time Antiques, Southampton, p. 134
Antique Center at Shirley, Shirley, p. 134
Baycrest Antiques & Design, Huntington, p. 126
Browsery, The, Huntington Station, p. 127
Carriage Trade, The, Cedarhurst, p. 119
Dower House Antiques, Southampton, p. 135
Elaine's Room Antiques, East Hampton, p. 121
Gail's Treasures & Trifles, St. James, p. 138
Glass Slipper Antiques, Northport, p. 130
Legacy Antiques Inc., Bay Shore, p. 114
LI Doll Hospital/Jan Davis Antiques, Southold, p. 136
Mickey Mikiter, Port Washington, p. 132
Mill Pond Antiques, Bridgehampton, p. 118
Nostalgia Collectibles, Southold, p. 137
Second Chance, Southampton, p. 136
Things I Love, The, Southampton, p. 136
Victorian Heart, The, Sag Harbor, p. 133
William Roberts Company, Garden City, p. 124
Willow Hill Antiques, Southold, p. 137

Holiday Collectibles

Barbara Trujillo, Bridgehampton, p. 117
Country Junque Shop, Bayport, p. 114
Old School House Antiques, Greenport, p. 126

Hooked Rugs

Let Bygones Be Antiques, Glen Cove, p. 124

Jewelry

Antique Pavilion, Bellmore, p. 115
Antiques Center of East Hampton, East Hampton, p. 120
Country Junque Shop, Bayport, p. 114
End Shop, The, Bay Shore, p. 114
Faces Antiques, East Hampton, p. 121
Joanne's Antiques, Bay Shore, p. 114
Ragamuffins, The, East Port, p. 123
Second Chance, Southampton, p. 136
Succotash Oddments, Watermill, p. 138

Jewelry/Costume

Jewelry/Estate

Kitchen Collectibles

Lace & Linen

Lighting Devices & Fixtures

Majolica

Maps

Militaria
Ray's Antiques, Bellmore, p. 116

Mirrors
Ambiance Antiques Ltd., Westhampton, p. 138
Antiques Center of East Hampton, East Hampton, p. 120
Cugino Antiques, Cedarhurst, p. 119
Early & Co., Inc. Antiques, Locust Valley, p. 128
Elaine's, Southampton, p. 121
Epel & Company Inc., Locust Valley, p. 129
Harbor Lights Antiques, Northport, p. 130
Hodge Podge Antique Emporium, East Moriches, p. 122
Mill Pond Antiques, Bridgehampton, p. 118

Movie Memorabilia
Filmart Galleries, Old Bethpage, p. 131
Just Kids Nostalgia, Huntington, p. 127

Nautical/Marine
Kapell's Antiques, Greenport, p. 125
Lyman Thorne Enterprises, Ltd., Cold Spring Harbor, p. 119
Ray's Antiques, Bellmore, p. 116
Young America, Sag Harbor, p. 133

Needlework
Elaine's, Southampton, p. 121
Grand Acquisitor, The, East Hampton, p. 121

Oriental Arts
Carls Antiques Ltd., Cedarhurst, p. 119
Rene's Antiques, East Hampton, p. 122

Oriental Carpets/Rugs
A & D Ctr of Cold Spring Hills Ctr, Huntington, p. 126
Cracker Barrel Gallery Inc., Huntington, p. 126
Joanne's Antiques, Bay Shore, p. 114
Tempus Fugit Antiques-Bay Gallery, Babylon, p. 113

Paintings
Antiques by Addie, Bellmore, p. 115
Arthur T. Kalaher Inc., Southampton, p. 134
Barbara Trujillo, Bridgehampton, p. 117
Birch Hill Antiques, Locust Valley, p. 128

Epel & Company Inc., Locust Valley, p. 129
Hamptique Antiques, East Hampton, p. 121
Kapell's Antiques, Greenport, p. 125
Lars Bolander Ltd., East Hampton, p. 121
Mill Pond Antiques, Bridgehampton, p. 118
Montauk Antiques & Art Gallery, Montauk, p. 130
Pine Street Antiques, Southampton, p. 136
Prilik Galleries, Garden City, p. 124
R. E. Kinnaman & B.A. Ramaekers, Inc., Bridgehampton, p. 118
Sterling & Hunt, Bridgehampton, p. 118
Tempus Fugit Antiques-Bay Gallery, Babylon, p. 113
Things I Love, The, Southampton, p. 136
Valdemar F. Jacobsen Antiques, Cold Spring Harbor, p. 119

Political Memorabilia
Nostalgia Collectibles, Southold, p. 137

Porcelain
Antique Center at Shirley, Shirley, p. 134
Antiques at East Marion, Bridgehamton, p. 116
Antiques by Addie, Bellmore, p. 115
Antiques Center of East Hampton, East Hampton, p. 120
Babylon Antiques Shoppe, Babylon, p. 113
Baycrest Antiques & Design, Huntington, p. 126
Collectibles Antiques, Water Mill, p. 138
Cracker Barrel Gallery Inc., Huntington, p. 126
Glass Slipper Antiques, Northport, p. 130
Hide'n Seek Antiques, Bellmore, p. 116
Homestead House, Roslyn, p. 132
Huntington Antiques Center, Huntington, p. 127
Kings Point Antique Shop Inc., Great Neck, p. 124
L. Calderon Pink Wagon Antiques, Bellmore, p. 116
Showcase Antiques, Great Neck, p. 125
Somewhere In Time Antiques, Northport, p. 130

Postcards
Pickwick Shop, The, Southold, p. 137
Time Machine, The, Sag Harbor, p. 133

Pottery
Abbott & Jackson Inc., Easthampton, p. 120
Affordable Antiques, East Moriches, p. 122
Another Time Antiques, Southampton, p. 134

Silver
Antique Center at Shirley, Shirley, p. 134
Antique Pavilion, Bellmore, p. 115
Arthur T. Kalaher Inc., Southampton, p. 134
Baycrest Antiques & Design, Huntington, p. 126
Browsery, The, Huntington Station, p. 127
Carriage Trade, The, Cedarhurst, p. 119
Dower House Antiques, Southampton, p. 135
Elaine's Room Antiques, East Hampton, p. 121
End Shop, The, Bay Shore, p. 114
Faces Antiques, East Hampton, p. 121
Grand Acquisitor, The, East Hampton, p. 121
Hide'n Seek Antiques, Bellmore, p. 116
Huntington Antiques Center, Huntington, p. 127
Joan Bogart, Roslyn, p. 132
Kings Point Antique Shop Inc., Great Neck, p. 124
Mickey Mikiter, Port Washington, p. 132
Ragamuffins, The, East Port, p. 123
Scarlett's, Northport, p. 130
Second Chance, Southampton, p. 136
Showcase Antiques, Great Neck, p. 125

Sporting Equipment
Just Kids Nostalgia, Huntington, p. 127

Stoneware
Montauk Antiques & Art Gallery, Montauk, p. 130

Textiles
Antiques Center of East Hampton, East Hampton, p. 120
Chinalai Tribal Antiques & Interiors Ltd., Shoreham, p. 134
Discover Yesterday Antiques, Port Jefferson, p. 131
Fisher's, Sag Harbor, p. 132
Grand Acquisitor, The, East Hampton, p. 121
Ruby Beete, Bridgehampton, p. 118
Time Machine, The, Sag Harbor, p. 133
Wall St Antiques, Huntington, p. 127

Tools
Balasses House Antiques, Amagansett, p. 113

Toys
Another Time Antiques, Southampton, p. 134

Antique Freaks, The, Northport, p. 130
Antiques at Bayport, Bayport, p. 114
Just Kids Nostalgia, Huntington, p. 127
LI Doll Hospital/Jan Davis Antiques, Southold, p. 136
Nellies of Amagansett, Amagansett, p. 113

Tribal Art
Chinalai Tribal Antiques & Interiors Ltd., Shoreham, p. 134

Vintage Clothing
Antiques at Trader's Cove, Port Jefferson, p. 131
Discover Yesterday Antiques, Port Jefferson, p. 131
Furniture Store Antiques, Greenport, p. 125
Harbor Lights Antiques, Northport, p. 130
Victorian Heart, The, Sag Harbor, p. 133

Weathervanes
Sterling & Hunt, Bridgehamton, p. 118

Wicker
Affordable Antiques, East Moriches, p. 122
Another Time Antiques, Southampton, p. 134
Cat Lady Antiques, The, Port Washington, p. 131
Dee's Caning & Wicker Inc., Hampton Bays, p. 126
Hampton Antiques, Southampton, p. 135
Home Port Antiques, Shelter Island, p. 134
Let Bygones Be Antiques, Glen Cove, p. 124
Victory Garden Ltd., East Hampton, p. 122

ANTIQUE DEALERS AND CO-OP MANAGERS PLEASE SEE PAGE 342

Services—Long Island

Appraisals

Authentication

Cabinetry

China & Pottery Restoration

Clock Repair & Restoration

Crystal & Glass Restoration

Consignments
Another Time Antiques, Southampton, p. 134
Cracker Barrel Gallery, Inc., Huntington, p. 126
Dee's Caning & Wicker, Inc., Hampton Bays, p. 126
Filmart Galleries, Old Bethpage, p. 131
Glass Slipper Antiques, Northport, p. 130
Lyman Thorne Enterprises Ltd., Cold Spring Harbor, p. 119
Mill Pond Antiques, Bridgehampton, p. 118
Prilik Galleries, Garden City, p. 124
Ray's Antiques, Bellmore, p. 116
Second Chance, Southampton, p. 136
Time Machine, The, Sag Harbor, p. 133
Victorian Heart, Sag Harbor, p. 133
Young America, Sag Harbor, p. 133

Display Material
Somewhere In Time Antiques, Northport, p. 130

Doll Repair
Long Island Doll Hospital & Jan Davis Ant., Southold, p. 136

Electric Train Repair
Another Time Antiques, Southampton, p. 134

Finders Service
The End Shop, The, Bay Shore, p. 114

Frame Restoration
Affordable Antiques, East Moriches, p. 122
Antiques Center of East Hampton, East Hampton, p. 120

Furniture Refinishing
Affordable Antiques, East Moriches, p. 122
Dower House Antiques, Southampton, p. 135

Furniture Reproduction
Wall St Antiques, Huntington, p. 127

Furniture Repair & Restoration
Bernard's Antiques, Bellmore, p. 116
Cracker Barrel Gallery, Inc., Huntington, p. 126
Dee's Caning & Wicker, Inc., Hampton Bays, p. 126
Harry's Antiques, Bay Shore, p. 114

Lyman Thorne Enterprises Ltd., Cold Spring Harbor, p. 119
Morgan Macwhinnie Antiques, Southampton, p. 135
Prilik Galleries, Garden City, p. 124
Ray's Antiques, Bellmore, p. 116
Raymond B. Knight Corp., Locust Valley, p. 129
Young America, Sag Harbor, p. 133

Glass Matching Service
End Shop, The, Bay Shore, p. 114

Jewelry Repair
Antique Center at Shirley, Shirley, p. 134
Gem Quest Jewelry & Antiques Inc, Bellmore, p. 116

Lamp Repair & Restoration
Cracker Barrel Gallery, Inc., Huntington, p. 126
Dower House Antiques, Southampton, p. 135
Huntington Antiques Center, Huntington, p. 127
Orelians Lamp, Freeport, p. 123
Urban Archaeology, Bridgehampton, p. 118

Painting Restoration
Affordable Antiques, East Moriches, p. 122
Valdemar F. Jacobsen Antiques, Cold Spring Harbor, p. 119

Prop Rentals
Another Time Antiques, Southampton, p. 134
Antiques at Trader's Cove, Pt. Jefferson, p. 131
Collectibles Antiques, Watermill, p. 138
Friendly Spirits Antiques, Greenport, p. 125
Georgica Creek Antiques, Wainscott, p. 138
Urban Archaeology, Bridgehampton, p. 118

Quilt Repair & Restoration
Tom's Quilts, Southampton, p. 136

Radio Repair & Restoration
Friendly Spirits Antiques, Greenport, p. 125

Restoration (General)
Ray's Antiques, Bellmore, p. 116
Young America, Sag Harbor, p. 113
Urban Archaeology, Bridgehampton, p. 118

Wicker/Caning Repair & Restoration

Upstate Antique Dealers

ALBANY

Btrading
114 Quail Street (12206)
(518) 465-3497
Hours: Tues–Fri, 9:30–5;
Sat 9:30–3:30

Catering to the beginning as well as advanced collector of philately and deliotology (postcards), Btrading conducts quarterly auctions during February, May, August, and November which have a strong national and international following. The business, which has been in the same location for more than 15 years, is a strong buyer and seller of stamps, postcards, covers, and paper Americana. PR: $. CC: MC, V.

Dennis Holzman Antiques
240 Washington Avenue, 2nd floor (12210)
(518) 449-5414
(518) 478-7201 fax
Hours: Mon–Fri, 11–5;
Sat by chance or appointment

In this large shop filled with autographs, photographs, manuscripts, prints, paintings, political Americana, rare books, historically significant objects, whimsical items, select furniture, and accessories, a collector is as likely to find a Tiffany sterling vase as a 10 foot Corinthian column. PR: $$$. CC: No.

New Scotland Antiques
240 Washington Street (12210)
(518) 463-1323
Hours: Mon–Sat, 10:30–4
but call to be sure

Said to be the largest in the capital district, this shop carries a general line of antiques with an emphasis on art and jewelry. Appraisals can be done. Radios can be repaired and restored. PR: $$. CC: No.

Possibly Antiques
248 Lark Street (12210)
(518) 432-7554
Hours: Wed–Sat, 12–6

The owners, Bob Gulotty and Frances McGee, specialize in unique and unusual decorative arts and Art Deco with a special emphasis on rare toys and Christmas and holiday ornaments. They also maintain a booth at A Page in Time Antique Center in Saratoga Springs, NY. PR: $$. CC: MC, V.

Zeller's
32 Central Avenue (12210)
(518) 463-8221, 439-8020
Hours: Mon–Sat, 10–5

Well displayed offerings of period furniture, Americana, prints, rare books, autographs, and manuscripts are complemented by antique and estate jewelry and older, collectible stamps and coins.
PR: Low to high. CC: No.

ALBION

Fischer's Antiques
14049 West County House Road (14411)
(716) 589-7559
Hours: By appointment only

For more than thirty years, this business has been noted for having quality 18th and 19th century American country furniture in old paint and in as found condition, as well as refinished pine and cherry furniture, paintings, folk art, pewter, iron fireplace cooking implements, and decorative accessories.

ALFRED

Marack & Wood Antiques
24 High Street (14802)
(607) 587-9519
Hours: By appointment, mail order, and shows

These dealers specialize in pre-1850 Americana, English ceramics, American blown and pressed glass, and period furniture. Folk art, prints, and interesting accessories from the 19th and 20th century are also stocked. Research, estate liquidation, framing, and appraisals are done.

ALFRED STATION

Canacadea Country Store
599 Route 244 (14803)
(607) 587-8634
Hours: Daily 10–5:30
except major holidays

An eclectic collection ranging from period pieces and folk art to country furniture and decorative smalls is found on the upper floor of this 1860s building. Antique silver and jewelry are located on the first floor. PR: $$.
CC: MC, V.

Canacadea Sled Shop
676 Tinkertown Road (14803)
(607) 587-9450
Hours: By chance or appointment

Located on Route 244, this shop contains a wide assortment of restored and original sleds that are for sale. The owner will also repair and restore sleds. PR: $.
CC: No.

Hill Bottom Antiques
588 Main Street, Box 71 (14803)
(607) 587-9488
Hours: By chance or appointment

Established in 1971, this shop

offers textiles, vintage clothing, and American furniture. CC: MC, V.

ALLEGANY

Dutch Mill Antiques (MD)

3996 West State Road (14706)
(716) 373-3391
Hours: Tues–Sat, 11–5;
Sun, 1–5 in the winter

A relatively new shop, this multiple dealer co-op offers a wide selection of country antiques, linens, furniture, and both estate and costume jewelry. CC: No.

ALLENTOWN

Allentown Antique Mart (MD)

Main Street, Box 101 (14707)
(716) 593-6652
Hours: Daily 10–5

Seven dealers offer an assortment of furniture, glass, toys, tools, and collectibles in this 10 room country shop. PR: Reasonable. CC: No.

AMSTERDAM

C & D Antiques

4740 State Highway 30 (12010)
(518) 843-0744
Hours: Summer, Daily, 10–5;
winter Thur–Sun, 10–5

Housed in a large barn is an eclectic mix of furniture and collectibles from local estates. The emphasis is on Deco period kitchenware, china, and pottery. PR: $. CC: No. LOC: A little more than three and a half miles from Thruway Exit 27 on Route 30 North.

ANDOVER

Kitchen Cupboard Antiques

4563 East Valley Road (14806)
(607) 478-8060
Hours: Open when open,
phone call suggested

Painted furniture from the 1850s, mechanical nutmeg graters, early kitchen items, baskets, fireplace cooking items, and rare eggbeaters are found in this shop. PR: Moderate. CC: No.

ANGELICA

Angelica Antique Emporium

42 West Main Street, Box 453
(14709)
(716) 466-3712, 466-3380
Hours: Jan–April, Sat–Sun, 10–5;
May–Dec, Thur–Sun, 10–5

A fine assortment of antique furniture, paintings, and collectibles fill this shop. Services include the cleaning and restoration of oil paintings; custom, reproduction lighting; custom stained glass windows; woodworking; custom shelves; and furniture reproduction. CC: No.

ANGOLA

Southtowns Antiques
8488 Erie Road (14006)
(716) 549-3543
Hours: Sat–Sun, 10–5

In addition to a good variety of oak, mahogany, walnut, and cherry furniture, this shop specializes in very fine glass, china, Flow Blue, and sterling silver tableware.

ARDSLEY

Marvin's Antiques & Refinishing Center
645 Saw Mill River Road (10502)
(914) 693-5885
Hours: Mon–Sat, 9–5

Furniture from the 1800s to the 1930s and wall, mantel, and grandfather clocks fill this shop. A complete refinishing service, which includes clock repair, recaning of chairs, and restoration of furniture and chairs is available. PR: $$$. CC: AMEX, D.

ARGYLE

Century House Antiques
Rt. 40 (12809)
(518) 638-8908
Hours: Daily 10–6

In addition to pottery by Roseville, Hull, Weller, and McCoy, furniture, lamps, glass, agateware, tin, and collectibles are for sale in this shop.

Hoffis Farm Antiques
Barkley Avenue (12809)
(518) 638-8305
Hours: Daily 10–5
by chance or appointment

Established in 1978, this shop specializes in pattern glass, Flow Blue, and antiques in the country manner with an emphasis on furniture in old paint and in as found condition. Decorative smalls and architectural items which complement the country look are also available.
PR: Moderate. CC: MC, V.

ARKVILLE

Crossroads Antique Center (MD)
Route 28 (12406)
(914) 586-2121
Hours: Daily 11–6 except closed Tues; Jan–April also closed Wed

Featuring the wares of 18 dealers, this multi-dealer antique center offers everything from furniture and postcards to jewelry and dishes. Shipping services are available. Quality consignments are accepted. CC: No.

AUBURN

Ward's Antiques
Route. 20 (13021-4008)
(315) 252-7703
Hours: Mon–Sat and holidays, 10–6; Sun 1–6

Located in the historic Finger

Lakes region, this shop offers American, European, and Oriental antiques. Estate and insurance appraisals can be done.
CC: No.

AUSTERLITZ

Robert Herron Antiques
Route 22 (12017)
(518) 392-5478
Hours: Mon–Sat, 9–5; Sun 1–5

An impressive presentation of both country and formal furniture from the 18th century to the mid 1800s with appropriate accessories such as glass, china, rugs, metals, and art is the hallmark of this shop.
PR: $$. CC: No.

Suzanne Courcier * Robert W. Wilkins
Route 22 (12017)
(518) 392-5754
(518) 392-5754 fax
Hours: By appointment only and at major shows

Specializing in the furniture and accessories of the Shakers, these dealers also offer a high quality selection of painted and decorated furniture in original condition and textiles. Members of the Antique Dealers Association, they are noted for their authentic American antique furniture.
CC: No.

William A. Gustafson Antiques
Corner of Routes 22 & 203, P.O. Box 104 (12017-0104)
(518) 392-2845, (800) 542-0867
(518) 392-4436 fax
Hours: By appointment and mail order

Specializing in restoration tools and both antique and collectible tools of the trades, William Gustafson is the largest supplier of restoration tools through private sales, mail order, and auctions. Furniture repair and restoration, tool search, cabinetry work, and appraisals are also available. Quality consignments accepted. PR: $$$$$.
CC: MC, V, D, AMEX.

AVON

Avon Antique House (MD)
65 East Main St., Routes 5 & 20 (14414)
(716) 226-8360
Hours: Wed–Sun, 11–5

This 30 plus dealer group shop occupies more than 6,000 square feet in a beautiful 1830s home. A great mixture of furniture, country antiques, primitives, china, glass, tools, pottery, art, and linens is available. CC: MC, V.
LOC: Exit 10 off I-390.

"Adventure" by Bassett Lowke Ship Models, LTD, ca 1925. *(Courtesy North Star Galleries, New York City)*

BAINBRIDGE

Iroquois Antiques and Collectibles (MD)
5 Walnut Street, off Route 7 (13733)
(607) 967-3266
Hours: Daily 10–5

Something for everyone can be found in this multiple dealer shop, which contains more than 5,000 square feet of quality, affordable items for both collectors and dealers. PR: $$. CC: MC, V.

Old Hickory Antique Center (MD)
Route 7 & Guilford Road (13733)
(607) 967-4145
Hours: Mon–Sat, 10–5; Sun, 12–5

Twenty-five dealers offer a constantly changing stock of antiques, collectibles, and memorabilia. The emphasis is on country furniture with appropriate accessories, old pottery, china, tools, postcards, quilts, textiles, and cast iron. PR: $$. CC: No.

Susquehanna Antiques & Collectibles (MD)
R.D. 3, Box 21D, Route 7 (13733)
(607) 967-4100
Hours: Mon–Sat, 10–5, Sun 12–5

A multiple dealer shop which displays a general line of merchandise that includes furniture, glass, and collectibles. An appraisal service is available. CC: No.

BALDWINSVILLE

James William Lowery
30 Canton Street (13027)
(315) 638-1329
Hours: Anytime by appointment

Recognized for their investment

quality 18th and 19th century American formal, country, painted, and Empire furniture, miniatures, and appropriate accessories, the Lowerys have been purchasing and selling for and acting as a brokerage agent to museums, private collectors, and other dealers for the past 18 years. CC: No.

BALLSTON LAKE

Jasada Antiques Inc.

860 Saratoga Road, Route 50 (12019)
(518) 399-1199
Hours: Daily 12–5

A general line of merchandise which includes furniture, dolls, Hummels, Fiesta Ware, clocks, jewelry, books, linens, and Edison phonographs can be found in this shop. CC: No.

BARKER

Open Door

9142 Coleman Road (14012)
(716) 795-3078
Hours: April–January: Mon–Sat, 10–6; Sun by appointment; closed during the winter

In an 1893 cottage-type home, country antiques and collectibles and some Victoriana are displayed. Primitives, kitchen collectibles, oak and pine furniture, sheet music, and records await the collector. PR: $. CC: No.

BATH

Abbey's Antiques, Art, & Appraisals

12 Ganesevoort Street (14810)
(607) 776-6719
Hours: By appointment

Although a general line shop, art in every form is featured. One will encounter formal French furniture and decorative smalls, American primitives, glass, paintings on canvas, Oriental rugs, and estate jewelry. PR: $$$. CC: No.

Bath Antiques

43 Geneva Street (14810)
(607) 776-4399
Hours: Tues–Sat, 11–4:30

This is a single owner shop offering antiques and collectibles with an emphasis on items related to the Civil War and World War II. Clock and watch repairs are available. CC: MC, V.

Donna's Antiques

105 Maple Heights (14810)
(607) 776-3003
Hours: Open when home

A general line of antiques and collectibles which includes furniture, lamps, clocks, and china is available at this shop.

BEACON

Beacon Hill Antiques

474 Main Street (12508)
(914) 831-4577
Hours: Wed–Mon, 12–5
or by chance or appointment

Decorative, formal, and country furniture complemented by appropriate accessories such as paintings, prints, lighting, silver, books, and toys are found in this beautiful shop which is noted for its eclectic offerings. Consignments are accepted and appraisals are given. Dealers and browsers are welcome.
CC: MC, V.

Dickinson's Antiques (MD)

440 Main Street (12508)
(914) 838-1643
Hours: Daily 11–5, closed Tues

This multidealer shop located in a historic brick building offers a wide selection of quality antiques, collectibles, and furniture.
PR: $$. CC: MC, V.

Early Everything (MD)

468-470 Main Street (12508)
(914) 838-3014
Hours: Daily 11–5, closed Tues

A wide variety of antiques which includes mahogany, formal, and country furniture; cut glass; china; jewelry; and pottery is presented by seven dealers in a bright, attractive atmosphere. Consignments are accepted. Caning and doll repair are available. Appraisals can be given. PR: $$.
CC: MC, V.

BEDFORD HILLS

Antiques Of A Rare Bird

297 Bedford Road (10507)
(914) 242-9270, 232-3944
(914) 232-3944 fax
Hours: Tues–Sat, 11–5
or by appointment

This shop is filled with collectibles, vintage clothing, kitchenware, lamps, Deco glassware and furniture, coin-operated machines, and vintage linen and bedding. PR: $$.
CC: MC, V.

BELFAST

Warner's Antiques

12 River Road, Box 214, Route 19
(14711)
(716) 365-2590
Hours: By chance or appointment

Located in a redwood barn on Route 19, this shop offers a general line of furniture with an emphasis on oak in the varnish, some refinished, and some in the rough. Also available are frames with and without pictures, interesting memorabilia, and collectibles which include lanterns, toys, oil lamps, graniteware, and stoneware. PR: $$. CC: No.

BELMONT

Ivan's Antiques & Miscellaneous

RD 2, Box 35, Belvidere Road (14813)
(716) 268-5316
Hours: Fri–Sat, 11–5,
other days by chance or appointment

Located next to the fire hall, this large store contains both antiques and collectibles gathered from local estates. A second shop, which is one mile south of Scio on Route 19, contains antiques, collectibles, and architectural items. CC: No.

BERGEN

Old Red Mill (MD)

29 Lake Road, Route 19 (14416)
(716) 494-1757
Hours: In good weather,
Tues–Sun, 10–5;
December – March, Sat & Sun, 10–5

Located on two floors of a 100 year old granary, this ten dealer group shop features fine glass, china, paintings, furniture, post cards, ephemera including sheet music, and collectibles.

BINGHAMTON

Baran's Antiques Center (MD)

171-177 Clinton Street (13905)
(607) 724-2114, 722-5041
Hours: Mon–Fri, 10–5; Sat, 9–5;
Sun, 12–5

Occupying 14,000 square feet, 15 dealers offer a quality line of antiques and collectibles. Furniture restoration, upholstering, and an appraisal service are also available. This is the oldest and largest antique center in Broome county.

Bob & Sallie Connelly

205 State Street (13901)
(607) 722-9593, 722-3555
(607) 722-1266 fax
Hours: Mon–Fri, 10–5;
Sat, 10–2 or by appointment

Antiques and decorative arts from the 19th and 20th century are tastefully displayed in three showrooms located in a historic building. Furniture, rugs, oil paintings, prints, jewelry, clocks, toys, sterling, vintage clothing, glassware, porcelain, china, folk art, and holiday collectibles are featured. CC: MC, V.

Clinton Mill Antique Center (MD)

99 Clinton Street (13905)
(607) 773-2036
Hours: Mon–Sat, 9–5

This large, clean, and beautifully lighted group shop has five dealers who specialize in Oriental rugs, musical instruments, quality glass, china, pottery, fine art, and both period and semi-antique furniture. Fred's Budgetiques and Collectibles is located here.
PR: $$$. CC: No.

Curio Cupboard, Twin Rivers Antiques & Gifts
339 Clinton Street (13905)
(607) 798-9395
Hours: Mon–Sat, 10–5

Located on Binghamton's Antique Row, this shop contains two floors of American furniture, linens, oil lamps, kitchen collectibles, glass, china, and mirrors. CC: MC, V.

For Your Listening Pleasure
368 Clinton Street (13905)
(607) 797-0066
(607) 797-0013 fax
Hours: Mon–Fri, 9:15–5:15 & Thur till 8:15; Sat, 9:15–2:15

Located on two floors, one will find a large collection of restored vintage radios, phonographs, and televisions with related memorabilia and tubes. Dedicated to the restoration and servicing of vintage radios, televisions, and phonographs that operate with electric valves (tubes) or mechanical reproducers manufactured from the early 1900s to the early 1960s, these dealers carry an extensive line of parts and literature including material for antique automobiles from the 1930s to 1969. CC: MC, V, AMEX.

Larry Gottheim Fine Photographs
33 Orton Avenue (13905)
(607) 797-1685
(607) 797-4775 fax
Hours: By appointment

Featuring photographic imagery of the 19th and early 20th century, this dealer specializes in important derrotypes and other early forms of photography with historical or photographic historical importance. Ephemera and books related to this field are also available. BE-HOLD, a catalog of early photographic imagery, is issued twice a year. PR: $$$$. CC: MC, V.

M. L. Baran
173 Clinton Street, 2nd floor (13905)
(607) 724-2114
Hours: Mon–Fri, 10–5; Sat, 9–5; Sun, 12–5

This art gallery specializes in fine art, paintings, engravings, lithographs, and sculpture of the 19th and 20th century. PR: $300+. CC: No.

Mad Hatter Antiques
284 Clinton Street (13905)
(607) 729-6036
Hours: Mon–Sat, 10:30–5:30

Quality country, Victorian, oak, and cherry furniture and accessories such as quilts, stoneware, and architectural antiques are displayed in showroom settings in this 5,000 square foot shop. PR: $$. CC: MC, V, AMEX.

Mary Webster Frames
12 Edwards Street (13905)
(607) 722-1483
Hours: By appointment and mail order

This business specializes in

antique picture frames and mirrors. Both archival and period framing services are available. CC: No.

Midtown Antiques & Auction Service
34 Chenango Street (13901)
(607) 723-8860
(607) 723-5768 fax
Hours: Mon–Sat, 11–4:30

Antique furniture, estate jewelry, antique phonographs, records, sheet music, and player piano rolls can be found in this shop. PR: $$. CC: MC, V, AMEX.

Silver Fox
304 Clinton Street (13905)
(607) 729-1342
Hours: Mon–Sat, 11–5

This shop features a general line of antiques and collectibles which includes early 20th century furniture and accessories such as pottery, glassware, dishware, kitchenware, and paintings. Custom framing is available. PR: $$.

Sweetcheeks
130 Clinton Street (13905)
(607) 771-0476
Hours: Tues–Fri, 1–5; Sat, 11–3

Established in 1974, this personal service costume shop specializes in the odd piece for stage productions. Interesting period pieces are available for rental or purchase.

Treadwell Farm Enterprises
10 Treadwell Road (13905)
(607) 648-6747
Hours: By chance or appointment

Two buildings are full of antiques, collectibles, miscellaneous, and "stuff in the ruff." As everything is in as found condition, this place is a paradise for the do it yourself type of person. CC: No. LOC: 10 Treadwell Road is located two miles up W. Chenango Road from Route 11.

BLOOMFIELD

Jan's Early Attic (MD)
6900 Route 5 and Route 20 (14469)
(716) 657-7446
Hours: Mon–Sat, 10–5; Sun, 12–5

Displaying the merchandise of more than 50 dealers, this group shop has furniture of all periods, primitives, tools, and early pottery. CC: MC, V.

BLOOMINGBURGH

Bloomingburgh Antique Center & Treasure Hunters of Yore (MD)
56 Main Street, P.O. Box 263 (12721)
(914) 733-1111
Hours: Daily 11–5

Pottery, porcelain, and furniture are among the antiques and collectibles that one will find in this multidealer shop. LOC: Exit 116 off the Quickway, right off the ramp then right at the next cross street.

BREWSTER

Brewster Station Antiques and Lighting
14 Main Street (10509)
(914) 279-2863
Hours: Thur–Sun, 12–6

Although some antiques and collectibles are available, this shop specializes in the sale and service of all kinds of lighting. Hundreds of oil, kerosene, gas, and electric lamps are available. The old and new parts and globe department is the most extensive in a 30 mile radius. Lamp repair, restoration, rewiring as well as lighting consultations are available. PR: $. CC: No.

Olana Gallery
#2 Carillolin Road (10509)
(914) 279-8077
(914) 279-8079 fax
Hours: Appointment only

Many antiquarians are of the opinion that this dealer has the largest selection in the world of books and catalogs on American paintings and sculpture. About 10 percent of the available titles are in print; the remaining titles no longer are. A search service for books on both the fine and decorative arts is available. CC: No.

Second Time Around Antiques
92 Main Street (10509)
(914) 278-7176
Hours: Wed–Mon, 11–4

This shop contains a large and beautiful selection of American furniture in mahogany, oak, pine, walnut, and cherry in excellent to mint condition. Collectibles from the 1900s to the 1960s are also stocked. Furniture and clock repair and lamp rewiring are available. PR: $$. CC: MC, V.

Seventy Nine Wistful Vista Ltd.
43 Main Street (10509)
(914) 278-4223
Hours: Wed–Mon, 11–5

Two adjoining stores offer a broad selection of Victorian and country furniture, restored antique frames with appropriate graphics, china, Art Pottery, vintage linens, jewelry, doll clothes, and collectibles. PR: $$. CC: AMEX, D.

BRIARCLIFF MANOR

Country Antiques Unlimited
1247 Pleasantville Road (10510)
(914) 945-0499
Hours: Tues–Fri, 11–6; Sat, 11–4; Sun by appointment

This shop carries a little of

A group of English and Continental brass and delftware. *(Courtesy Mark & Marjorie Allen, Putnam Valley)*

everything but the emphasis is on imported Danish country pine furniture and accessories. In addition to furniture, one will find boxes, lamps, costume and estate jewelry, pottery, stoneware, cast iron, books, and pantry items in the shop.
PR: $$$. CC: D.

Yellowplush Antiques (MD)
1192 Pleasantville Road (10510)
(914) 762-0594
Hours: Tues–Sat, 11–4

In a yellow Victorian house, four dealers offer American, English, and French furniture complemented by appropriate accessories which include lamps, mirrors, fireplace fenders and tools, porcelain, pottery, prints, oils, crystal, and glass. CC: No.

BRONXVILLE

Guest House, The (MD)
27 Pondfield Road (10708)
(914) 337-5150
Hours: Mon–Sat, 10:30–5:30; Sun, 11:30–4:30

Stocked by five dealers, this group shop offers quality 19th and 20th century furniture, paintings, prints, nautical material, china, glass, porcelain, silver, and decorative accessories. Furniture refinishing, repair, and restoration as well as appraisals are available. CC: No.

Morley
Box 422 (10708)
(914) 664-2105
Hours: Shows only

This dealer specializes in the finest quality musical boxes, musical bird boxes, and Moser and Bohemian glass.

Pierce-Archer Antiques
82 Kraft Avenue (10708)
(914) 337-0120
Hours: 10:30–4:30

This shop specializes in English antiques that the proprietors directly purchase in England. Formal furniture, brass accessories, steel and brass fireplace equipment, pottery, and porcelain which are mostly from the 18th to the early 19th century are featured. PR: $$$. CC: No.

Pug Crossing Antiques
63 Park Avenue (10708)
(914) 961-7799
Hours: By appointment only, shows, and mail order

This dealer specializes in pug dog porcelains, terra cottas, bronzes, Staffordshire, paintings, and prints. In among this impressive assemblage of pug dog material, one will also find decorative smalls, 19th century accessories for the home, and formal Continental porcelains. PR: $$. CC: No.

BUFFALO

Assets Antiques and Collectibles
140 Elmwood Avenue (14201)
(716) 882-2415
Hours: Tues–Sat, 12–6 or by appointment

In addition to specializing in vintage costume jewelry and accessories, these dealers offer decorative smalls, glass, and fine furniture.

Buffalo's Attic
927 Elmwood Avenue (14222)
(716) 884-3757
Hours: Mon–Sat, 12–6

Buttons, Depression glass, estate and costume jewelry, and pottery can be found in this shop. Appraisals are available, props can be rented, and consignments are accepted. CC: MC, V, D.

Great Lakes Artifact Repository
79 Perry Street (14203)
(716) 849-0149
(716) 852-0093 fax
Hours: Daily 9–4:30

Not an antique shop, this business specializes in appraisals and identification, conservation of paper and objects, brokering of large collections, and both long and short term storage of cultural property in a climate-controlled, secured vault with compactor storage for boxed objects and flat art. Interested parties should call to discuss their needs.

Horsefeathers Architectural Antiques
346 Connecticut Street (14213)
(716) 882-1581
(716) 882-1581 fax
Hours: Mon–Fri, 10–5; Sat, 10–3

Stocking something for everyone, this shop specializes in architectural antiques such as doors, mantels, lighting, and stained glass. Horsefeathers also carries a complete line of furniture in finished and unfinished condition, garden accessories, and cast and wrought iron. Appraisals and prop rentals can be arranged. This 35,000 square foot shopping experience is minutes away from the Peace Bridge. CC: MC, V.

Mix
611 Elmwood Avenue (14222)
(716) 886-0141
Hours: Tues–Sat, 11:30–5:30

Since 1979, this shop has offered reasonably priced home furnishings and accessories from the 1930s to the 1960s.
PR: Reasonable. CC: MC, V.

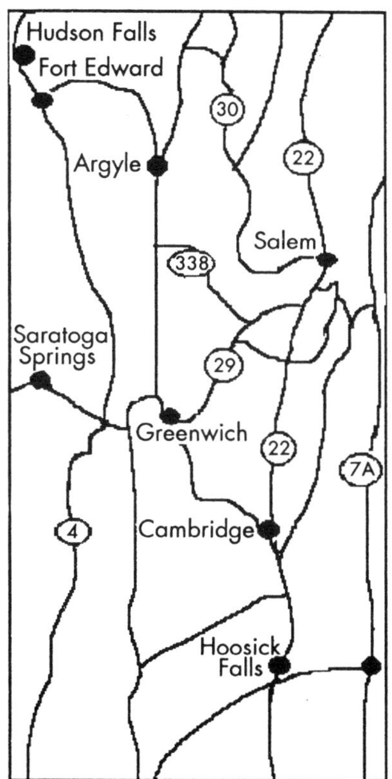

Cambridge-Saratoga Springs Area

Red Balloons
42 Allen Street (14202)
(716) 881-2727
Hours: Mon–Sat, 12–5 or by appointment

Established in 1984, this shop specializes in quality vintage clothing, hats, linens, lace, and early textiles. CC: No.

CALEDONIA

Curious Goods (MD)
3113 Main Street (14423)
(716) 538-6775
Hours: Tues–Sun, 10–5

With more than 25 dealers, this

antique collective which was established in 1989 carries a nice variety of antiques and collectibles.

CAMBRIDGE

Black Smith Shop Antiques

Box 398, Route 372 (12816)
(518) 677-2346
Hours: Daily 9–5, except Tues.
Call to be sure.

Located in a two story, brick, historical building this newly established shop contains a wide spectrum of quality antiques and collectibles which are very tastefully displayed. Caning, rushing, and splinting are available. PR: $$. CC: No. LOC: 1 mile west of Cambridge, NY on Route 372.

Jack's Out Back

30 West Main Street (12816)
(518) 677-8972
(518) 786-7139 fax
Hours: Open daily by chance or appointment

Featuring early cupboards, cabinets, and tables in old paint, this shop offers the collector an interesting line of country primitives and collectibles. Nineteenth century Americana and fun stuff can also be found. Jack's Out Back is also located in Glens Falls at Glenwood Manor on Quaker Road. PR: $$. CC: No.

Roberta Stewart Antiques

30 East Main Street (12816)
(518) 677-5666
Hours: Thur–Sat, 10–5; Sun, 1–5; Mon, 10–5 (From December 24th to May 1st open weekends only)

Baskets, boxes, silver, jewelry, furniture, glass, china, treenware, furniture, and other appropriate accessories from the 18th, 19th, and early 20th century can be found in this shop. PR: $$. CC: No.

Sheaf of Wheat (John Sheaf)

Route 22, RD 2, Box 152A (12816)
(518) 677-5562
Hours: Tues–Sat, 10–5
from April through October

American furniture, lighting devices and fixtures, country antiques, and antique tools are on display in this shop.

CAMPBELL HALL

Gramm-O-Phone Antiques

Route 207, Box 1 (10916)
(914) 427-2606
Hours: Mon–Sat, 9–7
and by appointment

Advertising, bottles, ephemera, furniture, glass, lighting fixtures, maps, prints, phonographs, and radios are available at this shop. In addition to matting and framing services, repair and restoration is available for furniture, lighting fixtures, phonographs, and radios. Consignments are accepted. PR: Moderate. CC: No.

Reminiscences
Route 208, RD 1, Box 317 (10916)
(914) 496-1243
Hours: Thur–Sun, 11–5 or by chance or appointment

Two floors of quality 19th century furniture complemented by decorative textiles, porcelains, and appropriate accessories are the hallmark of this shop.
CC: MC, V.
LOC: Route 208, ½ mile south of 207/208 intersection.

CANAAN

Iris Cottage Antiques
Route 295 and County Route 5 (12029)
(518) 781-4379
Hours: By appointment only and weekends May through Oct

Established in 1968, this business specializes in early American pressed glass. Research, glass matching, and glass identification services are available.
CC: MC, V. LOC: Route 22 between B2 and B3 of the Berkshire spur of the NYS Thruway.

CANANDAIGUA

Antiques Unlimited (MD)
168 Niagara Street (14424)
(716) 394-7255
Hours: Mon–Sat, 10–5; Sun, 12–5

Located in a restored 19th century railroad building, 50 quality dealers offer fine antiques within booths, showcases, and room settings. A constantly rotating stock of period and country furniture, wicker, decoys, china, glass, paintings, silver, clocks, toys, and baskets are offered. Layaways are available. CC: MC, V.

Cheshire Union Antique Center (MD)
Route 21 South-Cheshire (14424)
(716) 394-3043
Hours: Daily 10–5 with summer and holiday evening hours

Located in an old country school house, this co-op has 12 dealers who display their merchandise in individual classrooms. In addition to country and formal furniture and appropriate accessories, the various dealers offer lawn and garden furniture, holiday collectibles, advertising, Americana, and lighting devices and fixtures. Lamp repair and restoration are available. The co-op sponsors the 100 dealer Annual Cheshire Union Folk Fair on the last Saturday of July and the hundred dealer Annual Cheshire Antique Show held on the second Saturday of August. PR: **$$**.
CC: MC, V.

Cuddeback Antiques (MD)
47 Saltonstall Street, P.O. Box 352 (14424)
(716) 394-2297
Hours: Daily 10–5

An antique center displaying the merchandise of 30 dealers.

Harvest Mill
40 Parrish Street (14424)
(716) 394-5907
Hours: Tues–Sat, 10–5; Sun, 12–5

This large shop offers a variety of mahogany, pine, and country furniture complemented by appropriate decorative smalls in room settings. In addition to a country store and Christmas shop, a lamp shop offers fixtures and shades for the refurbishing of old lamps. CC: No.

Heir-loom House Antiques
2032 Route 21 North (14424)
(716) 289-4173
Hours: Thur–Tues, 11–5

Offering a wide variety of objects from local homes and estates, this shop specializes in tealeaf and white Ironstone. Formal and country items are available for both collectors and dealers. LOC: Three miles south of NY Thruway exit 43 or four miles north of Canandaigua.

Kipling's Treasures and Antiquities
116 Main Street South (14424)
(716) 396-7270
Hours: Mon–Fri, 10–6; Sat, 10–5; Sun, 12–5

Fine 18th and 19th century antiques and art are tastefully displayed in a gallery setting. An emphasis is placed on Empire, Eastlake, and rare furniture from England and Europe. Ancient artifacts from Egypt and the Holy Land add a touch of romance and mystery. PR: $$. CC: MC, V.

Petticoat Junction Antiques
103 Leicester Street (14424)
(716) 396-0691
Hours: Tues–Sat, 10–5; Sun, 12–5

This shop specializes in country antiques, collectibles, glass, and both American and Oriental furniture. CC: MC, V. LOC: From the intersection of Main St. and Niagara St., go all the way to the end of Niagara St. and turn right on Leicester St.

Silent Woman Antiques (MD)
221 South Main Street (14424)
(716) 396-0327
Hours: Tues–Sat, 10–5; Sun, 12–5

This multidealer shop features primitives, furniture, ephemera, decoys, quilts, glass, and more. CC: MC, V.

CARMEL

Erik Johns Associates
Old Peckslip Road (10512)
(914) 878-9369
Hours: By appointment

In addition to an interior design service, this dealer offers antique furniture, paintings, and decorative accessories. CC: No.

CATSKILL

Kathleen Seibel Antiques
40 North Jefferson Avenue
(12414)
(518) 943-2256
Hours: Thursdays or by appointment

This 18th century Hudson Valley Dutch house is stocked with painted furniture and accessories with an emphasis on cupboards, textiles, stoneware, hooked rugs, and painted wooden objects. PR: Moderate. CC: No.

CAZENOVIA

Lakeside Antique Galleries
11 Albany Street (13035)
(315) 655-8663
Hours: By chance or appointment

Located in a restored Victorian mansion, this shop specializes in Victorian furniture, paintings, jewelry, and decorative accessories—both American and Continental. Appraisals can be done for both estimates and insurance. PR: $$$. CC: MC, V.

CENTRAL BRIDGE

Dapper Frog Antiques Center, The (MD)
Route 7 and Junction Road (12035)
(518) 868-4228
Hours: Wed–Mon: 10–5
except Sun 12–5; Tues closed
(closed Tues & Wed during January and February)

Exhibiting the merchandise of more than 20 dealers, this multi-dealer shop has a nice selection of antiques, collectibles, furniture, old toys, jewelry, glass, and smalls. CC: MC, V. LOC: Take I-88 to exit 23 (Schoharie) Central Bridge then ½ mile west on U.S. Route 7.

CHAMPLAIN

Hayloft Antiques
53 Dudley Road (12919)
(518) 298-8406
Hours: Chance or appointment

A general line of smalls which include kitchen collectibles, glass, and decorative items can be found in this shop. PR: $. CC: No.

CHAPPAQUA

Charles L. Washburne
P.O. Box 78 (10514)
(914) 238-4130
Hours: By appointment only and shows

In addition to offering other pottery and porcelain, this dealer specializes in majolica of the highest quality. PR: $$$$$. CC: No.

Crown House Antiques
297 King Street (10514)
(914) 238-3949
Hours: Tues–Sat, 10–5

In the same location for 30 years, this shop which carries a full

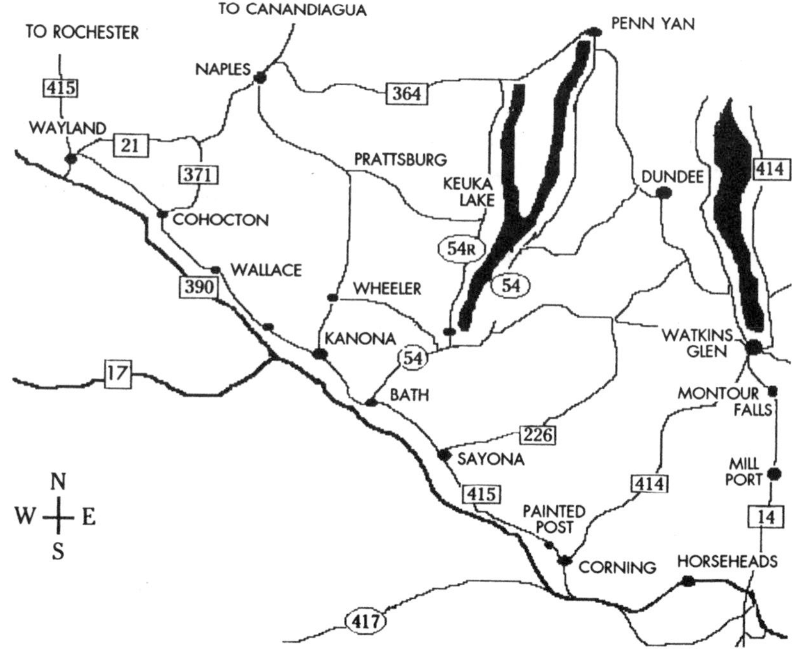

Corning-Horseheads-Painted Post Area

range of antiques, reproductions, gift items, and seasonal gifts specializes in lamp accessories, especially shades. Both lamp and clock repair and restoration are available. Appraisals can be done. CC: MC, V, AMEX.

CHATHAM

Anderson American Antiques
Box 163, East Chatham (12060)
(518) 392-3956
Hours: Sat–Sun, 12–4:30;
anytime by appointment

In this shop, the emphasis is on quality and condition. Formal and country American furniture of the late 18th and early 19th century, American landscape paintings, hooked rugs, and lighting are offered. CC: MC, V.

Birge Hill Farm Antiques
Birge Hill Road, RR 2, Box 2032 (12037)
(518) 392-9720
Hours: Fri–Sun, 10–5;
other times by chance or appointment

This shop specializes in country antiques, glassware, furniture, and decorative smalls. LOC: A half mile off Route 295 between Chatham and East Chatham on Birge Hill Road.

Country Store Antiques
Route 295, East Chatham, Box 32 (12060)
(518) 392-5157
Hours: Daily during the summer;
weekends during the winter
or by chance or appointment

Located in a rustic old barn, this

shop offers a wide variety of antiques and collectibles. Country furniture, quilts, pattern glass, Flow Blue, and early china are some of the items you will find. Chair seating repair and restoration in cane, rush, splint, and other materials is a specialty.
CC: No.

Greenwillow Farm Ltd.
Raup Road (12037)
(518) 392-9654
Hours: Sat–Sun, 10–4
or by appointment

This shop offers Art Deco-Moderne furniture and appropriate accessories plus a smattering of Shaker and Japanese pieces.
LOC: One mile north of Route 203 on County Route 9.

John Sideli
Route 295 (12037)
(518) 392-2271
Hours: Open by appointment
or chance

American country furniture in original finish as well as folk art, weathervanes, cupboards, Windsor chairs, architectural elements, trade signs, and unusual decorative items can be found in this shop. All of the pieces have been carefully selected for quality, condition, color, and design. Bottles, books, and redware are also available. PR: $$$$$.
CC: No.

Richard & Betty Ann Rasso Antiques
Village Square, East Chatham (12060)
(518) 392-4501
Hours: By chance or appointment

American painted furniture in original condition from the 18th and 19th century, Shaker furniture and accessories for the beginning to advanced collector, as well as American folk art with an emphasis on weathervanes and sculptural pieces are offered by these dealers who have been in business since 1973. Appraisals and authentication services are also available.
CC: No.

Skevington-Back Antiques
County Route 9 between Route 203 and Route 66 (12037)
(518) 392-9056
Hours: Open all year,
call ahead for an appointment

This shop specializes in period 17th and 18th century English, American, and Continental furniture. A selection of sporting and botanical prints; some fireplace equipment and garden accessories; and decorative and useful items of brass, iron, glass, and pottery are also available.
CC: No. LOC: One and a quarter miles from Route 203 exit on the Taconic Parkway. Go east on Route 203 toward Austerlitz for ¼ mile. Turn right onto Co. Route. 9. Shop 1 mile on right.

Yesteryears
3 Railroad Avenue (12037)
(518) 392-3949
Hours: Mon–Sat, 11–5; Sun, 12–5

An ever-changing variety of furniture, paintings, linens, glassware, silver, collectibles, and decorative smalls is the hallmark of this shop. PR: $$. CC: MC, V.

CHESHIRE

Cheshire Union Antique Center
See Canandaigua

CHESTER

Antique Alley
139 Main Street (10918)
(914) 469-5622
Hours: Daily 10–5

This shop carries a general line of antiques and collectibles. Ephemera, furniture, and country antiques are emphasized. PR: $. CC: No.

Chester Square Antiques (MD)
112 Main Street (10918)
(914) 469-9754
Hours: Daily 10–5

This group shop of seven dealers offers a fine selection of 17th, 18th, and 19th century American antiques and related accessories. Twentieth century items are excluded from this shop. CC: No.

76 Barn
42A Brookside Avenue, Route 17M (10918)
(914) 469-9222
Hours: Daily 10–5

Established in 1983, this business offers a wide variety of collectibles and antiques such as furniture, primitives, and country items. Furniture repair, restoration, and refinishing as well as home restoration are available. PR: $20+. CC: No.

Ver-Del's Collectibles
161 Main Street (10918)
(914) 469-9556
Hours: Daily 11–4 or by appointment

Lighting fixtures, lamps, miniatures, kitchen collectibles, and both gas and electric globes are to be found in one room in an old barn. CC: No.

CIRCLEVILLE

Alfred's Antiques
P.O. Box 31 (10919)
(914) 361-3655
Hours: Afternoons but call first

In addition to specializing in gold and silver antique and estate jewelry and sterling and coin flatware, these dealers also offer a general line of antiques which includes small furniture. This business was established in 1966. LOC: Exit 119 on Route 17, turn right and travel one and a half miles north on Route 302.

Tramp Art mirror/frame on pedestal, double sided with finger like projections, eight layers deep, ca. 1930. *(Courtesy Paper Moons, New York City)*

CLARENCE

Muleskinner

10626 Main Street (14031)
(716) 759-2661
(716) 759-2661 fax
Hours: Mon–Fri, 10–5; Sat–Sun, 12–5

Considered to be one of western New York's finest Americana galleries, this shop specializes in American country furniture in original finish, folk art, Native American items, and other appropriate decorative arts.
CC: MC, V.

Tschopp Stained Glass

10830 Main Street (14031)
(716) 759-6010
Hours: Tues–Sat, 10–5; Sun, 12–5

This shop is primarily involved in the restoration of stained glass lamps and windows, panel lamps, and figural metal lamps. Services include panel bending, patina, and electric and metal repair. Antiques in the above categories plus decorative furniture, pottery, jewelry, and pictures from the 1880s to the 1940s are available.
PR: $$. CC: No.

Uncle Sam's Antiques
9060 Main Street (14031)
(716) 626-9931
Hours: Daily 10–6

Located in the Clarence antique district, this shop carries a large inventory of oak and country furnishings plus advertising, toys, and collectibles. It is the only local shop with a Steiff and bear related display.
CC: MC, V, AMEX.

Vi & Si's Antiques
8970 Main Street (14031)
(716) 634-4488
Hours: Daily 10–5

Although these dealers specialize in Buffalo Pottery and Buffalo China, their shop contains a wide variety of antiques and collectibles. Railroadiana, glass, silver, china, and porcelain are among the many items that can be found. CC: MC, V.

CLAVERACK

Dutch House, The
Route 23, Box 50 (12513)
(518) 851-2011
Hours: Summer, Daily 10–5; winter by appointment

This shop offers a wide selection of country furniture that includes tables, chairs, and cupboards in pine, maple, and cherry. Appropriate accessories such as baskets, quilts, textiles, pottery, stoneware, cast iron, lamps, and both old and new Steiff bears are also available. Taconic baskets are a specialty. PR: $. CC: No.

CLINTON CORNERS

Dolores Rogers Murphy Antiques
218 Bulls Head Road (12514)
(914) 266-5707
(914) 266-4312 fax
Hours: By appointment or chance

An in-home setting is used to tastefully display American furniture, antiques, and accessories such as mirrors and decorative smalls. This business was established in 1979. PR: $$. LOC: One mile west of Bulls Head Road exit of the Taconic State Parkway off County Route 19 (five miles east of Rhinebeck).

COBLESKILL

Patent, The (MD)
Route 145, Exit 22 off of Route 88 (12043)
(518) 296-8000
Hours: Wed–Sat, 10–5; Sun, 12–5, Mon 10–5

Located in a restored 1935 Cobleskill State Grange Hall, this 15 dealer co-op offers a wide selection of antiques and collectibles that will please everyone. If not, they have a referral service. CC: MC, V.

COLD SPRING

Country Clocks
145 Main Street (10516)
(914) 265-3361
Hours: Mon–Fri by appointment; Sat–Sun, 12–4:30

Fine examples of all types of clocks are available for the collector to purchase. Each clock comes with a one year guarantee. Restoration work which includes face and case work is available. Repair work is also guaranteed for one year, and house calls can be made. PR: $$$. CC: MC, V.

Dew Drop Inn Antique Center (MD)
Route 9 (10516)
(914) 265-4358
Hours: Daily, 11–5
except closed Tues

Located on two floors, this 40 dealer group shop offers a wide selection of silver, china, furniture, toys, ephemera, advertising, pottery, books, jewelry, and other interesting antiques and collectibles. CC: MC, V.
LOC: On Route 9, one mile north of Route 301 or five miles south of Exit 13 on I-84.

Mrs. Hudson's Emporium
89 Main Street (10516)
(914) 265-4577
Hours: Mon, Wed, Thur, & Fri, 12–5; Sat–Sun, 12–6

Housed in a two story, 1820s building, Mrs. Hudson's offers an eclectic mix of antiques and collectibles from American to African. The shop features fascinating books, primitives, Victoriana, Orientalia, tools, and ephemera. PR: $.
CC: MC, V, AMEX.

Pig Hill Antiques
73 Main Street (10516)
(914) 265-9247
(914) 265-2155 fax
Hours: Mon, Thur–Sun, 11–6

This nine room inn has armoires, beds, dressers, country furniture, and decorative gifts for sale. PR: Medium. CC: MC, V, AMEX.

Sarabeck Antiques
Route 9 (10516)
(914) 265-4414
(914) 228-1418 fax
Hours: Thur–Sun, 11–6
or by appointment

This quality shop specializes in furniture and 19th and 20th century lighting, sterling, and porcelain. In addition to furniture repair and restoration, leaded and panel glass shades can be repaired. Patina work is also done. PR: $$. CC: MC, V.

Sugar Loaf Antiques
290 Main Street (10516)
Hours: Thur–Sun, 12–6

This shop contains 19th century classical furniture, appropriate accessories, paintings, and textiles. Expert appraisal services are available by appointment. In business for more than 10 years, this is one of the finest shops in the Cold Spring area. CC: No.

COLLIERSVILLE

Vintage House Antique Center (MD)

Route 7 (13747)
(607) 433-4772
Hours: Daily 10–5

On two floors of a farmhouse, 23 dealers offer a large selection of furniture ranging from country to Depression with accessories that include lamps, linens, glass, and jewelry. There is also a wide selection of collectibles with an emphasis on baseball memorabilia. Delivery services and layaways are available. Consignments are accepted. A lamp repair service is offered. CC: MC, V. LOC: Exit 17 off I88 to Route 7, left on Route 7 for a quarter mile.

COOPERSTOWN

Cooperstown Antiques Center (MD)

73 Chestnut Street (13326)
(607) 547-2435
Hours: Daily 11–6

This group shop has eight dealers who offer a general, eclectic line of antiques and collectibles with an emphasis on restored lighting, furniture (1750-1950), Oriental rugs, nostalgia, and vintage decorative accessories. PR: $$. CC: MC, V.

Frog Hollow Shop, The

92 Pioneer Street (13326)
(607) 547-8631
Hours: Year round by chance or appointment

This shop carries country antiques, Americana, and appropriate accessories such as glass, china, textiles, decorative smalls, and primitives.

CORFU

Hen's Nest

8945 Allegheny Road (14036)
(716) 599-6417
Hours: Summer: Tues–Sat, 10–5; fall & winter: Sat, 10–5; Sun, 12–5

Country antiques, primitives, cupboards, and collectibles are complemented by dried arrangements and gifts.

CORNING

Blake's Antiques

Baron Steuben Place (14830)
(607) 962-1859
Hours: Daily 10–5 or by appointment

This shop specializes in Art Glass, Steuben, Tiffany, cut glass, sterling, hand painted china, and jewelry.

Carder Steuben Glass Shop/The Rockwell Co.
Baron Steuben Place,
5 West Market (14830)
(607) 962-7807
Hours: Mon–Sat, 10–5

In this shop, one will encounter a very impressive collection of Carder Steuben Glass made from 1903 to 1933. Price estimates can also be given. CC: MC, V.

Dimitroff's Antiques
140 East First Street (14830)
(607) 962-6745
Hours: By appointment

Specializing in fine American glass with an emphasis on both pre and post 1932 Steuben glass, this business also offers an appraisal and authentication service and will accept consignments. Purchases can be made by mail order.

Margaret S. King Quality Antiques
10 East First Street (14830)
(518) 962-0876
Hours: By appointment only

This dealer is noted for stocking fine quality 18th and 19th century furniture with appropriate decorations.

CORNWALL-ON-HUDSON

Butter Hill Antiques
211 Hudson Street, Route 218 (12520)
(914) 534-2361
Hours: Fri–Sun, 1–5

Offering a general line of antiques and the decorative arts, this shop features American furniture, paintings, watercolors, old prints, and good quality glass and china. In addition to an appraisal service, cane and rush chair seat repair is available. CC: MC, V.

CORTLAND

Cracker Barrel Antiques
Route 11, Box 3908 (13045)
(607) 756-7643, 749-3490
Hours: Wed–Fri, 12–4; Sat, 10–5; Sun, 12–5

One will find an eclectic blend of antiques and collectibles ranging from glass, china, and jewelry to furniture, pottery, buttons, rugs, and prints. CC: No.

Frank Hoxie
6 Main Street (13045)
(607) 756-2192, 756-1923
Hours: Daily 9:30–5

In addition to a mixture of antique furniture, glassware, china, and miscellaneous goods, this shop carries both antique and estate jewelry. Loose gems, new jewelry, and some gift items are also stocked. Jewelry repairs and both household and jewelry appraisals can be done. PR: $$. CC: MC, V, AMEX, D.

Wilson's Antique Services
1732 East Homer Road, Route 13N (13045)
(607) 753-1076
Hours: Fri–Sat, 9:30–4
or by chance or appointment

In a barn and two rooms in the adjacent house, one will find furniture, advertising, collectibles, dolls, glassware, pottery, and toys. Estates are purchased. Dolls can be repaired. Appraisals and show management services are available. PR: Wide. CC: MC, V.

CROSS RIVER

Yellow Monkey Antiques
Yellow Monkey Village, Route 35 (10518)
(914) 763-5848
(914) 763-8832 fax
Hours: Tues–Sun, 10–6

Displayed in a 7,000 square foot 19th century homestead, one will find authentic antique English and Irish stripped pine and original paint country furniture and accessories. PR: $$$. CC: MC, V.

CUBA

Antiques at the Inn
28 Genesee Parkway (14727)
(716) 968-3335
Hours: Daily 9–5

Antiques at the Inn, located on the grounds of the Rocking Duck Inn Bed and Breakfast, offers smalls, wall art, and contemporary Pairpoint Crystal from Cape Cod. Situated in the heart of the country, the shop has access to a wide variety of rural artifacts and collectibles. Glass, pottery, paper items and fun and funky treasures round out the collection at this shop. CC: MC, V.

CUDDEBACKVILLE

B.J. Antiques
946 Route 209, P.O. Box 336 (12729)
(914) 754-8417
Hours: By chance or appointment

Located eight miles north of Port Jervis, this shop has a general line of antiques and collectibles such as glass, china, country items, post cards, and costume jewelry. PR: $$. CC: No.

"Heirlooms with a Background"
1018 Route 209 (12729)
(914) 754-8136
Hours: By chance or appointment

Established in 1972, this shop

has a general line of antiques and collectibles including quality china, glass, and jewelry.

DELHI

Heirlooms
76 Main Street (13753)
(607) 746-3434
Hours: Mon–Sat, 10–5; Sun, 12–5; Tues closed

This shop has a constantly changing inventory of furniture and accessories which includes antique linens, vintage clothing, jewelry, books, and smalls. Western, hunting, and fishing collectibles are also available.
CC: MC, V.

DELMAR

James K. Van Dervort Antiques
Delaware Avenue (12054)
(518) 439-2143, 439-6576
Hours: Mon–Sat, 12–5
or by appointment;
call if coming a distance.

These dealers specialize in quality American formal and country furniture, early glass, ceramics, porcelain, brass, pewter, textiles, paintings, prints, estate jewelry, and appropriate accessories.
CC: No. LOC: One and a half miles from the intersection of Delaware Avenue and Cherry Avenue.

Maria C. Brooks Antiques
RR 1, Box 322A,
Delaware Turnpike (12054)
(518) 768-2920
Hours: By appointment only

This shop offers authentic furnishings and accessories with a specialization in Shaker.
PR: $$$. CC: No.

DEPOSIT

Axtell Antiques
1 River Street (13754)
(607) 467-2353
Hours: Mon–Sat, 10–5; Sun, 12–5

Quality offerings of 18th and 19th century furniture in original paint and surface, treenware, baskets, folk art, redware, stoneware, early lighting, and hearth accessories fill this shop. PR: $$$$$.

DUANESBURG

Black Sheep Antiques Center (MD)
U.S. Route 20 West (12056)
(518) 895-2983
Hours: Daily 10–5 except closed Tues & Wed during Jan & Feb; closed major holidays

More than 70 dealers offer a diverse assortment of antiques, accessories, and collectibles from the late 18th through 20th century. CC: MC, V. LOC: Three miles west of Duanesburg.

Fine 17th century Continental carved and giltwood figure of a lamb, probably German. *(Courtesy Georgian Manor Antiques, Inc., New York City)*

DURHAM

Mulberry Bush Antiques Bed & Breakfast

Route 22, Susquehanna Turnpike (12422)
(518) 239-4563
Hours: Daily 10–? or by chance

Furniture, decorative smalls, collectibles, and custom ordered reproduction furniture made on the premises are on display throughout this historical bed & breakfast. PR: $400+. CC: MC, V.

EAST AURORA

Roycroft Campus Antiques (MD)

37 South Grove Street (14052)
(716) 655-1565
Hours: Mon–Sat, 11–5

Five dealers offer a general line of antiques that includes primitives to 1950s items. The group shop emphasizes Roycroft pieces. Estate sales and auctions are conducted. PR: $$$. CC: MC, V.

EDMESTON

Ingeborg Quitzau, Antiquarian Books

Route 80, P.O. Box 5106 (13335)
(607) 965-8605
Hours: By appointment, mail order, and shows

Miniature books, books in German, children's books, and illustrated books are the specialty of this dealer. Mail order and a search service are available. CC: No.

ELMIRA

Maple Avenue Antiques

352 Maple Avenue (14904)
(607) 734-0332
Hours: Tues–Sat, 11–5;
Sun & Mon by chance

Quality antiques and collectibles have been assembled in a historical, Victorian home. Depression ware, Mission furniture, cut glass, Deco, and oak furniture fill this newly expanded shop. PR: $$$. CC: No.

Mark Twain Country Antiques (MD)

220 South Main Street (14904)
(607) 734-0916
Hours: Daily 10–5

Established in 1985, the group shop offers a general line of quality antiques, furniture, ceramics, art objects, and decorator pieces. Appraisals, as well as furniture care products, are available. PR: $$$. CC: MC, V.

Oldies But Goodies

Route 352 & Carpenter Road (14903)
(607) 562-3916, (800) 479-7416
Hours: Mon–Sat, 10–5

Using an old-fashioned mercantile shop as a setting, this 10,000 square foot shop offers heirloom quality refinished furniture, especially oak and mahogany. Rugs and lighting devices and fixtures are some of the accessories that are also stocked. PR: $$. CC: MC, V.

Touch of Country, House of Shops (MD)

1019 Pennsylvania Avenue (14904)
(607) 737-6945
Hours: Tues–Fri, 10–6 with Thur till 8; Sat, 10–5; Sun, 12–3; Nov & Dec, Fri till 8 & Sun till 5

Located in a Victorian farmhouse, this group shop has 15 dealers who offer a wide assortment of antiques, collectibles, gifts, and home decorating items. Furniture refinishing is available. CC: MC, V, D.

FAIR HAVEN

Black Creek Farm

P.O. Box 390, Mixer Road (13064)
(315) 947-5282
Hours: April 20–December 20, Wed–Sat, 11–4 or call

This shop offers Victorian furniture, appropriate accessories, vintage children's clothing, and some cut glass. Furniture refinishing and caning are available. CC: MC, V.

FAIRPORT

Donald Naetzker Antiques

205 South Main Street (14450)
(716) 223-6634
Hours: By appointment only

In addition to specializing in 18th and 19th century American country furniture, this dealer also offers early brass lighting, candlesticks, and whale oil lamps. A full line of pottery from 1760 to 1850 with some emphasis on historical

American views on Staffordshire also is offered. PR: $$. CC: No.

Wagonjack and Holly Cobbles Antiques
9 North Main Street (14450)
(716) 388-0134
Hours: Tues–Fri, 11–5; Sat, 10–5

This shop offers country furniture, quilts, lamps, kitchenware, and accessories that the owners feel are affordably priced to personalize a country setting. CC: No.

Windy Acres Antiques
2518 Huber Road, off Route 441 (14450)
(716) 377-2207
(716) 377-8145 fax
Hours: Fri–Sat, 11–5
or by appointment

This shop is stocked with country antiques, decorative smalls, folk art, decoys, pine and painted furniture, holiday collectibles, mirrors, and primitives for both collectors and dealers. PR: $$. CC: No.

FAYETTEVILLE

Seymour June House Art & Antiques (MD)
203 South Manlius Street (13066)
(315) 637-1749
Hours: Mon–Sat, 11–5; Sun, 12–4

Located in a restored 1838 Greek Revival mansion, this group shop offers fine art and antiques of the 18th, 19th, and 20th centuries. A 3,000 square foot display area offers an eclectic collection of interesting quality pieces from every continent. Consignments are accepted. Authentication and appraisal services are available.
PR: $$$$$. CC: No.

FISHKILL

Noah's Ark Antique Center (MD)
2213 Route 9 North (12524)
(914) 896-0654
(914) 896-4008 fax
Hours: Tues-Sun, 10-5

More than 35 dealers have filled 6,000 square feet with glass, furniture, military antiques, pocketwatches, clocks, collectibles, and a wide range of antiques for both interior and exterior decoration. In addition to accepting consignments and offering prop rentals, repair work can be done on marble, metal, glass, stained glass, bronze, cast iron, furniture, paintings, and pewter. Appraisals can also be given. CC: MC, V.

FLINT

Willowen Antiques
2348 Route 5 & 20 (14561)
(716) 526-4405
Hours: Mon-Sat, 10-5; Sun 12-5

This shop which is located in a 1850s carriage factory carries a wide range of glass, china, linens,

and assorted country antiques and collectibles. Consignments are accepted. CC: No.
LOC: Midway between Canandaigua and Geneva.

FLORIDA

Randallville Mill Antiques

65 Randall Street (10921)
(914) 651-7466
Hours: By chance or appointment, open most Sunday afternoons

In three room settings, one will find pine and oak furniture on display with complementary accessories. Furniture repair, refinishing, and restoration are available. PR: $$. CC: No.
LOC: A half mile east of the village of Florida on Route 94.

FRANKLINVILLE

Once Upon A Time Country.... Furniture and Antique Market (MD)

22 Park Square (14737)
(716) 676-2728
Hours: Tues–Thur, 11–6; Fri, 11–7; Sat, 10–5; Sun 12–5

Fifteen dealers offer a wide variety of antiques and collectibles such as furniture, glassware, and country items. There is also a gallery featuring new country furniture in oak and a variety of new and antique upholstered furniture. Consignments are accepted. Furniture refinishing and reproduction services are available. Appraisals can be given. CC: MC, V, in-store revolving credit with 90 day interest free program.

FRIENDSHIP

Anntiques

18 West Main Street (14739)
(716) 973-7921
Hours: Mon–Sat, 10:30–5 except closed Wed;
Sun, 1:30–5 or by appointment

This cozy little shop has a basement filled with kitchen collectibles, bottles, floor lamps, postcards, lighting fixtures plus gas and electric parts, and other neat stuff. CC: No.

Circus Barn Antiques with Chairs Upstairs

18 West Main Street (14739)
(716) 973-7921, 973-7975
Hours: Mon–Sat, 10:30–5 except closed Wed; Sun, 1:30–5

This two story barn is full of furniture and other items from all eras. Upstairs are more than 500 chairs: sets, singles, parts—both refinished and not. Cane, rush, split, and Shaker tape seat repair are available. CC: No.

Good Trade Farm

W. Main & Sunnyside St. (14739)
(716) 973-2441
Hours: Tues–Sat, 10–5
or by appointment

In addition to offering repair and

restoration services for wood and painted antiques, this deal also has folk art, unique gifts, bowls, turnings, and Dover books. An extensive research library helps bring custom and reproduction furniture work to life. CC: D.

Pink Church Antiques, The
39 West Main Street (14739)
(716) 973-7921
Hours: Mon–Sat, 10:30–5 except closed Wed; Sun, 1:30–5

Located one mile from Exit 29 on Route 17, this shop offers quality antiques and collectibles such as Depression glass, vintage clothing, primitive to Victorian furniture, books, and Scouting items. CC: No.

FULTONVILLE

Hillcrest House Antique Mall (MD)
Corner of Routes 30A & 5S (12072)
(518) 853-4550
Hours: Daily, 7:30–5

Twenty-two dealers present a full line of antiques and collectibles which include American furniture, glass, and marbles. CC: No.

GARDINER

The Country Store Antique Center (MD)
132 Main Street (12525)
(914) 255-1123
Hours: Mon–Sat, 10–5; Sun, 11–5

Located in an old country store, 25 dealers offer a vast array of antiques and collectibles such as furniture, estate and costume jewelry, and furniture. PR: $$. CC: MC, V.

GENEVA

Calhoun's Books
1510 Routes 5 & 20 West (14456)
(315) 789-8599
Hours: Mid–April to Mid–November, Daily 11–5; other times by appointment

More than 50,000 books and 75,000 postcards can be found in this shop. Areas of specialization include Americana, literature, maps, and decorative bindings. The postcards are arranged for easy viewing. PR: $$. CC: MC, V. LOC: Three miles west of Geneva on Routes 5 & 20.

GERMANTOWN

Blue Stores Antiques (MD)
2120 Route 9 (12526)
(518) 537-6518, 537-4209
Hours: Daily, 9–5

Six dealers are located in an old country store and two barns which are brimming over with refinished furniture, bedroom and kitchen sets, blanket chests, kitchen utensils, jelly cupboards, tables and chairs, crocks, books, china closets, yellow ware, folksy objects, and objects from the 18th through the 20th century. Refinishing work is also available. PR: $$. CC: MC, V.

GHENT

Jenny Hall, Asian Antiques

Box 219, R.D.2 (12075)
(518) 672-4902
Hours: By appointment, shows, and mail order

This dealer specializes in Chinese furniture, vases, porcelain, bronzes, netsuke, textiles, screens, paintings, and calligraphy. Consignments are accepted. A decorating service is available.

GILBERTSVILLE

Jill Fenichell

Gilbertsville
(607) 783-2930
(607) 783-2948 fax
Hours: Shows and mail order only

English pottery and porcelains from the mid 1700s until 1930 including 18th century Worcester and Derby, Aesthetic period pottery, parian ware, and Susie Cooper pottery of the 1920s and 1930s are this dealer's areas of specialization. Appraisals, research, and authentication services are available. PR: $100+. CC: MC, V.

GILBOA

Day-Barb Antiques

RD 1, Box 329 (12076)
(607) 588-9435
Hours: Open by chance or appointment

Established in 1977, this shop has a broad selection of antiques and collectibles that will satisfy everyone's taste. Architectural items; lighting devices and fixtures; fine china; oak, pine, and mahogany furniture; decorative smalls; glass; and furniture in old paint fill this shop. CC: No.
LOC: Route 145 to Cooksburgh, west on Route 362, then bear left on Route 354.

GLENS FALLS

Glenwood Manor Antiques (MD)

Bay & Quaker Road, Route 254 (12801)
(518) 798-4747
Hours: Mon–Sat, 10–5; Sun, 12–5

In an elegant Manor House, 40 dealers on four floors offer an extensive line of antiques and collectibles that range from estate jewelry, fine glass, toys, and pottery to country collectibles, American furniture, and books. CC: No.
LOC: Exit 19 on I-84, one mile east on Route 254.

GLOVERSVILLE

Bayberry House

P.O. Box 174 (12078)
(518) 725-1954
Hours: Shows only

This dealer offers American coin silver, silver plate holloware, and 19th century furniture and accessories such as quilts and mirrors.

One of a kind birdhouse with spires and steps from Iowa, 32" x 21' x 20". *(Courtesy American Primitive Gallery, New York City)*

Brickwood Antiques
103 Woodlawn Drive (12078)
(518) 725-0230
Hours: Appointments, mail order, and shows only

This dealer specializes in Chinese Export Porcelain, pewter, pottery, and porcelain. Appraisals can be arranged.

Olde Clocks
4 Mountain View Avenue (12078)
(518) 725-5779
Hours: By appointment only

This shop which specializes in American clocks also offers a repair and restoration service. CC: No.

GREENE

Collectors' Showcase
78 Genesee Street
(13778)
(607) 656-8805
Hours: Wed–Mon, 10–5

This is a fun shop specializing in baby boomer nostalgia: political items, collectible toys and premiums, and a large selection of Hess trucks and other station promotional trucks. A selection of collector display cases in wood and acrylic is also available. PR: $$. CC: MC, V.

Lady Paydacker
Elmer Smith Road, Box 243 (13778)
(607) 656-9433, 754-3776
Hours: Seasonal, May through September; best to call ahead

This shop carries a general line of antiques and collectibles such as country furniture, wicker, linens, costume jewelry, advertising, kitchenware, dinnerware, Depression glass, and fishing and sporting collectibles. CC: No.

Old Country Store, The
2 South Chenango Street (13778)
(607) 656-9070
Hours: Wed–Sun, 10–5

In an 1803 country store, one will find country antiques and collectibles. Quality primitives plus 19th and early 20th century furniture and accessories are tastefully displayed in room settings. PR: $$. CC: No.

Pheasant Farm Antiques (MD)
7 Foundry Street (13778)
(607) 656-9188
Hours: Daily 10–5

In this two story 9,000 square foot co-op, 35 dealers offer a nice selection of antiques, collectibles, books, jewelry, and furniture. Also, The Booktree Bookshop, which deals in new books, is at this location. CC: MC, V.

GREENFIELD PARK

Apple Tree Antiques
233 Caston Road Ext. (12435)
(914) 647-7651
Hours: Fri–Sun, 10–5; other days by chance or appointment

In addition to furniture in as found or refinished condition, decorative smalls, and carnival glass, one will find most patterns of Depression glass. All this merchandise is housed in two buildings. CC: No.

GREENWICH

Country Books
RD #1 Cottrell Road (12834)
(518) 692-2585
Hours: Please call to check

This shop specializes in illustrated editions, children's books, and books concerning the Adirondacks. In addition to these offerings, the shop carries a general stock. PR: $$. CC: No. LOC: Route 40, three miles north of Route 29.

Old Greenwich Hardware Antiques
120 Main Street (12834)
(518) 692-7745
Hours: Wed–Fri, 11–5; Sat, 10–5; Sun 1–5

A general line of antiques; country, early American, and Victorian furniture; and decorative smalls including early iron, tin, woodenware, prints, mirrors, quilts, and lighting are offered on three floors in an 1870s village building. CC: MC, V, D.

O'Wagon Antiques
RD #1 (12834)
(518) 692-9427
Hours: Daily 10–5 except closed Thur

In addition to primitives, country items, and furniture in old paint, this shop contains Victorian, Deco period, and oak furniture. There is also a large selection of dolls, toys, country smalls, and Christmas related items. PR: $$. CC: No. LOC: On Route 40, 1.5 miles north of town.

Owl Pen Books
Riddle Road (12834)
(518) 692-7039
Hours: May 1 through November 1, Wed–Sun, 12–6

This large general antiquarian bookstore stocks 75,000 books plus prints and ephemera in two buildings. Since this business is located on a back road off another back road, it is best to call for directions. CC: No.

GUILFORD

Praiseworthy Antiques
Merchant Street & Main Street
(607) 895-6278
(607) 895-6211 fax
Hours: Wed–Sun, 10–5

Located in a former, small, gothic style, stone church, one will find Empire and other period furniture, Art Glass and Art Pottery, outdoor furniture in cast iron and stone, and elegant smalls. An interior design decorating service is available. Appraisals can be given. Estates are also purchased. PR: $$$. CC: No.

HAMILTON

Ingrid Migonis Antiques
at the Veranda Antique Center, Madison
(315) 824-3029

This dealer offers quality country furniture, quilts, samplers rugs, and paintings.

HAMMONDSPORT

Antiques at the Warehouse
8091 County Route 88 (14840)
(607) 569-3655
Hours: April–Oct, Daily 10–5; Nov–March, by chance or appointment

Refinished country antiques and good quality smalls are always available in this warehouse-type setting. CC: MC, V.
LOC: Between Bath and Hammondsport, near the entrance to the Taylor Wine Co.

Opera House Antiques (MD)
61-63 Sheather Street (14840)
(607) 569-3525
Hours: January to Memorial Day, Sat–Sun, 10–5; Memorial Day to Christmas, Daily 9–5

Located just off the square in

Hammondsport, this group shop with 15 dealers offers a general line of antiques and collectibles. Primitives, jewelry, sterling silver, prints by both Parrish and Nutting, kitchen items, furniture, advertising pieces, linens, toys, and decorative items are just a few of the many items that one will find. PR: $$. CC: MC, V.

HANCOCK

Hancock Antiques
50 West Main Street (13783)
(607) 637-2704
Hours: Thur–Mon, 11–5
or by chance or appointment;
a call ahead is suggested

This shop specializes in quilts and country furniture, paintings and prints, textiles, linens, and rugs. Decorative smalls to complement a country setting are also available. PR: Moderate to Expensive. CC: No. LOC: Exit 87 on Route 17, one block east of McDonald's restaurant.

HARTSDALE

Memory Lane Antiques & Collectibles
210 East Hartsdale Avenue (10530)
(914) 723-7974
Hours: Daily 10–7

This shop specializes in Victorian furniture, art, collectibles of all types, vintage clothing, and Depression glassware. About half the items in this shop are on consignment. Furniture, lamp, oil painting, china, and pottery repair services are available. PR: $$. CC: MC, V, AMEX.

HERKIMER

2+4 Antiques (MD)
212 North Main Street (13350)
(315) 866-1861
Hours: Mon–Sat, 10–4:30;
Friday till 6:00

In this group shop, seven dealers present an interesting selection of antiques and collectibles which includes both oak and mahogany furniture, glass, stoneware, pottery, and glass. PR: $$. CC: MC, V.

HIGH FALLS

Tow Path House Antiques (MD)
Second Street (12440)
(914) 687-0615
Hours: Thur–Mon, 11–5

This eight dealer shop features a constantly changing selection of furniture, collectibles, and accessories. One is likely to encounter country antiques, folk art, Americana, and Art Pottery. PR: $$. CC: No.

HILLSDALE

K & K Quilteds
Route 23, P.O. Box 23 (12529)
(518) 325-4502
Hours: Fri–Sat, 10–4; Sun, 1–4;
Mon, 10–4

With five rooms of floor to ceiling coded vintage fabrics that result in an 80 percent chance of exact fabric match plus a national network of vintage fabric collections throughout the United States, this is the largest quilt restoration service on the East Coast. In addition, three retail rooms are filled with antique quilts and gift items. There is an annual sale the last weekend of July averaging about three hundred quilts. PR: $$. CC: MC, V.

Red Fox Antiques
9768 State Route 22 (12529)
(518) 325-3841
Hours: Fri–Mon, 11–5;
other times by chance

Established in 1988, this shop specializes in quality Americana and folk art in the country manner. Furniture in old paint, Shaker smalls, Native American items, decorative smalls, textiles, primitives, and ceramics are featured. Appraisals can be given, and furniture repair and restoration are available. PR: Moderate. CC: MC, V. LOC: Two miles north of Route 23.

HOLCOMB

Rader's Antiques
7235 Gauss Road (14469)
(716) 657-6213
Hours: By appointment only,
please call ahead

Since its establishment in 1977, this shop has specialized in country furniture with an emphasis on cherry, tiger maple, and paint plus appropriate accessories.
CC: MC, V.

HOMER

Pheasant Hill Antiques
77 Route 281 (13077)
(607) 749-7293
(607) 749-7293 fax
Hours: Mon–Sat, 10–5;
Sun by chance or appointment

In addition to having the largest offering of refinished wood frames in the area, this shop specializes in quality 19th century refinished country and period furniture in pine, cherry, mahogany, and walnut. There is also a fine selection of decorative accessories to complement any setting or give as gifts. PR: $$. CC: MC, V.

HONEOYE

Bristol Antiques
P.O. Box 728 (14471)
(716) 229-5727
Hours: Closed shop, shows only

This business specializes in sporting equipment, medical collectibles, yellow ware, and garden accessories. PR: $. CC: No.

HOOSICK

Hoosick Antique Center (MD)
New York Route 7 (12089)
(518) 686-4700
Hours: Daily 10–5

Located in a restored 1820s post

and beam farm house and country store, 62 dealers have assembled a magnificent offering of quality antiques and selected collectibles spanning the 18th to 20th century. Furniture repair and restoration, as well as appraisals, are available. PR: $$. CC: MC, V.

HOPEWELL JUNCTION

Hopewell Antique Center (MD)
638 Route 82 (12533)
(914) 221-3055
Hours: Daily 11–5

This is a group shop stocked by twenty dealers who feature furniture, collectibles, glassware, pottery, linens, fine and costume jewelry, paintings, ephemera, postcards, and many other interesting items. A paperback book exchange is also on the premises. PR: $$. CC: MC, V.

John Laing's Yesteryear Antiques
8 Schoolhouse Lane (12533)
(914) 223-3083
Hours: Closed shop:
mail order, and shows

In the antique business since 1977, this dealer carries a general line of antiques with an emphasis on porcelains, dog figurines, American Brilliant Period cut glass, and Victoriana. Consignments are accepted. Appraisals and estate sales are conducted.

R & M Leed Antiques
27 Warren Farm Road (12533)
(914) 897-2282
Hours: By appointment only

In addition to offering fine American and Continental furniture and accessories especially from the Neoclassical period, these dealers also stock all types of pre-1840 items. There are no collectibles in this shop. All items are guaranteed as represented. PR: $$$$$. CC: No.

Wiccopee Antiques, Inc.
Route 52 and Old Grange Road (12533)
(914) 896-7956
Hours: Sat–Sun, 10–4
and by appointment

This shop is filled with antique wicker, furniture, collectibles, glassware, and decorative accessories. PR: $. CC: No.

HORSEHEADS

Cider Mill Antiques
160 Ithaca Road (14845)
(607) 739-1768
Hours: April–December,
Tues–Sat, 12–5

This shop offers a unique blend of carefully chosen antique furniture, lamps, and accessories as well as reproduction upholstered furniture, Windsor chairs, and lighting fixtures.

HOWES CAVE

Cavern View Antiques
4678 Barnerville Road, RD 1,
Box 23 (12092)
(518) 296-8052
Hours: Summer: Tues–Sat, 10–4; year round by chance or appointment

This three room shop features 19th century furniture and decorative items including English white ironstone and other 19th century ceramics. PR: $. CC: MC, V.

HUDSON

Antiquities
415 Warren Street (12534)
(518) 822-1207
Hours: Daily 10–5

American and Continental furniture, oil paintings, ship models, and mahogany furniture can be found in this shop. PR: $$$. CC: No.

Atlantis Rising
545 Warren Street (12534)
(518) 822-0438
Hours: Daily 11–4

Although specializing in all types of collectible smalls which are mainly from the 20th century, this shop also carries a significant stock of primitive and antique objects. PR: $. CC: No.

Beata Baird Antiques
612 Warren Street (12534)
(518) 828-0575
Hours: Thur–Mon, 11:30–5

This shop contains an eclectic mixture of country furniture and accessories, jewelry, textiles, and items with character. PR: $$. CC: MC, V.

Doyle Antiques
711 Warren Street (12534)
(518) 828-3929
Hours: Thur–Mon, 11–5; Tues, by appointment or chance; Wed, closed

This large shop carries a wide range of 19th and early 20th century American, English, and Continental furniture complemented by paintings, decorative accessories, cast iron, silver, lighting, boxes, and engravings. Appraisals can be done. CC: AMEX.

Foxfire Limited
538 Warren Street (12534)
(518) 828-6281
Hours: Daily 11–5 except closed Wed

This shop carries an interesting mix of English and American antiques complemented by prints, rugs, porcelain, and Oriental items. PR: $$$. CC: No.

Hudson Photographic Center
611 Warren Street (12534)
(518) 828-2178
Hours: Mon–Fri, 9–5; Sat, 9–4:30

This dealer specializes in antique and unusual cameras and all types of photographic memorabilia. At least 200 cameras and hundreds of early photos are always in stock. PR: $$. CC: MC, V.

Irish Princess, The
537 Warren Street (12534)
(518) 828-2800
Hours: Thur–Tues, 11–5

This large two story shop features 19th century English, Continental, and American Empire formal furniture, porcelain, paintings, and vintage jewelry. PR: $$$$. CC: MC, V.

Lawrence P. Kohn
624 Warren Street (12534)
(518) 822-1924
Hours: Thur–Tues, 11–5

This dealer offers an eclectic assortment of paintings, furniture, toys, and decorative arts.

Lou Marotta
430 Warren Street (12534)
(518) 822-0604
Hours: Thur–Tues, 11–5

Inspired by both humor and nature, this dealer has assembled an interesting assortment of 18th, 19th, and 20th century furniture and furnishings, especially French and Italian complemented by garden accessories and decorative smalls. An interior design service is available. PR: $$$. CC: No.

Savannah Antiques
512 Warren Street (12534)
(518) 822-1343
(518) 822-1343 fax
Hours: Sat–Sun, 10–5; otherwise by chance of appointment

A Victorian townhouse is the setting for a mixture of architectural and garden elements, formal and country furnishings, decorative art, and accessories. All of the offerings are of the highest quality. Estates can be appraised and consignments are accepted. PR: $$$. CC: AMEX, OPT.

707 Warren Street Antiques
707 Warren Street (12534)
(518) 766-5395, 766-3937
Hours: Fri–Sun, 11–5; Thur & Mon by chance.

This dealer oriented shop specializes in country antiques, architectural items, collectibles, cast iron, and the unique. CC: No.

Townhouse Antiques
306 Warren Street (12534)
(518) 828-8939
Hours: Thur–Tues, 12–5

One will find Art Pottery, collectibles, ephemera, toys, games, trains, and puzzles in this shop. CC: No.

Vincent R. Mulford
711 Warren Street (12534)
(518) 828-5489
Hours: Fri–Mon, 11–5

In addition to unusual and one of a kind objects and high style furnishings from the 18th to the

Thirty-two plate russet iron kabuto with mempo and gilt figural maedate, ca. 1750. *(Courtesy Flying Cranes Antiques, Ltd., New York City)*

20th century that include both country and formal, this shop also has cast iron, mahogany, art, and upholstered furniture.

HUGHSONVILLE

Art Book Services
P.O. Box 360 (12537)
(914) 297-1312
(914) 297-0068 fax
Hours: 9–5

As reflected by the company name, this business deals in books on the fine and decorative arts. Two catalogs are issued per year that list all important new books on antiques. It is worth having your name on their mailing list. PR: $$. CC: MC, V, AMEX.

HURLEY

Van Deusen House Antiques
11 Main Street, two blocks off Route 209 (12443)
(914) 331-8852
Hours: Tues–Thur, 10–5 and most weekends but call

This old fashioned single owner shop that welcomes both dealers and browsers offers country and formal furnishings, early porcelain, glass, Orientals, tools, and ephemera. CC: MC, V, D.

HURLEYVILLE

Edward & Judith Keiz Antiques

318 Bowers Drive, Divine Corners
(12747)
(914) 434-0057
Hours: By appointment or chance—a call ahead is advised

These dealers specialize in good early country furniture in original paint, tiger maple, cherry, and walnut. Cupboards, blanket chests, assorted tables from the 19th century, and appropriate accessories such as stoneware, treenware, and textiles are some of the items that one regularly finds in this shop. LOC: Six miles east of Route 17, Exit 100.

HYDE PARK

Findings Antiques (MD)

644 Albany Post Road, Route 9
(12538)
(914) 229-9667
Hours: Sun, 12–6; Fri–Mon, 10–6; Tues–Thur, 11–5

In this shop, six dealers present an eclectic and constantly changing mixture of furniture, antiques, and collectibles at realistic prices. Reproduction hardware, refinishing supplies, waxes, and polishes are also available. PR: $. CC: MC, V.

Hyde Park Antiques Center (MD)

544 Albany Post Road, Route 9
(12538)
(914) 229-8200
Hours: Daily 10–5

Fifty-five dealers have filled this 10,000 square foot co-op with fine antiques and collectibles. Featured items include country and period furniture, silver, porcelain, Art Pottery, majolica, glass, tramp art, toys, dolls, advertising, and estate, vintage, and costume jewelry. PR: $$$$. CC: MC, V, AMEX, D.

Village Antique Center (MD)

597 Albany Post Road, Route 9
(12538)
(914) 229-6600
Hours: Daily 10–5

An incredible variety of antiques, collectibles, and a select group of classic reproductions are presented by 35 dealers. CC: MC, V.

ILION

Steele Creek Antiques

Johnston Road, RD 1, Box 485
(13357)
(315) 822-5180
Hours: By chance or appointment, days or evenings

Established in 1991, this shop which is in an 1800s red grist mill contains a general selection of antiques and collectibles. PR: $. CC: No.

INTERLAKEN

Bob and Ginny's Treasures

8355 Main Street, P.O. Box 285
(14847)
(607) 532-4260
Hours: Tues–Sat, 12–5
or by appointment

Specializing in Elegent and Depression glassware, these dealers also carry a nice selection of oak, pine, and painted furniture plus some unexpected surprises. PR: $. CC: MC, V.

Simply Country

8381 Main Street (14847)
(607) 532-9290
Hours: By chance or appointment, shows, and mail order

This dealer offers restored brass chandeliers, wall sconces, and a large selection of glass shades. Graniteware, treenware, and country decorative smalls but not furniture are also stocked. A repair and restoration service for all types of electric lamps is available, and a complete line of homespun plaid lamp shades is carried. PR: $. CC: MC, V.

Turn of the Century

8406 Main Street (14847)
(607) 532-8822
Hours: Tues–Sun, 12–5

This shop contains two large showrooms of furniture and thousands of unusual, affordable collectibles, antiques, and nice old things. Dealers always shop this shop. CC: MC, V.

IRVINGTON-ON-HUDSON

Rags and Rarities

51 Main Street (10533)
(914) 591-6277
Hours: Daily, 10–6

This shop contains a collection of estate jewelry, American paintings, and antique accessories. Consignments are accepted. Appraisals can be done. CC: MC, V, AMEX. LOC: One and a half miles south of the Tappan Zee Bridge, just off Route 9.

ITHACA

Collection, The

See Trumansburg

Pastimes

Dewitt Building (14850)
(607) 277-3457
Hours: Mon–Sat, 10–5:30

Located in a renovated 1912 schoolhouse, Pastimes has been specializing in small antiques and collectibles since 1979. A large selection of vintage jewelry, postcards, buttons, beads, pens, photographica, political buttons, tins, marbles, and ephemera is offered. PR: $. CC: MC, V.

JASPER

Hickory Bend Antiques
2995 Drake Hill Road (14855)
(607) 792-3343
(607) 792-3309 fax
Hours: Business conducted by appointment only

In addition to specializing in brass cash registers, these dealers also offer barbershop collectibles, coin-operated machines, and soda fountain collectibles. Parts and restoration services for old cash registers are available. Metal repair and restoration are also done. CC: MC, V.

JEFFERSON

Justin Thyme Antique Center (MD)
Star Route, Route 10 (12093)
(607) 652-7624
Hours: Wed–Mon, 10–6;
Jan 1–May 1, closed Tues & Wed

Consisting of 5,000 square feet of display space on two floors in a 13-sided barn, this nine dealer shop features pottery, furniture, collectibles, postcards, toys, clocks, prints, jewelry, and advertising. PR: $. CC: No.

JEFFERSON VALLEY

Oldies But Goodies Antiques
3635 Hill Boulevard, #510 (10535)
(914) 887-5272
Hours: Shows and mail order only

In addition to specializing in antique perfume bottles and their restoration, Tiffany Studios desk sets and Art Glass by Tiffany, R. Lalique, Galle, Loetz, and Moser are also available. China and pottery restoration services are available.
PR: $$.
CC: MC, V, AMEX, D, DC.

JOHNSON CITY

Frantiques
205 Main Street (13790)
(607) 770-7103
Hours: Mon–Sat, 11–5, except Thur till 8

In addition to a general line of antiques that includes jewelry, furniture, glass, books, and sheet music this dealer stocks a large selection of Blue Willow ware. PR: $$.
CC: MC, V.

JORDANVILLE

Paul L. Baker Antiques
RR 1, Box 42 (13361)
(315) 858-2784
Hours: Appointment, chance, or shows

This dealer carries primitives, country, and pre Victorian period pieces in original finish. In addition Flow Blue china, ironstone, stoneware, and red ware are stocked.
CC: No.

KATONAH

Ana Maria Recouso Antiques

P.O. Box 386 (10536)
(914) 232-8316
Hours: By appointment

This dealer offers a general line of antiques that span several eras and cultures such as North American, South American, and Asian. In addition to antiques and folk art, decorative accessories such as lamps, china, glass, eclectic furniture, Asian ceramics and art, paintings, prints, rattan of the 1930s, jewelry, and fireplace equipment are offered. PR: $$$. CC: No.

Barbara F. Israel Enterprises

296 Mt. Holly Road (10536)
(914) 232-4271
(212) 744-2188 fax
Hours: By appointment only and shows

This dealer specializes in antiques for the garden: statuary, fountains, benches, urns, gates, lanterns, sundials, and birdbaths in a variety of stones and metals. Also stocked are a few larger pieces such as gazebos and architectural columns, all in old or old looking finishes and more often than not with classical inspirations. PR: $$$$$. CC: No. LOC: Two and a half miles from the junction of 684 and Route 35.

Elmantiques

10 Woods Bridge Road (10536)
(914) 232-4765
Hours: Spring, summer, and fall; Fri–Sat, 12–5 and by appointment; winter by appointment

In addition to specializing in antique bottles, insulators, and collectibles, this shop offers quilts and a limited selection of furniture and Oriental pieces.
PR: Low to Moderate. CC: No.

KINDERHOOK

Binder, Joiner, & Smith

(518) 758-7563
Hours: By appointment

Early American formal and country furniture and appropriate accessories are offered by these dealers. Special wants are handled by appointment. Otherwise, they exhibit at the Kinderhook Antique Center. Mail order except for furniture is available. Some consignments are accepted. PR: $$. CC: MC, V.

Kinderhook Antique Center (MD)

Route 9H (12106)
(518) 758-7939
Hours: Summer, Daily 10–5; winter, Daily 10–4

Sharing an old barn, 12 dealers offer a wide range of American furniture (country, primitive, painted, and formal), stoneware, china, books, glass, tools, and textiles with an emphasis on the 18th and 19th century. A finders service is available, prop rentals can be arranged, and a delivery service within 50 miles (further by arrangement) is provided. PR: $$. CC: MC, V.

KINGSTON

Boulevard Attic
400 Boulevard (12401)
(914) 339-6316
Hours: Thur–Mon, 11–5

Collectibles, decorative smalls, kitchen collectibles, and a general line of furniture can be found in this shop. PR: $. CC: No.

Catskill Mountain Antique Center (MD)
Route 28, two miles west of Thurway Exit 19 (12475)
(914) 331-0880
Hours: Sun, 11–5; Mon–Sat, 10–5 but closed Tues

Stocked by 20 dealers, this large two story group shop deals in furniture, early jewelry, porcelain, silver, paintings, American Indian material, and glass. Consignments are accepted. Oriental rug repair is available. Appraisals can be done. PR: Varied. CC: MC, V.

Fred J. Johnston Antiques/ Robert A. Slater, Prop.
63 Main Street, P. O. Box 3235 (12401)
(914) 331-3979
Hours: Mon–Sat, 9:30–4:30 usually, appointment advised

Established 68 years ago, this business is noted for its large inventory of period, quality 18th and early 19th century American furniture and accessories. CC: No. LOC: Minutes from Exit 19, NYS Thruway.

Holiday Hill Antiques
66 Holiday Lane (12401)
(914) 331-4983
Hours: Summer, Mon–Thur, 8–12 (noon); winter, Mon–Fri, 8–12 (noon); other times by appointment

Although placing an emphasis on American country furniture and accessories, this shop also has ephemera, period hardware, collectibles, and a general line of 19th and 20th century furnishings. CC: No. LOC: From Washington St. to Lucas, left on Millers, fifth right off Millers, 2nd house on left.

Jack & Maryellen Whistance
288 Route 28 (12401)
(914) 338-4397
Hours: By chance or appointment

Located one mile west of NYS Thruway Exit 19, this shop is filled with 18th and 19th century country furniture, paintings, glass, marbles, bottles and collectibles. CC: No.

Rondout Art and Antiques
35 Broadway (12401)
(914) 339-1844
Hours: Thur–Sun, 11–9; Mon, 11–5 or by appointment

In addition to offering a wide selection of quality antiques and collectibles, this dealer specializes in paintings, prints, sculpture, and musical instruments.

Skillypot Antique Center (MD)
41 Broadway (12401)
(914) 338-6779
Hours: Jan 1st–April 30th, Daily 11–4 except closed Wed; May 1st–Oct 31st, Daily 11–6

This multidealer shop has a wide range of antiques and collectibles and features glassware, estate and costume jewelry, oak and primitive furniture, vintage clothing, and Depression glass. Shipping can be done for small items. PR: Moderate. MC: MC, V, D.

Vin-Dick Antiques
2545 Route 209 (12401)
(914) 338-7113
Hours: By chance or appointment

In this carpeted and well lit store, one will find English and American formal and country furniture with various appropriate accessories. PR: $$. CC: No. LOC: Five miles south of Kingston.

Wall Street Antiques
333 Wall Street (12402)
(914) 338-3212
Hours: Mon–Sat, 9–5

Different types and styles of furniture, antiques, and collectibles fill this eclectic shop that has something for everyone. PR: $$. CC: AMEX, D.

KRUMVILLE

Old Mill Antiques
327 Sahler Mill Road (12447)
(914) 657-8235
Hours: Fri–Mon, 12–5

Furniture in oak, pine, mahogany, and walnut and a full range of decorative and useful accessories such as light fixtures, mirrors, pottery, and glassware can be found in this shop. CC: No.

LAKE CARMEL

Fieldstone Antiques
150 Smadbeck Avenue (10512)
(914) 225-2690
Hours: Tues–Sun, 10–5

These dealers carry a general line of antiques and collectibles with an emphasis on oak furniture and brick-a-brac. PR: Varied. CC: No.

LAKE GEORGE

Antiques & Such
Route 9, Lake George Road, R.R. #3, Box 3354 (12845)
(518) 668-4710
Hours: Mon–Sat, 10–4

Occupying two floors, this shop contains oak, Victorian, and pine furniture with an emphasis on European pine armoires and decorative smalls for every taste—all at affordable prices. PR: $. CC: MC, V.

LAKE PLACID

Allan Pereske Antiques
81 Saranac Avenue (12946)
(518) 891-3733
Hours: In season, Daily 12–5:30; Off season, Tues–Thur by chance or call ahead

In addition to specializing in rustic furnishings, Mission, formal, and painted furniture, this shop also has a large selection of oil paintings, rugs, garden and architectural accessories, and interesting smalls. Appraisals can also be done. CC: MC, V.

Heritage Hill Antiques
161 Saranac Avenue, Crestview Plaza (12946)
(518) 523-2435 (afternoons)
Hours: Mon–Sat, 12–5

In this shop, one will find estate jewelry, smalls, paintings, prints, coins, linens, and Olympic memorabilia. PR: $$. CC: Yes.

Lake Placid Antique Center (MD)
103 Main Street (12946)
(518) 523-3913
Hours: Daily 10–5

Four dealers offer a general line of antiques and collectibles that includes memorabilia, glass, lamps, pottery, hunting and fishing collectibles, decorative arts, and quilts. PR: $$. CC: MC, V.

LANSING

Oak Ridge Antiques
96 Lansing Station Road (14882)
(607) 533-7329
Hours: Tues–Thur, 1–7 and shows, please call for schedule

These dealers feature Classical mahogany furniture (circa 1800-1840), walnut and cherry Victorian furniture (circa 1860-1880), and paintings, lighting, and accessories appropriate to those eras. Decorative smalls such as pottery, garden statuary and furniture, and Oriental carpets are also available. Consignments are accepted. Estates and collections are purchased. Research, a finders service, and furniture repair and restoration are available. CC: MC, V.

LARCHMONT

American Flyer

2074 Boston Post Road (10538)
(914) 833-1353
Hours: Tues–Sat, 11–5

Antiques and memorabilia from the 1930s to the 1950s fill this shop. The sale, purchase, repair, and restoration of older radios is of special interest to these dealers. PR: $$. CC: MC, V.

Dualities Gallery

2056 Boston Post Road (10538)
(914) 834-2773
(914) 834-2773 fax
Hours: Mon–Sat, 10:30–5:30

One will find a vast selection of quality antiques and collectibles from the 1700s to the 1950s in this shop. Paintings, sculpture, Art Glass, Art Pottery, porcelain, ceramics, silver, and jewelry are only some of the items for sale. Consignments are accepted. PR: $$$$. CC: MC, V, AMEX.

Post Road Gallery

2128 Boston Post Road (10538)
(914) 834-7568
(914) 834-9245 fax
Hours: Mon–Sat, 10–5

Specializing in 19th century American and European Fine and Decorative Arts, this shop has an extensive selection of quality paintings, sculpture, furniture, and clocks. These items are also actively purchased.

Woolf's Den Antiques

2138 Boston Post Road (10538)
(914) 834-0066
Hours: Tues–Sat, 11–6

This shop offers both collectibles and fine antiques such as paintings, china, glass, jewelry, rugs, military items, and fixtures. Appraisals can be done and consignments are accepted. PR: $$$. CC: No.

LEROY

Carriage House Antiques

7895 Main Street (14482)
(716) 768-4987
Hours: Sat–Sun, 10–5
and by appointment

This shop is noted for carrying a large selection of furniture from Victorian to oak. China, silver, prints, paintings, Oriental rugs, early lamps, cast iron, and estate jewelry are also offered. PR: $$. CC: No.

Lone Gable Emporium

7991 East Main Road, Route 5
(14482)
(716) 768-8349
Hours: Daily 10–5,
closed major holidays

This is a full line, full service, old fashioned shop where you deal directly with the owners who specialize in as found and refinished furniture complemented by smaller items. Appraisals, furniture repair and refinishing, and

caning are available.
CC: MC, V, AMEX, D.

Old Broadway Antiques, The (MD)
8509 East Main Street (14482)
(716) 768-7538
Hours: Tues–Sun, 10–5

This group shop has 20 dealers who have brought together items that run from primitive to the 1950s. Quilts, Depression glass, furniture, advertising, jewelry, toys, silver, glassware, country items, and toys fill two floors.
CC: MC, V.

Vintage Antique Center (MD)
62 Main Street (14482)
(716) 768-7540
Hours: Tues–Sun, 10–4

On two floors, 50 dealers offer a wide selection of antiques and collectibles. Furniture from country to the 1950s, kitchenware, china, glassware, jewelry, ephemera, advertising, and cast iron are some of the items that are available.
CC: MC, V, AMEX, D.

LEWISTON

Mimi Pyne's Antiques
175 Niagara Street (14092)
(716) 754-8560
Hours: Wed–Sat, 12–5;
other times by chance

Located in an 1824 carriage house, this shop specializes in smaller items such as antique furniture, glass, jewelry, and collectibles. PR: $. CC: No.

Stimson's Antiques and Gifts
1727 Ridge Road, Route 104
(14092)
(716) 754-7815
Hours: Daily 1–5

Established in 1973, this shop specializes in antique country furniture plus china, glass, pottery, folk art, primitives, and collectibles. Appraisals, estate sales, lamp repair, and chair caning services are available. PR: $$.
CC: No.

LIBERTY

Antique Palace Emporium, Incorporated, The
300 Chestnut Street (12754)
(914) 292-2270
Hours: By chance or appointment

Three floors are filled with collectible and antique furniture. A large selection of refinished 1920s dining room and bedroom suites is offered. PR: $$$.
CC: MC, V, AMEX, D.

LIMA

Crossroads Country Mall (MD)
7346 East Main Street, P.O. Box 476 (14485)
(716) 624-1993
Hours: Wed–Mon, 11–5

On two floors of a renovated

1850s church, 40 dealers offer fine glass, furniture, collectibles, and antiques.

Maxwell's Treasures Books
7303 Main Street (14485)
(716) 624-4550
Hours: Sat, Sun, Wed, Thur, 11–4:30; closed January

More than ten thousand books—out of print, used, and antiquarian—can be found in this shop. Also, there is a selection of photographs, paper items, and prints. PR: $. CC: No.

LODI

Caywood Antiques
1525 Caywood Road (14860)
(607) 582-6100
Hours: Thur–Tues, 12–5

In addition to a general line of antiques with an emphasis on American Empire and oak furniture, this dealer offers a large selection of kerosene and early electric lighting. PR: $. LOC: Three and a half miles south of Lodi in the hamlet of Caywood.

MABBETTSVILLE (12545)

Calico Quail Antiques and Bed & Breakfast
Route 44, P.O. Box 748, Millbrook, NY 12545
(914) 677-6016
Hours: By appointment or chance

Period furniture and accessories are found in the house. Other furniture, smalls, prints, paintings, and accessories are located in a barn. Framing and custom furniture reproduction as well as furniture repair and restoration can be done. CC: No.

MACEDON

Woodshed Antiques
344 Sheldon Road (14502)
(315) 986-7930
Hours: By chance or appointment

In an 1820s home, early to Depression era furniture in both finished and in as found condition, glass, lamps, clocks, and primitives are presented in room setting displays. A finders service is available. PR: Low to high. CC: No.

MADISON-BOUCKVILLE

Bittersweet Bazaar
Route 20, Bouckville (13310)
(315) 893-7229
Hours: March through December, Thur–Tues, 10–5;
January and February by chance.

Located next to the Landmark Tavern, this quaint shop in an 1850s building features country furniture and accessories. One will also find Old Village Paints, fabric shades, new tin lighting, and rag rugs. CC: MC, V.

Chelsea Antiques
P.O. Box 215, Route 20, Madison (13402)
(315) 893-7766
Hours: Daily 10–5

This 5,000 square foot shop carries a very fine selection of items that range from country to the Victorian Era with a smattering of Art Deco. In this eclectic presentation, one will uncover everything from furniture and mirrors to paintings and prints. Furniture repair, restoration, and stripping can be done. PR: $$$. CC: MC, V, D.

Cobblestone Store, The (MD)
Corner of Routes 20 & 46N, Box 83, Bouckville (13408)
(315) 893-7670
Hours: March through December, Daily 10–5

Fifteen dealers offer a wide selection of antiques and collectibles. In addition to primitive, country, and oak furniture, one is likely to find old tools, fishing tackle, ephemera, linens, bottles, ironstone, kitchen items, and Art Pottery. CC: MC, V, D.

Depot Antiques Gallery, The (MD)
Route 20, Box 57, Bouckville (13310)
(315) 893-7676
Hours: March through December, Daily 10–5; January and February, Fri–Mon, 10–5 or by appointment

From their charming, elegant gallery that once served as a railroad station, 30 dealers offer a wide range of antique furniture, lighting, toys, glassware, china, Oriental rugs, estate jewelry, musical instruments, military items, and collectibles. CC: MC, V, D.

Gallery Co-op, The (MD)
Route 20, Bouckville (13310)
(315) 893-7279
Hours: Daily 10–7, except open December through February, Fri–Mon, 10–5

This 20 dealer shop features a wide range of antiques and collectibles. In addition to early period furniture, oak, walnut, and mahogany pieces are available. Accessories and collectibles include glassware, china, lamps, jewelry, kitchen items, stoneware, Disneyana, and much more. CC: MC, V.

Grasshopper Antiques Center
Route 20, Madison (13402)
(315) 893-7664
Hours: Daily 10–5 or by appointment

Located in a red barn, this shop has everything from American Indian items, paintings, and furniture to African art, fish decoys, and graniteware. CC: No.

J & R Ferris Antiques
P.O.Box 121, Madison (13402)
(315) 893-7006
Hours: Mail order & shows only, available by phone daily 10–4

Specialties are: Medical items

from the pre-sterilization period; militaria, especially pre-1900 weapons; scientific instruments; and both antique and contemporary folk art.

Jackie's Place

Route 20, P.O. Box 113, Bouckville (13310)
(315) 893-7457
Hours: April through November, Daily 10–5 or by appointment

This eclectic shop of interesting smalls carries items mostly from the 1930s to the 1950s. One can find everything from circus chalkware to a TV lamp. PR: $. CC: No.

Jem Shop, The

7201 Route 20, Madison (13402)
(315) 893-7921
Hours: May Through October, Sat, Sun, & holidays, 9–5 and by appointment

This shop carries a little bit of everything but is heaviest into clocks, watches, jewelry store items, coins, music boxes, and books. PR: $. CC: No.

Madison Inn Antiques (MD)

7417 Route 20, Madison (13402)
(315) 893-7639
Hours: April through December, Daily 10–5; January through March, Fri–Mon, 10–5

This group shop which is stocked by 25 dealers features a wide range of antiques and collectibles with an emphasis on glassware, china, pottery, and early American furniture and antiques. CC: MC, V, D.

Pine Woods Antique Shop

Corner of Routes 20 & 46N, Box 21, Bouckville (13310)
(315) 893-7405
Hours: May through December, Mon–Sat, 10–5

This shop has a good selection of oak, cherry, pine, mahogany, and maple furniture complemented by appropriate accessories.

Purdy's

Corner of Route 20 & Indian Opening Road, Bouckville (13310)
(315) 824-1980
Hours: Summer, Sat–Sun, 10–5; winter, Sat–Sun, 10–4; 10–5, off season call to be sure

Oak furniture, tins, bottles, tools, toys, and automobilia are offered in this 1834 Federal two story house. CC: No.

Stone Lodge Antiques

Rte. 20, Bouckville (13310)
(315) 893-7263
Hours: 10–5

Located on the East End, this 1834 federal two story house contains oak furniture, tins, bottles, toys, tools, and aoutomobilia. CC: No

Timothy's Treasures

Route 20, Madison (13409)
(315) 893-7008
Hours: Sat, 11–5; Sun closed; weekdays by chance or appointment

This high quality shop specializes in refinished pine and cherry country and period furniture.

Veranda, The (MD)
Route 20 & 12B South, Bouckville (13310)
(315) 893-7270
Hours: Daily 10–5; Jan–Feb, weekends only

This 20 plus dealer group shop is noted for the very high quality antiques and collectibles that are available. Country furniture and appropriate accessories, advertising, folk art, ephemera, Orientalia, and jewelry are featured; all items are from the eighteenth to early twentieth century only. Well worth the trip. PR: $$$$$. CC: MC, V.

Willow Hill Antiques
7585 Route 20, Madison (13402)
(315) 893-7696
Hours: Sat–Sun, 10–5; weekdays by chance or appointment

Established in 1982, this shop specializes in restored oak and country furniture from the late 19th century to the early 20th century and appropriate accessories such as lamps, rare graniteware, kitchen collectibles, blown glass, Christmas ornaments, and the like. Furniture repair, restoration, and refinishing are available. CC: MC, V, D.

MAHOPAC

Yellow Shed Antiques
571 Route 6 (10541)
(914) 628-0362
Hours: Tues–Sun, 10–5

This 8,000 square foot shop is filled with furniture, glassware, jewelry, stamps, coins, collectibles, Oriental porcelain, silver, ephemera, clocks, lighting fixtures, marcasite jewelry, and quality reproductions. A jewelry repair service is available. PR: $$$. CC: MC, V, AMEX, D, CB, DC.

MALDEN BRIDGE

Claudia Kingsley Quilts & Antiques
Route 66, in the post office complex (12115)
(518) 766-4759
Hours: By chance or appointment

In addition to an impressive grouping of quilts, this shop offers a general line of antiques such as country furniture and pottery and personalized floral arrangements in antique accessories.

MAMARONECK

Chatsworth Auction Rooms
151 Mamaroneck Avenue (10543)
(914) 698-1001
Hours: Tues–Sat, 8–6

Considered by many to be the largest buyer and seller of antiques and used furniture in Westchester County, this business which was established in 1924 has three floors packed with merchandise. Dining room sets, occasional tables, bedroom sets, and accessories are their specialty areas. Purchases are delivered free. PR: $$$. CC: No.

Lorraine's Antiques
128 Mamaroneck Avenue (10543)
(914) 381-4454
Hours: Tues–Sat, 10–4

Offering the unique, obscure, and hard to find for the serious collector, this shop contains furniture, prints, paintings, lithographs, books, textiles, pottery, porcelain, silver, glass, china, and hardware. CC: No.

Michael Kessler Antiques Ltd
124A Palmer Avenue (10543)
(914) 698-6013
Hours: Mon & Thur, 10–5
or by appointment

This shop specializes in European furniture and accessories. CC: No.

MARATHON

Cross's Antique Center (MD)
Route 11 North (13803)
(607) 849-6605
Hours: Daily, 10–5

Thirty-one dealers offer everything from glass, china, furniture, frames, and jewelry to reference books, Civil War era pieces, early country, primitives, and Victoriana. CC: MC, V.

Peck Street Antiques (MD)
7 Peck Street (13803)
(607) 849-6367
Hours: Wed–Sun, 10–5:30

In a quaint Victorian decorated shop, 12 dealers offer a variety of large and small antiques and collectibles. A year-round Christmas booth with hand-made Santas is on the premises. A bridal registry service is available. CC: No.

Riverbend Antique Center (MD)
79 Cortland Street, Route 11N (13803)
(607) 849-6305
Hours: Tues–Sun, 10–6

This group shop of more than 40 dealers on two floors features quality items from period to collectible with a strong emphasis on period furniture, Staffordshire portrait figures, majolica, country furniture, yellow ware, and everything delightful under the sun. PR: $$$$$. CC: MC, V.

MARLBORO

Eagle's Roost Antiques
Box 56, Old Post Road (12542)
(914) 562-2362
Hours: By chance or appointment

In business since 1970, this shop is located in a large two story building which is brimming over with furniture, dolls, postcards, glass, linens, and the like. CC: MC, V. LOC: One mile off Route 9W, north of Newburgh.

McGRAW

Old Time Trappings
34 Main Street, P.O. Box 423 (13101)
(607) 836-6069
Hours: Wed–Fri, 12–4; Sat, 10–5; Sun, 12–5 or by appointment

Since 1980, this shop has specialized in quality 18th and 19th century Americana such as furniture, glass, porcelain, and mirrors at reasonable prices. Mail order is available. CC: No. LOC: One mile east off I-81, Exit 10, on Route 41.

MIDDLETOWN

Memory Lane Antiques and Etceteras

1 Sprague Avenue (10940)
(914) 343-5544
Hours: Tues–Wed, 10–5; Thur, 12–5; Fri–Sat, 10–5

Priced for the local trade, this shop offers an eclectic mix of collectibles, decorative smalls, kitchen collectibles, and costume jewelry. Consignments are accepted. A card file system for individual pieces or catagories is available. Appraisals can be done. CC: No.

Stepping Stone Inn Antiques

RD #3, Box 900, Goshen Turnpike (10940)
(914) 361-2261
Hours: Mon–Sat by chance or appointment; a call ahead is advised

Doing business since 1973, this country antique shop specializes in Flow Blue china and 18th and 19th century furnishings such as kitchen and hearth items, furniture, glass, linens, and decorative accessories in many catagories. CC: No. LOC: Located on the Goshen Turnpike, near Circleville, between Routes 302 & 211.

MILFORD

Brockman's Antique Center (MD)

RD #1, Box 104 (13807)
(607) 547-9192
Hours: Daily 10–5 except Sun, 12–5; call for winter hours

Located five miles south of Cooperstown on Route 28, this 20 dealer shop with both booths and showcases offers a complete line of antiques and collectibles. Consignments are accepted. Furniture refinishing and caning services are available. PR: $$. CC: MC, V.

Wood Bull Antiques

Route 28 (13807)
(607) 286-9021
Hours: Daily 10–5

In this huge barn that comprises four floors and 64 room settings, one can find oak, pine, cherry, Victorian, Mission, Deco, and painted furniture; 1600 chairs; sports and hunting collectibles; kitchen, bedroom, and dining room sets; tools; cupboards; chests; musical instruments; jewelry; wood stoves; and scientific instruments. PR: $$. CC: MC, V.

MILLBROOK

Millbrook Antiques Center, The (MD)

Franklin Avenue, Route 44 (12545)
(914) 677-3921
Hours: May through October, Mon–Sat, 12–6 except Sun and legal holidays 1–5; November through April, Mon–Sat, 11–5 except Sun and legal holidays 1–5

In the original antique center of Dutchess County, 44 dealers offer fine collections of antiques and collectibles for both collectors and dealers. PR: $$. CC: MC, V.

Millbrook Antiques Mall (MD)

Franklin Avenue, P.O. Box 1267 (12545)
(914) 677-9311
Hours: Mon–Sat, 11–5; Sun, 1–5

This 30 dealer shop specializes in quality 18th and 19th century furniture and appropriate accessories such as quilts, folk art, paintings, fireplace equipment, jewelry, and Persian and kilim rugs. Some consignments are accepted. Appraisal and interior design services are available. Chair caning and rush seats can be done. PR: $$$$$.
CC: MC, V.

Village Antique Center (MD)

Franklin Avenue, P.O. Box 388 (12545)
(914) 677-5160
Hours: Mon–Sat, 11–5; Sun, 1–5

Fifty dealers offer an eclectic mixture of furniture, accessories, and collectibles ranging from early American to Art Deco and beyond. Country and formal items, glassware, porcelain, postcards, sterling silver, quilts, jewelry, pottery, ephemera, furniture, prints, and paintings are among the diverse offerings. Furniture refinishing and jewelry repair can be done.
CC: MC, V.

Wicker's Antiques, The

P.O. Box 288 (12545)
(914) 677-3906
Hours: Mail order or by appointment

These dealers who are members of the National Early American Glass Club specialize in early American Pattern Glass.

MILLERTON

Green River Gallery

RD 2, Box 130, Boston Corners Road (12546)
(518) 789-3311
Hours: Sat, 10–5 or by appointment

In addition to specializing in 19th and 20th century American art with an emphasis on the American West and the works of Eric Sloane, this gallery also offers selected furniture and accessories from the period 1680 to 1860. Appraisals and authentication services are available. Consignments are accepted. Painting restoration and research services are also available. CC: No.

MILLPORT

Millport Mercantile

5476 Main Street (14864)
(607) 739-3180
Hours: April through December, Daily 10–6, January through March, Fri–Sun, 10–6

Located in a renovated 1854 general store, this shop offers the finest in American antiques, American-made crafts, and confections. CC: MC, V.
LOC: Midway between Watkins Glen and Elmira on Route 14.

Samuel R. Page House

2010 Crescent Street (14864)
(607) 796-5260
Hours: Daily 10–6 but closed December through March

Specializing in decorating ideas of the 1800s, this shop offers furniture, primitives, Griswold and Wagner pots and pans, cupboards, tools, prints, and folk art. Coca Cola items are also available. PR: $. CC: MC, V.

Serendipity II (MD)

4905 Route 14 (14864)
(607) 739-9413
Hours: Mon–Fri, 10–5;
Sat–Sun, 11–4; closed major holidays

Ten dealers offer a variety of glass, china, books, furniture, linens, collectibles, tin, and paper. PR: $. CC: No.

MINERVA

Mountain Niche Antiques

P.O. Box 955, Route 28N (12851)
(518) 251-2566
Hours: May–Sept, Daily 10–5;
Oct–April, same hours by chance

In a unique Adirondack setting, this shop carries a general line of antiques and collectibles with an emphasis on country furniture, quilts, glassware, folky/funky collectibles, and Adirondack items. PR: $. CC: No.

MOHAWK

Back To Granny's Day Antiques

32 East Main Street (13407)
(315) 866-8479
Hours: Mon–Fri, 10–5; Sat, 10–4

This shop stocks an interesting variety of glass, furniture, picture frames, advertising items, bottles, and various other odds and ends. PR: $. CC: No.

Shedd's Antiques

Route 28 South, Vickerman Hill (13407)
(315) 866-1758
Hours: Daily, call to be sure

This shop is filled with furniture in restored ready for your home condition and unusual antiques and collectibles. There is a kitchen area which features Hoosier cabinets and kitchen collectibles. CC: MC, V.

LOC: One and a half miles south of Mohawk.

Treasure Chest, The
24 East Main Street (13407)
(315) 866-1255
Hours: Mon–Sat, 10–6; Sun, 1–6

Three cozy rooms contain small antiques and collectibles, especially country items and cupboards that are priced to sell. CC: No.

MONROE

Marilyn in Monroe
Route 17M (10950)
(914) 782-8757
Hours: Fri–Sun, 12–5

In addition to having the largest costume jewelry selection in the area, this shop specializes in 1950s clothing, purses, and accessories. These items are nicely complemented by a small selection of 1950s furniture and many lamps and collectibles. Prop rental and window display services are available. PR: Very reasonable. CC: No.

Monroe Antiques
163 Stage Road (10950)
(914) 783-6347
Hours: Daily 10–5,
a call ahead is advised

This shop has an interesting collection of art and antiques displayed in room settings in a Federal Period house. Furniture is in as found condition. Most of the items are from local Hudson Valley homes. PR: $$$$$. CC: No.

MONTGOMERY

Antiques at Ward's Bridge (MD)
87 Clinton Street (12549)
(914) 457-9343
Hours: Fri–Tues, 11–5

A general line of antiques which includes furniture, china, glass, silver, books, bric-a-brac, and linens is offered by 16 dealers. Consignments are accepted. Prop rentals, appraisals, and repairs are offered. CC: MC, V.

Buy-Gone Days
16 Collabar Road (12549)
(914) 361-5216
(914) 361-3605 fax
Hours: By appointment

This lovely country shop specializes in vintage textiles, trimmings, cloth, and accessories. Select consignments are accepted. Appraisals can be given. CC: No. LOC: Just off Route 17K, four and a half miles west of the village.

Clinton Shops Antique Center (MD)
84 Clinton Street (12549)
(914) 457-5392
Hours: Fri–Tues, 11–5

Specializing in the unusual, 12

A grouping containing a Gustav Stickley library table, Gustav Stickley latter chair, and an E. & J.G. Stickley frame. *(Courtesy Peter-Roberts Antiques, New York City)*

dealers offer a broad and eclectic range of antiques and collectibles for all tastes. Both dealers and collectors will always find items that range from primitive and country to Victorian, Deco and beyond. Furniture, pottery, glass, jewelry, books, fabrics, lamps, and distinctive decorator accessories are always available.

Montgomery Antique Mall (MD)
40 Railroad Avenue (12549)
(914) 457-9393
Hours: Tues–Mon, 10–5

Oak, pine, Empire and Victorian furniture, costume and estate jewelry, pottery, advertising, toys, cast and wrought iron, and textiles are offered by the 15 dealers in this co-op. PR: $. CC: MC, V.

MONTICELLO

Antiques at Cedarwood (MD)
140 Bridgeville Road (12701)
(914) 791-6339
Hours: Summer, Wed–Sun, 10–5; after Labor Day, Sat–Sun, 11–5

On two floors, five dealers feature textiles, costume jewelry, fine glass, porcelain, pottery, books, mirrors, crazy quilts, smalls, decorative accessories, and furniture from the Victorian Period through the 1950s. PR: $$. CC: MC, V. LOC: Exit 107 off Route 17.

MONTOUR FALLS

Guild Brothers Antiques

232-234 West Main Street (14865)
(607) 535-7463
Hours: Mon–Sat, 9–5
or by appointment

This shop carries the area's largest selection of professionally refinished Victorian, oak, and country furniture. In addition to caning and seat weaving, furniture repair, restoration, and refinishing are available. CC: MC, V.

MORRIS

Gatehouse, The

2-4 West Main Street (13808)
(607) 263-5855
Hours: Wed–Sat, 10–4 or call (607) 263–5746 for other times

These dealers specialize in early lighting including kerosene and also offer furniture, ceramics, and prints from the same period. Patented items with their attached patents are also available. CC: No.

Mary Ann Thompson

South New Berlin Road, Route 23, P.O. Box 327 (13808)
(607) 263-5431
Hours: By appointment or chance, mail order, and shows

This dealer offers china, glassware, vintage clothing, linens, picture frames, prints, and small furniture. A search service for specific items is available. CC: No.

Victoria's Garden

22 South Broad Street (13808)
(607) 263-5179
Hours: Evenings and weekends
or by appointment

Located in an 1873 Victorian home, one will find selected furnishings, decorative accessories, and collectibles of the Victorian era. CC: No.

MT. KISCO

Apple Antiques Ltd

205 & 477 Lexington Avenue (10549)
(914) 242-5365
Hours: Mon–Sat, 10:30–5;
Sun, 12–5

This shop offers antique bleached pine, country French, and formal furniture for both the retail and wholesale trade. PR: $$. CC: MC, V.

Curiosity Shop Inc., The

35 Main Street (10549)
(914) 666-5860
Hours: Tues–Sat, 10–5

This large consignment shop features furniture, mirrors, clocks, china, silver, toys, dolls, prints, paintings, and collectibles. CC: No.

MT. VERNON

Trend, The
154 South 4th Avenue (10550)
(914) 664-4478
Hours: Mon–Sat, 11–6

This eclectic shop carries something for everyone—1930s and 1940s furniture, Depression glass, and porcelain.
CC: AMEX.

NAPLES

Semmel Antiques
11798 Lewis Road (14512)
(716) 374-2179
Hours: By chance or appoinment and shows

Established in 1986, this shop specializes in both refinished and professionally upholstered antique furniture complemented by appropriate collectibles and glass. CC: No.

NEVERSINK

Hamilton's Antiques Shoppe
Route 55, P.O. Box 491 (12765)
(914) 985-2671
Hours: June–Sept, Daily 10–5; Oct–May call or by chance

This shop offers refinished oak furniture, loads of glassware with an emphasis on Depression glass, and antique jewelry. CC: MC, V.
LOC: Seven miles from Liberty, NY on Route 55.

NEW HAMPTON

Four Winds Center & Steve's Antiques (MD)
Route 17M (10958)
(914) 374-7272, 374-6111
Hours: Thur–Tues, 11–5; Wed by chance

This group shop offers a wide variety of toys, refinished trunks, postcards, collectibles, oak furniture, and railroadiana.
CC: No.

NEW HARTFORD

Owens' Collectibles
12 Bonnie Avenue (13413)
(315) 735-8789
Hours: By appointment

Although specializing in beer advertising, other types of advertising such as Coke, Pepsi, and McDonalds are featured. Some glassware, kitchen collectibles, and painted soda bottles are also available. PR: $$. CC: No.

NEW LEBANON

Golden Eagle Antiques
Corner of County Routes 5 & 20 (12125)
(518) 794-9809
Hours: Thur–Mon, 10:30–5:30

This shop contains a constantly changing assortment of antiques and collectibles such as linens, laces, cut glass, furniture, books, paintings, prints, pottery, jewelry,

Hummels, and primitives. PR: $$. CC: MC, V.

NEW PALTZ

Country Charm Antiques
201 DuBois Road (12561)
(914) 255-7916
Hours: By chance or appointment

Located in a barn, this shop offers country accessories, tinware, and the unusual antique. The arrangement of floral designs in your antique containers can be done. CC: No. LOC: Located off Route 32 South, approximately five miles from New Paltz.

Fred Hansen Antiques
27 North Chestnut Street (12561)
(914) 255-0928
Hours: Daily 9–5

This shop which is well worth a visit specializes in European and American armoires and has a very strong offering of clocks and barometers. PR: $$$$. CC: MC, V.

Jenkinstown Antiques
520 Route 32 South (12561)
(914) 255-8135
Hours: Thur–Mon, 11–5
or by appointment

This shop is stocked with country and formal furniture, paintings, and appropriate accessories displayed in period settings. Consultation on 18th and 19th century home restoration and painting restoration are available. PR: $$$. CC: No. LOC: Four miles south on New Paltz on Route 32.

Marna Anderson Gallery
(914) 255-1132
Hours: By appointment

This dealer specializes in quality 19th century American folk art such as weathervanes and wood carvings, Amish quilts, hooked rugs, and garden and architectural ornaments. Appraisals are done. CC: No.

NEW WINDSOR

Antique Center at Forge Hill Village, The (MD)
815 Blooming Grove Turnpike, Suite 109 (12553)
(914) 569-0406
Hours: Daily 11–5

Stocked by 27 dealers, this group shop offers a wide selection of furniture, glass, pottery, ceramics, books, collectibles, country items, rustic furniture and accessories, jewelry, lace, linens, quilts, lighting, and antiquarian books. PR: $$. CC: MC, V, D.

NEWARK

Carol's Antiques
104 Myrtle Avenue
(14513-1840-01)
(315) 331-3330
Hours: By appointment or chance

Established in 1970, this shop

contains a wide range of eclectic offerings which include early flint and Sandwich glass, Orientalia, Art Glass, miniatures, primitives, and Americana. Appraisals can be done.
CC: No.

NEWBURGH

Broadway Antiques & Interiors
90 Broadway (12550)
(914) 565-9519
Hours: Thur–Fri, 11–4; Sat–Sun, 11–5

Located in a Belle Epoque building, this shop features an extensive collection of American and European furniture arranged in vignettes to complement the period. Located one mile from I-84 across from City Hall, this business also offers interior design services, Oriental rug restoration and cleaning, appraisals, and a consignment service. Estate sales are also conducted. CC: MC, V.

Esther-Bernard Antiques
75 Susan Drive West (12550)
(914) 562-7020
Hours: By appointment only

These dealers specialize in American furniture from the Federal Period through Deco with appropriate accessories that include lighting, glass, porcelain, and silver. CC: No.
LOC: North of Newburgh, call for directions.

Ruggiero Antiques
605 Route 9 West (12550)
(914) 561-1756
Hours: Tues–Mon, 11–5

This 3,000 square foot barn is filled to the rafters with antiques and collectibles for the beginning to advanced collector.
CC: No.

NIAGARA FALLS

McMullen Lasalle Antiques
7724 Buffalo Avenue (14304)
(716) 283-2900
Hours: Mon–Fri, 9–5; Sat, 10–4

Nine thousand five hundred square feet of floor space is filled with oak furniture, old linens, primitives, glass, lighting fixtures and devices, quilts, pottery, and various collectibles. PR: $$$.
CC: MC, V, D.

NORTH COHOCTON

Beehive Antique Co-Op (MD)
7 Wayland Street, Route 21, P.O. Box 143 (14868)
(716) 534-5770
Hours: Daily 10–5

More than 40 dealers occupying 14,000 square feet of selling space offer a wide variety of antiques

and collectibles.
CC: MC, V, AMEX, D.

NORTH SALEM

Artemis Gallery

Wallace Road (10560)
(914) 669-5971
(914) 669-8604 fax
Hours: Any time by appointment

This shop presents a very strong collection of American furniture and decorative arts of the Federal Period—Hepplewhite, Sheraton, and Neoclassical—and a fine selection of American paintings of the 19th and early 20th century. Painting restoration, appraisals, and furniture repair and restoration can be done. LOC: Near the intersection of I-84 and I-684, one hour north of New York City.

Kathy Schoemer American Antiques

Route 116 at Keeler Lane (10560)
(914) 669-8486
Hours: Wed–Sat, 12–5; Sun by chance or appointment

Established in 1971 and in Westchester County for 12 years, this dealer offers an impressive array of American country furniture and accessories such as textiles, hooked rugs, and folk art in a large mid-19th century store. PR: $$$. CC: AMEX.

NORTH TROY

Sullivan's Antiques & Collectors Items

657 2nd Avenue, near 118th Street (12182)
(518) 233-7126, 283-2365
Hours: Tues–Sat, 12–5
or by appointment

This shop contains an impressive amount of antiques and collectibles. Appraising and auctioneering can be done. PR: $$$. CC: No.

NORWOOD

John Sholl Antiques

Route 1, Box 107, Austin Ridge Road (13668)
(315) 353-2474
Hours: By appointment only

John Sholl is noted for offering a funky, eclectic, and high-quality selection of folk art. Although specializing in all forms of tramp art, he also deals in popsicle art, matchstick art, bottle whimseys, bottle cap art, spool decorated items, shop art, memory items, and rustic furniture. PR: $$$. CC: No.

NYACK

Dagmar's Antiques

37 South Broadway (Hudson Valley Emporium) 10960
(914) 353-5564
Hours: Sat–Sun, 11–6
or by appointment

This shop specializes in fine

American and Continental antique furniture, paintings, and accessories. Furniture repair and restoration which includes carving repair, veneer work, guilding, and French polishing and painting restoration and cleaning are available. Appraisals can be given. CC: No.

Elayne's Antiques
6 South Broadway (10960)
(914) 358-6465
Hours: Wed–Sun, 11:30–5

Carrying a large selection of antiques and collectibles, this shop features porcelain, dinnerware, stemware, furniture, and the unusual. CC: AMEX.

Franklin Antique Center (MD)
142 Main Street (10960)
(914) 353-0071
Hours: Wed–Sun, 11–5

Considered to be the Tri-State's largest indoor antique center with 25,000 square feet, the multidealer center consists of 32 individual shops which offer fine quality antiques, art, rugs, collectibles, jewelry, and much, much more. CC: Yes.

Gloria Paul Antiques
152 Main Street (10960)
(914) 358-1859
Hours: Wed–Sun, 12–5
and by appointment

This shop offers an eclectic mix of American and Continental furniture from the 19th century to the 1950s and accessories such as silver, paintings, lamps, and rugs. PR: $$$. CC: MC, V, AMEX.

Memories
142 Main Street (10960)
(914) 358-3373
Hours: Daily 11–6

In this large warehouse-type shop, one will find a wide variety of furnishings from formal to country plus decorative smalls, pottery, silver, estate jewelry, vintage watches, radios, and collectibles. CC: MC, V.

Now & Then Antiques & Gifts
292 Main Street (10960)
(914) 353-1797
Hours: Wed–Sun, 11–5

This shop contains oak and mahogany furniture from period to modern; old, Steiff, Gund, Merry Thought, and artist bears; antique to modern dolls by various makers; old, custom-made, and new quilts; vintage clothing; and clocks. Clock repair is available. Estate sales are conducted. CC: MC, V.

Remembrances
85 Main Street (10960)
(914) 358-7226
Hours: Tues–Sun, 12:30–5:30

A wide, eclectic selection of antiques, collectibles, and used furniture, which includes decorative smalls, porcelain, silver,

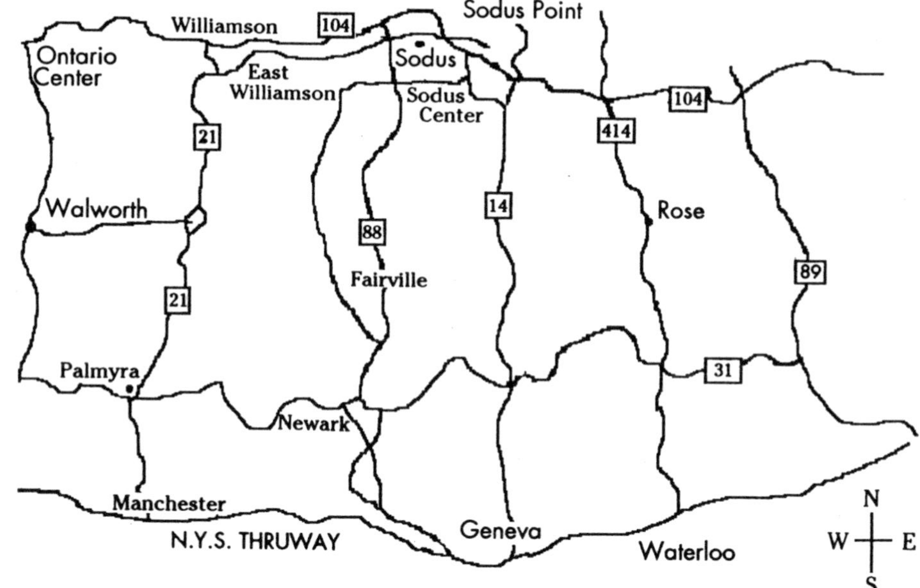

Palmyra-Geneva-Sodus Area

lamps, country things, prints, and mirrors is offered. PR: $. CC: MC, V, AMEX.

OAK HILL

Cheritree Antiques (MD)
Route 81 (12460)
(518) 239-4081
Hours: Daily as available

This multidealer shop offers an extensive array of the unusual such as primitives, militaria, and decorative smalls. Consignments are accepted. CC: No.

Country Kitchen Antiques
Durham Road (12460)
(518) 239-4076
Hours: Open by chance or appointment all year

Housed in an old horse barn, one will find old kitchenware, glassware, linens, jewelry, and other collectibles. PR: Very Affordable. CC: No.

DeWitt Hotel Antiques (MD)
Route 81 (12460)
(518) 239-6960
Hours: Thur–Mon, 10–5; also open Wednesday from July through October

In a historic, 19th century hotel, 20 dealers offer an eclectic collection of furniture from primitive to formal, choice collectibles, brass, porcelain, baskets, textiles, and folk art. Authentication, prop rentals, and home restoration services are available. Featured in "Architectural Digest," this shop is a quality source for decorators, designers, collectors, and dealers. CC: No.

OLEAN

Country Gentleman Antiques (MD)
1562 East State Road, Route 417 (14760)
(716) 373-2410
Hours: Mon–Sat, 10–5; Sun, 1–5

In a beautifully restored inn, seven dealers present a wide range of antiques and collectibles. CC: MC, V.

Jerry's Antique Co-Op (MD)
1217 Union Street (14760)
(716) 373-3702
Hours: Mon–Sat, 11–5; Sun, 1–5; closed major holidays

In addition to having the largest offering of railroad items in Western NY, this multidealer shop offers early sleds, country furniture, estate and costume jewelry, pottery, stoneware, oak furniture, cast iron, quilts, and linens. PR: $$$. CC: No.

Olean Antique Center (MD)
269 North Union Street, Route 16 (14760)
(716) 372-8171
Hours: Mon–Sat, 10–5; Sun 1–5

This group shop of 24 dealers in an 8,000 square foot building carries a wide range of antiques and collectibles. One will find furniture, lamps, quilts, jewelry, glassware, books. pottery, stoneware, and vintage clothing. PR: $$. CC: MC, V.

OLMSTEDVILLE

Board 'N Batten Antiques
Main Street, Box 19 (12857)
(518) 251-2507
(518) 251-2101 fax
Hours: June–October, Daily 10–5; other times by appointment

Located in the heart of the Adirondack Mountains, this general line shop focuses on glassware, furniture, steins, and postcards. PR: Low to Medium. CC: MC, V. LOC: Six miles from Exit 26 on Interstate 87.

ONEONTA

Silversmith & Goldsmith Jewelers, The
81 Chestnut Street (13820)
(607) 432-9091
Hours: Tues–Fri, 10–6; Sat, 10–5 except June through August, 10–2

Established in 1972, this shop specializes in silver and gold estate jewelry, small antiques, stamps, coins, reproductions, and custom service. Appraisals can be done for estates and insurance. Engraving work is available. CC: V, MC, D. LOC: On Routes 23 & 7, three blocks from Main Street.

Southside Antique Center Inc. (MD)
R.D. 2, Route 23, Box 377 (13820)
(607) 432-1662
Hours: May to Christmas, Daily 11–6; Christmas through April closed Tues & Wed

Forty-four individual shops

occupy 7,000 square feet in this multidealer shop. A vast array of bronzes, Art Glass, china, porcelain, ephemera, American Indian items, furniture from period to the 1950s, toys, reference and antiquarian books, folk art, country store items, Victoriana, Handel and Steuben are only some of the antiques and collectibles that fill the shops. PR: $$$. CC: MC, V. LOC: Four miles east of Oneonta on Route 23.

ONTARIO

Route 104 Antiques Center (MD)

6275 Dean Parkway (14519)
(716) 265-3280
(716) 265-1390 fax
Hours: October–February, Daily 9–5; March–September, Mon–Fri, 9–8; Sat–Sun, 9–5

This is a showcase only shop. Forty showcases contain quality antiques such as porcelain, glass, silver, silverplate, bottles, Americana, decoys, dolls, carnival glass, pewter, prints, primitives, and miniatures.
CC: MC, V, AMEX, D.

ORCHARD PARK

Shades of the Past Antiques

4264 North Buffalo Road (14127)
(716) 662-0035
Hours: Mon–Sat, 11–5

In addition to featuring fine Victorian furniture in mahogany, cherry, rosewood, and oak, this shop also has decorative smalls and accessories to complement any decor. A finders service is available. Appraisals are given.

OSSINING

American Jazz

Box 302 (10562)
(914) 762-5519
(914) 762-5519 fax
Hours: By appointment only and shows

Although specializing in fine childhood antiques such as toys, ephemera, dolls, banks, and optical material, this dealer also offers a variety of quality American and international objets d'art with an emphasis on unusual folk art, aesthetic pieces, and jazz memoribilia. Appraisals can be done.
PR: $$$$$. CC: No.

Centennial Corner Antiques

217 Main Street (10562)
(914) 762-3636
Hours: Tues–Sat, 10–5:30; Sun, 12–5

Offering antiques and collectibles from the 18th through early 20th century, this dealer has something for everyone. Furniture, lamps, porcelains, pottery, glass, jewelry, and art fill this shop. PR: $$.
CC: No.

OTEGO

John and Lynn Gallo

75 Main Street (13825)
(607) 988-9963
Hours: Open by chance
or appointment

In business since 1970, these dealers specialize in yellow ware, redware, and other decorative pottery. Strongly complementing these offerings are country furnishings in original paint and condition, decorative smalls, advertising tins, and hooked and braided rugs. John Gallo is the author of *Nineteenth and Twentieth Century Yellow Ware*. PR: $$$$. CC: No.

OVID

You Want What!

2125 West Seneca Street (14521)
(607) 869-9286
Hours: Mon–Fri, 2–5; Sat–Sun, 11–5

This shop contains collectibles, Depression glass, costume jewelry, and glass. PR: $. CC: No.

OXFORD

Cider Mill Antiques

RD #2, Box 38 (13830)
(607) 843-8985
Hours: 10–5 or by chance
or appointment

Cider Mill Antiques carries a general line of antiques and collectibles that range from primitives and jewelry to glassware and kitchenware. PR: $. CC: No.

PATTERSON

Fanny Doolittle

Route 22, Box 157 (12563)
(914) 878-6766
Hours: Sat–Sun, 11–5;
call for weekday hours

This shop offers an assortment of Victorian and turn of the century antiques and collectibles. PR: $. CC: MC, V.

White Lion Antiques

RR #3, Route 22 (12563)
(914) 278-4541
Hours: Mon–Sat, 10–4

Located five miles north of the I-684 and I-84 interchange on Route 22, this shop specializes in glassware, china, and collectibles and, also, offers a general line of antiques. PR: Moderate. CC: No.

PAWLING

Hob Nail Antiques

571 Route 22 (12564)
(914) 855-1623
Hours: Daily 9–5

In business since 1970, this dealer offers all sizes of refinished turn of the century brass and brass and iron beds. Even king and queen size beds are available.

PELHAM

Terry Sheldon Calhoun/ Fifth Estate

106 Harmon Avenue (10803)
(914) 738-1806
(914) 738-1806 fax
Hours: Anytime by appointment

Specializing in antiques and art, this dealer offers a wide range of merchandise that includes furniture, jewelry, paintings, and sculpture. Consignments are accepted. Decorating, repair and restoration, and appraisal services are available. PR: $$$$. CC: No.

PENN YAN

Belknap Hill Books

106 Main Street (14527)
(315) 536-1186
Hours: Mon–Fri, 10–5; Sat, 10–3; Sun 10–2

With more than 30,000 used, rare, and out of print books in stock, this store is a browsers delight. Children's books, Americana, and murder mysteries are specialty areas. Prints, maps, and postcards are also in stock. A book search service, appraisals, and book binding and restoration are available. CC: No.

Deacon's Bench Antiques, The

114 Main Street (14527)
(315) 531-8155
Hours: Wed–Fri, 10–12:30 & 1:30–4; Sat, 10–12

This shop specializes in china and glass with an emphasis on R.S. Prussian china, cut glass, Flow Blue, and sterling silver.

Necia Smith Antiques & Collectibles

113 Sunset Avenue (14527)
(315) 536-8778
Hours: May 15th to September 30th by chance or call

This shop is stocked with antique buttons, kitchen collectibles, linens, doilies, and postcards.

Paul Coon

R.D. #2 (14527)
(315) 536-8546
(315) 536-8546 fax
Hours: By appointment only and shows

In addition to pre 1840 American country furniture in either original paint or refinished condition, this dealer also offers appropriate accessories such as quilts, stoneware, decoys, and folk art. PR: $$. CC: No.

PHOENICIA

At Home Antiques

46 Route 214 (12464)
(914) 688-5063
Hours: Sat–Sun, 10:30–5 or by appointment

With an accent on country, this shop contains furniture and appropriate accessories such as quilts and textiles. In a separate section, The Pantry offers bever-

ages, pastries, gourmet items, and contemporary gifts which are made in America.
CC: MC, V.

Phoenicia Antique Center (MD)
Route 28
(914) 688-2095
Hours: Daily 11–5, closed Wed

This 30 dealer shop which occupies 7,000 square feet contains antiques, collectibles, furniture, jewelry, toys, glass, and baseball cards. It has something for everyone. Auctions are conducted every two to three weeks.
CC: MC, V.

PIERMONT

Decades Inc.
210 Ash Street (10968)
(914) 365-3940
Hours: Wed–Sun, 12–6; Summer; open till 10, Thur–Sat

This shop is divided into two sections. In the first, one will find items from the 1930s, 1940s, and 1950s: memorabilia; Fiestaware; Chase Chrome; baseball pictures of the Brooklyn Dodgers, Yankees, and Giants; movie lobby posters; ephemera; quilts; and Art Deco furniture. In the other section is a classic 1950s ice cream parlor that offers such delights as a Lime Rickey, Egg Cream, and Charlotte Roux. PR: $.
CC: MC, V.

PINE BUSH

Coffee Grinder
70 Main Street, P.O. Box 358 (12566)
(914) 744-3946
Hours: Tues–Sat, 11–5; Sun, 12–5

In addition to carrying a line of farmhouse antiques, this shop offers various blends of coffee and related accessories, gift baskets, crafts, and Old Sturbridge paints. The Book Worm, which offers a full line of books, is also here.
PR: Affordable. CC: MC, V.

Country Heritage Antique Center
Route 302, Box 519 (12566)
(914) 744-3792
Hours: Thur–Sun, 11–5
or by appointment

This dealer has had 20 years of experience specializing in Victorian furniture, which is tastefully displayed in four showrooms. All of the shop's large inventory is in either excellent or refinished condition. Federal and country period antiques plus quality reproductions are also offered.
CC: MC, V.

Kelso Antiques
Maple Avenue (12566)
(914) 744-2828
Hours: Wed–Sun, 10–5

In addition to a sizeable collection of early American pattern glass and kitchen collectibles, the shop also has primitive prints on canvas. PR: $. CC: No.

Second Time Around
Route 52 (12566)
(914) 744-9934, 744-2151
Hours: Mon–Sat, 11–5

Established in 1979, this 2,500 square foot shop contains furniture, collectibles, antiques, glassware, and jewelry that will please everyone. PR: $$. CC: MC, V, D. LOC: Two tenths of a mile west of the traffic light in Pine Bush.

Willow Parva Antiques
2918 Route 52 (12566)
(914) 744-3771
Hours: Daily 10–6

Within an Edwardian barn, carriage house, and ice house located on an 1880s Victorian estate, one will find a large selection of fine antiques such as formal/country furniture, porcelain, lighting, decorative arts, and architectural items. PR: $$. CC: MC, V.

PINE CITY

Proud American Shoppe
1828 Pennsylvania Avenue (14871)
(607) 733-1043
Hours: Mon–Sat, 10–5 or by appointment

Specializing in Americana, this shop contains a fine selection that ranges from cupboards, quilts, and stoneware to primitives, classical, and formal with a excellent selection of appropriate accessories. CC: MC, V.

Woodshed, The
1647 Pennsylvania Avenue (14871)
(607) 733-2897
Hours: Most days, 10–5
or by appointment

This shop contains painted and refinished country furniture plus primitives and collectibles. CC: No. LOC: One half mile off Route 328S in Webb Mills.

PINE HILL

Cloudspinners Antiques
Elm Street, off of Route 28
(12465)
(914) 254-4838
Hours: Daily 9–5, call to be certain

Stressing craftmanship in both repairs and refinishing, this shop specializes in fully restored furniture and lighting. Decorative smalls are also available. CC: D.

PITTSFORD

Audree & Bryce Chase's Collector's Corner
3 Spruce Lane (14534)
(716) 385-8957
Hours: Shows only & some special request items from their home

In business since 1965, these dealers carry anything that may have been used to furnish the American home before 1850: furniture, rugs, paintings, prints, pottery,

A poplar corner cupboard, probably Midwestern origin, ca. 1860, with exhuberant original grain painted shades of orange over yellow. *(Courtesy Webb & Brennan American Antiques Pittsford)*

porcelain, earthenware, lighting devices, cooking equipment, brass, iron, copper, globes, barometers, sewing tools, bed covers, clocks, guns and the like. Consignments are accepted and authentication is available. PR: $$$$. CC: No.

Rainbird, The
7 Schoen Place (14534)
(716) 385-5690
Hours: Mon–Sat, 10:30–4:30

This shop directly imports antique English country pine furniture and china. There is an extensive selection of hutches, dressers, tables, chests of drawers, collectibles, garden accessories, decorative accessories and tools. PR: $$$. CC: MC, V.

Strawberry Hill Bookshop
50 State Street—Northfield Common (14534)
(716) 586-8707
(716) 359-0561 fax
Hours: Mon–Sat open; Sun closed

This bookstore specializes in old, used, and rare books with an emphasis on literature, history, poetry, children's books, cookbooks, biography, business, and marketing. A book search service is available. CC: MC, V.

Webb & Brennan American Antiques
84 Washington Road (14534)
(716) 442-9011, 385-3954
Hours: Show exhibitors only

These dealers offer fine formal, country, and painted furniture from the 18th and 19th centuries with appropriate accessories such as paintings, watercolors, silhouettes, textiles, and folk art. All items are guaranteed as represented.

PLATTSBURGH

Bargaineer, The
39 Bridge Street (12901)
(518) 561-3525
Hours: Mon–Sat, 9–5; Sun, 11–3

This shop carries anything old or collectible. CC: No.

Black Bear Antiques
5452 Peru Street, Route 9 (12901)
(518) 562-0577
Hours: Evenings, Weekends, and Summers

This small shop carries about 400 items which are mostly Victorian smalls such as Art Pottery and majolica. PR: $. CC: No.

Bridge Street Antique Emporium (MD)
60 Bridge Street (12901)
(518) 563-6658
Hours: Daily 12–6

Twelve dealers present a wide variety of antiques and collectibles. In addition to many items of local interest, pottery, china, jewelry, primitives, smalls, and furniture can be found. PR: $$$. CC: MC, V.

Third Eye Antiques
5114 North Catherine Street (12901)
(518) 563-3047
Hours: Daily 10–4:30

This shop offers a wide selection of prints and paper Americana such as illustrated books, colored engravings, and photographs. CC: No.

POND EDDY

Anthony S. Werneke Antiques
Hollow Road, Box 99 (12770)
(914) 856-1037
(914) 856-1037 fax
Hours: By appointment

In addition to specializing in 17th and 18th century American furniture and English Delft, brass, and drinking glasses, this dealer also offers accessories which are appropriate to the period. Estate work, appraisals, and buying services are done. CC: No.

PORT JERVIS

J. Gardner
4 South Street (12771)
(914) 856-0900
Hours: Mon–Fri, 11–4:30; Sat–Sun, 12–5; Wed closed

This shop specializes in country furniture in original paint and high country forms in original surface. In addition to country accessories, architectural elements which are both decorative and functional, Victorian Era garden furniture, windows, and fencing are always available. CC: No.

POTSDAM

Birchbark Bookshop, The
Ashton Road, Route 4 (13676)
(315) 265-3875
Hours: Thur–Sun, 1–6

Specializing in Adirondack Mountains, St. Lawrence River area, and New York State material, this used bookshop has more than 15,000 volumes. PR: $. CC: No.

POUND RIDGE

Alan Y. Roberts, Inc.

27 Westchester Avenue (10576)
(914) 764-5427
Hours: Mon–Sat, 9:30–5; Sun closed

This has been one of the region's largest and busiest shops for the past 24 years. There are nine showrooms of American and English antique furniture and decorations with a emphasis on dining room pieces and desks of all types. The shop frequently receives new shipments of merchandise.

Antiques & Tools of Business & Kitchen

Westchester Avenue, Scotts Corner (10576)
(914) 764-0015
(914) 764-5348 fax
Hours: Tues–Sat, 10–5; Sun, 12–5, Monday closed

From wall to wall and floor to ceiling, this shop is an organized clutter of funky, familiar, old "stuff" from barns, kitchens, attics, farms, hospitals, ships, and workshops. Metal repair and restoration services are available. PR: $. CC: MC, V.

Dora Landey Antiques

Westchester Avenue, Scotts Corner, Route 124 (10576)
(914) 533-2643
Hours: Thur–Sat, 11–5; Sun, 1–5; Mon closed; Tues–Wed by chance or appointment

This shop contains an impressive offering of blue and white Staffordshire china plus pink, black, brown, green, and purple. Historical Staffordshire, English china, and country smalls are also available. CC: No.

Elizabeth de Bussy, Inc.

67 Westchester Avenue (10576)
(914) 764-1247
Hours: Tues–Sat, 11–5

This small shop is full of quality period items that are hand picked by the owner in Continental Europe. PR: $$$. CC: No.

Strap Hinge (MD)

Scotts Corners (10576)
(914) 764-1145
Hours: Call for hours

This four dealer shop specializes in antique wicker, Christmas ornaments, country furniture, and china.

Voss Beringer, Ltd.

Corner of Lower Trinity Pass & Westchester Avenue, Scotts Corner (10576)
(914) 764-1923
(914) 241-7028 fax
Hours: Wed–Sun, 12–5, by chance or appointment, best to call ahead.

In addition to fine 18th and 19th century American furniture and accessories and antique Oriental rugs, this dealer specializes in high country items and sandpaper paintings. A selection of toys from the 1920s is also offered. Consignments are accepted, and an interior decorator service is available. PR: $$$$$. CC: No.

PRESTON HOLLOW

Antique Center of Preston Hollow (MD)

961 Main Street (12469)
(518) 239-4251
Hours: May through September, Daily 10–5; October & November, Sat–Sun, 10–5

Twenty-four dealers and numerous consignors offer antiques and collectibles in four quaint buildings with more than 8,000 square feet of space. Reasonably priced, a wide range of period furniture, glassware, pottery, jewelry, toys, tools, sports memorabilia, and general antiquities is always available. PR: $$. CC: MC, V.

Green Acres Antique Center (MD)

960 Main Street (12469)
(518) 239-4891
Hours: May 1st through Labor Day; Daily 10–5

Although the Empire and Victorian Periods are emphasized at this 12 dealer co-op, other antiques and collectibles are also for sale in this large two-level barn. A fine assortment of primitives, advertising, costume jewelry, bottles, and decorative smalls make this a must stop for browsers. Consignments are accepted. PR: $$. CC: MC, V.

PUTNAM VALLEY

Karen Kaufer Antiques

319 Oscawana Lake Road (10579)
(914) 526-2425
Hours: Weekends and by appointment

Housed in a two story red barn is a presentation of quality country pieces such as cupboards, tables, and chairs. Complementing these antiques are a fine selection of country smalls, yellow ware, old iron, stoneware crocks, baskets, and quilts.
PR: $$. CC: No.

Mark & Marjorie Allen

29 Marsh Hill Road (10579)
(914) 528-8989
Hours: Appointment preferred

Established in 1968, this shop specializes in pre 1780 American furniture and appropriate accessories with an emphasis on brass and Delftware. All of which is tastefully presented in a period setting. CC: No.

RED HOOK

Annex Antique Center (MD)

23 East Market Street (12571)
(914) 758-2843
Hours: Daily 11–5

Twenty-six dealers feature glassware, toys, oak and pine furniture, primitives, country furniture, and a decorating with antiques service in the balcony.

A representative selection of mid 17th and 18th century brass and delft.
(Mark & Marjorie Allen, Putnam Valley)

Custom curtains, fabrics, and decorating services are available. Estate sales are also conducted. PR: $. CC: MC, V.

Cider Mill Antiques
5 Cherry Street (12571)
(914) 758-2599
Hours: Fri–Mon, 11–5

Located in a 1750s building, this country antique store is filled with primitive furniture, accessories, yellow ware, textiles, and teddy bears. Handmade country reproduction furniture is also available. Furniture repair can be done. CC: MC, V. LOC: Off Route 9, the first right north of light behind the Elmendorf Inn.

Lafayette House Antiques Center, The (MD)
North Road, Route 199, Box 269A (12571)
(914) 758-6024
Hours: Daily

Ten dealers offer antiques and collectibles that range from country furniture and accessories, hooked rugs, pillows, miniatures, pottery, dolls, Victorian furniture, Depression and pattern glass, advertising, jewelry, prints, and paintings. A monthly flea market is held during the summer. Call for dates and times.

RENSSELAERVILLE

David Davis Antiques
P.O. Box 643 (12147)
(518) 432-0964, 496-1357
Hours: Closed shop, shows and mail order only

This dealer specializes in 18th, 19th, and 20th century decorative arts which are all picked home fresh.

Rensselaerville Antiques
Route 85, P.O.Box 153 (12147)
(518) 797-3499
Hours: Daily 10–5;
a call ahead is advisable

In a restored Federal Period church, one will find 18th and 19th century furniture complemented by silver, paintings, prints, export china, Staffordshire, jewelry, textiles, and metalware. Consignments are accepted. Appraisals are given. CC: MC, V.

RHINEBECK

Barbara Zitz Antiques
37 Wurtemburg Road (12572)
(914) 876-2652
Hours: By chance or appointment

This dealer specializes in 18th century furnishings featuring country furniture in old paint and in as found condition, country primitives, quilts, and yellow ware. PR: $$. CC: No.

Rare American musical tall case clock by Daniel Porter of Williamstown, MA, ca. 1795. The tunes play on a nest of ten bells every three hours; there is a selection of six tunes on the dial. *(Courtesy Fanelli Antique Timepieces, Ltd., New York City)*

Beekman Arms Antique Market (MD)
Beekman Square behind the Beekman Arms Hotel (12572)
(914) 876-3477
Hours: Daily 11–5

Thirty dealers offer Americana, period furniture, primitives, country items, jewelry, books, and accessories. CC: MC, V.

Dennis & Valerie Bakoledis Antiques
East Market Street (12572)
(914) 876-7944
Hours: By chance or appointment

Members of the Antique Dealers Association of America, these dealers specialize in Americana with an emphasis on folk art, weathervanes, cast and wrought iron, architectural elements, and decorative accessories.

Dolores Rogers Murphy Antiques
See Clinton Corners

Old Mill House Antiques (MD)
144 Route 9 North (12572)
(914) 876-3636
Hours: Daily 11–5, closed Wed

This pleasant group shop in a country setting offers a variety of antiques and collectibles for the collector, dealer, and decorator. Although specializing in country furniture and accessories, the dealers also offer unique items from other periods such as ephemera, books, artifacts, textiles, and lighting. PR: $$. CC: MC, V. LOC: Three miles north of Rhinebeck Village.

Rhinebeck Antique Center (MD)
7 West Market Street (12572)
(914) 876-8168
Hours: Thur–Tues, 11–5

This 40 plus dealer group shop specializes in showcase items that range from antiques to collectibles. PR: $$. CC: MC, V.

Susan Bean of Silhouette
24 East Market Street (12572)
(914) 876-4545
Hours: Mon–Sat, 11–5:30; Sun, 12–4

This combination gift and antique shop features vintage and antique clothing, handmade lace, fine linens, and old costume jewelry. A small selection of Native American silver and turquoise jewelry is also offered. PR:$$. CC: MC, V, AMEX, D.

RICHMONDVILLE

Bear Gulch Shop
Bear Gulch Road, Box 370, RD #1 (12149)
(518) 294-6567
Hours: Sat 10–5; Sun, 12–5 and by appointment

Set in an early barn, this shop contains antiques and collectibles for varied tastes. Glassware of all description, furniture, and primitives are only some of the items that can be found. CC: No.

ROCHESTER

Abacus Bookshop

350 East Avenue (14604)
(716) 325-7950
Hours: Mon–Sat, 12–6
except Thur till 8

Stocking used and rare books, this shop specializes in the fine arts, photography, architecture, and literature. Prints, autographs, and maps are also featured. Catalogs are issued periodically. Appraisals are given and archival matting can be done on prints. CC: MC, V.

Antique Barn (MD)

499 East Ridge Road (14621)
(716) 266-5520
Hours: Tues–Sat, 10–4; Sun, 12–4

This 11 dealer group shop offers nice, clean merchandise with an emphasis on Hummels, pottery, furniture, smalls, primitives, prints, quilts, and bottles. PR: $$. CC: No.

Antiques of Merritt

85 Bellevue Drive (14620)
(716) 271-0912
Hours: By appointment

Doing business since 1972, this dealer primarily does shows. However, she does sell her specialty, quilts and coverlets, from her home by appointment.

Bettiques

1697 Monroe Avenue (14618)
(716) 442-2995
(716) 442-2995 fax
Hours: By appointment or chance, shows and mail order

This shop specializes in silver, jewelry, Chinese Export porcelain, fine glass, and porcelains. Purchases can be made through mail order. CC: MC, V, AMEX.

Brennan Antiques

76 Rogers Parkway (14617)
(716) 544-7658
Hours: By appointment only and shows

These dealers are noted for their high quality cherry and pine furniture in paint with original surface, primitives, folk art, decorative smalls, and paintings. CC: No.

David Mouilleseaux Art and Antiques

60 Bradford Road (14618)
(716) 442-9011
Hours: Closed shop, shows and appointments

Established in 1991, this business offers 19th and early 20th century paintings, prints, and folk art as well as appropriate furniture. The cleaning and restoration of paintings can be done.

DeSimone and Yount Booksellers
274 North Goodman Street (14607)
(716) 242-9349
Hours: Daily 10–6, Thur & Fri till 8

Located in a factory turned mall, this shop services the needs of the collector of fine books especially on the Civil War and Americana. CC: Yes.

Kruggel Antiques
Unlisted
(716) 244-6475
Hours: By appointment only, shows, and mail order

Conducting business since 1988, this dealer specializes in early brass, wood, English pottery, glass, American furniture, and Art Glass. PR: $$. CC: No.

Miriam Rogachefsky Antiques
1905 Westfall Road (14618-2828)
(716) 256-3426
Hours: By appointment, shows, and mail order

In business since 1971, this dealer offers a fine selection of Chinese and Japanese porcelain, lamps, furniture, and cloisonne. Native American arts and wicker and wire furniture are also available. CC: No.

Mission Oak Antiques
378 Meigs Street (14607)
(716) 442-2480
Hours: Wed, Fri, & Sat, 12–5 or by chance or appointment

This shop specializes in furniture and decorative accessories from the American Arts & Craft Movement by names such as Stickley, Roycroft, Limbert's, and Rohlfs. One will find a fine offering of furniture, metalware, lighting, and pottery. PR: $$$. CC: MC, V, AMEX.

Richard Romberg
96 Richmond Street (14607)
(716) 546-3785
Hours: By appointment

This dealer features a small but choice selection of American folk sculpture, paintings, architectural fragments, antique garden furnishings, and country and period furniture in original surface. Appraisals and authentication can be done. CC: MC, V.

Upstate Gallery Antiques Ltd.
16 Gardiner Park (14607)
(716) 262-2089
Hours: Tues–Sat, 10–4

This full-time professional shop is owned by retired curators who specialize in American and Continental furniture, decorative and fine arts, and toys. A written guarantee is given for all items that are purchased. CC: No.

Yankee Peddler Bookshop, Vol. II
Village Gate Square, 274 North Goodman Street (14607)
(716) 271-5080
Hours: Mon–Sat, 11–6 except Thur till 8; Sun, 12–5

In addition to a large general

stock of books, this business features a selection of prints, paintings, photographica, and historical paper. Book, print, and painting restoration as well as appraisals can be done. Hand coloring, matting, and framing services are available. PR: $$$. CC: MC, V.

ROME

Brynilsen's Homestead Antiques
8497 Turin Road (13440)
(315) 337-1360
Hours: Nov–April; Wed–Fri, 12–5; Sat, 10–2

Located in a 200 year old farmhouse, this shop offers restored antique woodstoves, primitives, and collectibles. During the holidays, a Christmas shop contains ornaments, decorations, wreaths, and live trees. PR: Reasonable. CC: No.

Sue Evans—Antiques
217 South James Street (13440)
(315) 337-0027
Hours: Tues–Sat, 10–4 (generally)

At this shop, one will find a good selection of refinished pine and cherry furniture from the 19th century as well as complementary accessories, some glass, books, and decorative or useable horsedrawn carriages and sleighs.

ST. JOHNSVILLE

Pickle Hill & Co.
41 West Main Street (13339)
(518) 568-2005, 993-4166
Hours: By Appoinment

This shop carries a general line of antiques which includes decorative bric-a-brac, blanket boxes, and cupboards. Clock repairs can be done.

SALEM

Joe's Antique Tools
East Broadway, P. O. Box 309
(918) 854-3813
Hours: Mon–Fri, 10–5; Sat–Sun, 1–5

This dealer features antique wood working tools for the discriminating craftsperson and collector. A selection of antique costume jewelry is also available. PR: $.

SARATOGA SPRINGS

Antiques 400
400 Broadway (12866)
(518) 587-3433
Hours: Daily 10–5

This shop contains an eclectic blend of antiques, collectibles, and decorative accessories. One is likely to find estate jewelry, glassware, cast iron, Victoriana, furniture, bronzes, and lamps.
CC: MC, V, AMEX, D.

Broadway Antiques Gallery (MD)

484 Broadway (12866)
(518) 581-8348
Hours: Daily 11–6 with extended summer hours on Thur, Fri, and Sat evenings

This mall group shop has 11 dealers who offer quality American antiques at reasonable prices. This is a shop for both the trade and the collector. CC: MC, V.

Lyrical Ballad Bookstore

7 Phila Street (12866)
(518) 584-8779
(518) 584-6815 fax
Hours: Mon–Sat, 10–6; Sun, 12–4 except Jan & Feb

This general antiquarian bookstop has a large, select inventory of books in all fields but is especially strong in art, architecture, music, dance, literature, and fine bindings. A large selection of old prints and postcards is also available. PR: $$$$$. CC: MC, V.

Nine Caroline Antiques

9 Caroline Street (12866)
(518) 583-9112
Hours: Daily 11–5 with extended summer hours

This shop is noted for a very eclectic assortment of antiques which range from primitives to Art Deco to kitch. New items arrive daily. PR: $$. CC: No.

Old Stuff

493 Broadway (12866)
(518) 583-9680
Hours: Daily 10–6, July–August till 11

Located just north of the post office building, this shop is filled with antiques and collectibles. CC: No.

Page in Time, A (MD)

462 Broadway (12866)
(518) 584-4876
Hours: Mon–Sat, 10–6; Sun, 12–5

This 20 dealer group shop of offers glassware, china, heirloom linens, prints, pottery, planters, paperweights, estate and costume jewelry, vintage clothing, sterling and plate silver, toys, and Christmas decorations from the 1800s to the 1950s. CC: MC, V.

Regent Street Antique Center (MD)

153 Regent Street (12866)
(518) 584-0107
Hours: Daily 10–5

Located in a historic building and occupying 12,000 square feet, 30 dealers offer a wide variety of select antiques and collectibles. Stoneware, books, Art Deco items, quilts, prints, canes, china, silver, Hummels, holiday collectibles, furniture, and jewelry are some of the items for sale. On display are museum collections of Hummels, decorated stoneware,

Unusual English Regency tortoiseshell-veneered tea caddy in the Gothic manner, ca. 1815. *(Courtesy Georgian Manor Antiques, Inc., New York City)*

scrimshaw, canes, Saratoga memoribilia, and miniatures. PR: $$. CC: MC, V.

Ye Olde Wishin' Shoppe
353 & 355 Broadway (12866)
(518) 583-7782
Hours: Daily 10–5:30
with some seasonal hours

This shop features 1940s and older vintage clothing with an emphasis on dress for weddings, proms, and galas. One will also find linens, lace, Black Americana, and estate jewelry. PR: $$. CC: MC, V, AMEX, D.

SAUGERTIES

Anne Smith Antiques
249 Main Street (12477)
(914) 246-7766
Hours: Fri–Sun and
most Mondays, 11–5

Specializing in the unusual and the colorful, this shop contains an impressive offering of American paintings, doll houses, birdcages, decorative antiques, and antique jewelry. CC: MC, V.

Booktrader
252 Main Street (12477)
(914) 246-3522
Hours: Mon–Sat, 10–6; Sun, 12–4

Specializing in regional history, science fiction, children's books, and mysteries, this shop contains more than 25,000 new and used titles. About 90 percent of the books which include current romances, readers' copies, and sets from the late 18th and 19th century are used. This shop buys, sells, and trades books. PR: $. CC: MC, V.

Burning Lights
84 Partition Street (12477)
(914) 246-2306
Hours: Wed–Mon, 11–5

This shop carries all types of lighting—candle, oil, and keroscene—plus older electric lamps. Repair and restoration services are available. A full line of candles is stocked. PR: $. CC: No.

English Garden Antiques & Interiors
232 Main Street (12477)
(914) 246-1012
Hours: Daily 11:30–5

In addition to specializing in glassware, decorative smalls, costume jewelry, prints, small furniture, and an eclectic mix of other items, this shop offers custom picture framing. Also, the area's top designer is available for all types of window treatments from contemporary to Old English plus other design consultations. PR: Reasonable. CC: MC, V, D.

Fancy Flea, The
50 Market Street (12477)
(914) 246-9391
Hours: Fri–Tues, 11–5:30

In the heart of the village, this shop is crammed full of antiques and collectibles, things old and not so old.

Fed-On Antiques
Corner of Market and Livingston Streets (12477)
(914) 246-8444, shop;
(518) 678-3581, home
Hours: Fri–Sun, 12–5;
sometimes Monday but call

This shop specializes in lighting fixtures complemented by glass and refinished and in as found condition furniture that ranges in style from country to Deco. CC: No.

Glory Daze Antiques
105 Partition Street (12477)
(914) 246-7861, 336-5180
Hours: Daily 11–5

One will find a special blend of antiques and collectibles from primitive to Art Deco at affordable prices in this shop. CC: No.

Granny's Antiques
97 Partition Street (12477)
(914) 246-5527
Hours: Daily 10:30–5

In addition to featuring glassware and fabrics, this shop also contains furniture, lamps, collectibles, jewelry, and rugs. PR: Affordable. CC: No.

Old Stone House Antiques
5080 Kings Highway (12477)
(914) 246-7905
Hours: Any Time

In addition to specializing in salt dips (open salts) and spoons, this shop also carries a general line of antiques and collectibles that includes Depression and pressed glass, prints, paper, toys, and post cards. Some consignments are accepted and appraisals can be given. PR: $$. CC: No. LOC: Located a little more than a mile south of Thruway Exit 20.

Saugerties Antique Annex
243 Main Street (12477)
(914) 246-4363
Hours: Daily 11–5

A one owner shop featuring better quality antiques and collectibles with a specialty in Mission furniture and accessories, Art Pottery, art works, jewelry, and silver. Furniture repair, refinishing, and restoration can be done.

Saugerties Antique Center (MD)
220 Main Street (12477)
(914) 246-8234, 246-3227
Hours: Mon–Sat, 10–5; Sun, 12–5

Twenty-six dealers offer a wide assortment of affordable collectibles; Victorian, Deco, and primitive furniture; glassware; china; silver; lighting; paintings; and decorative accessories. PR: $. CC: No.

Saugerties Antique Gallery
104 Partition Street (12477)
(914) 246-2323
Hours: Daily, 10–5

This shop contains highly decorative antiques such as bronzes, Tiffany lighting, paintings, sterling silver, jewelry, and Art Glass. On the second floor, one will find 19th century furniture. CC: MC, V, AMEX, D.

Stone House Gallery
102 Partition Street (12477)
(914) 247-0827
Hours: Fri–Wed, 11–5:30

This shop contains a very eclectic selection ranging from primitives and good painted furniture to Art Deco items, designer furniture, and architectural fragments; all of which are chosen for their aesthetic value. One will find both large and small decorative items for indoors and out, paintings, sculpture, folk art, vintage clothing, and estate jewelry. In addition, appraisals can be done, consignments are accepted, a finders service is offered, and paintings can be restored.

Treasure Shop, The
78 Partition Street (12477)
(914) 247-0802
Hours: Wed–Mon, 11–5

From local attics, cellars, and barns, this shop contains tools, primitives, folk art, kitchen collectibles, country antiques, and paintings. PR: $. CC: No.

SCARSDALE

Arles Ltd. "Objects from a Finer Time"
1493 Weaver Street, Colonial Village Shopping Center (10583)
(914) 723-6464
Hours: Tues–Fri, 11–5;
Saturday by appointment

In addition to English and French furniture and accessories from the 18th and 19th century, one will find period pieces, mirrors, table appointments, and architectural items in this shop. PR: $$$. CC: AMEX.

Carol David Antiques
9 Harwood Court (10583)
(914) 723-2767
Hours: Mon–Sat, 10–5;
Sun by appointment

This shop offers a decorative mix of town and country English, French, and American furniture with appropriate accessories that include mirrors, porcelain, silver, glassware, paintings, prints, and chandeliers. This shop is well worth a detour. CC: MC, V, AMEX.

Lucky Strike Antiques
515 Central Park (10583)
(914) 472-2110
Hours: Wed–Sun, 12–5

Turn of the century oak and Victorian furniture and appropriate accessories including prints and lighting devices can be found in this shop. CC: No.

SCHENECTADY

Howard Bliss Antiques
205 Union Street (12305)
(518) 372-5856
Hours: Daily 10–5, but please call first

Located in an 18th century Sanders-Ellice house, this dealer specializes in Americana, textiles, needlework, and American furniture. PR: $100+. CC: No.

Tom Jardas Antiques
507 Union Street (12305)
(518) 374-4931
Hours: No set hours, call ahead

This dealer carries a general line with an emphasis on popular culture that includes ephemera, old

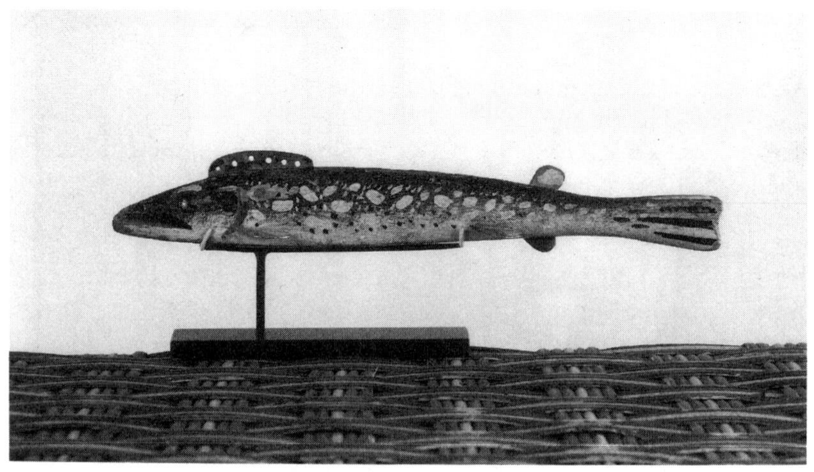

Pike fish decoy carved by Oscar Peterson in Michigan, ca. 1940.
(Courtesy American Primitive Gallery, New York City).

advertising, garden accessories, and collectibles.

SCHOHARIE

Partridge Run Antiques
Route 30 & Stony Brook Road
(12157)
(518) 295-7705
Hours: By chance or appointment

In addition to a nice selection of smalls, paintings, quilts, and the like, this shop specializes in country furniture in both paint and refinished condition. PR: $$. CC: No.

Selective Eye Antiques at the 1849 House (MD)
383 South Main Street (12157)
(518) 295-7070
Hours: Mon, Wed–Sat, 10–5;
Sun, 12–5

This group shop contains a quality eclectic mix that features a wide range of market fresh antiques and collectibles. The focus is on country, garden, and architectural elements. PR: $$$. CC: MC, V.

SENECA FALLS

Collection Agency, The
58 Fall Street, Routes 5 & 20
(13148)
(315) 568-5515
Hours: Tues–Sat, 11–5:30
or by appointment

This large single owner shop features a variety of furniture and smalls, a significant selection of paintings, graniteware, Indian items, china, and unique decorator items. CC: MC, V, AMEX, D.

Country Reflections
84 Cayuga Street, Routes 5 & 20
(13148)
(315) 568-4176
Hours: Open almost always

Located in an 1870s home, this

shop carries items to make your home look like *Country Living.* Kitchen tables, bowls, trunks, kitchen collectibles, and a general line of country antiques are offered. A country decorating service is available. PR: $$. CC: No.

SHOKAN

Gateway Antiques
Croswell Manor Drive (12481)
(914) 657-8502
Hours: Daily 10–5

Just off Route 28, this shop stocks quality porcelain, pottery, yellow ware, glass, textiles, linen, and lace. Nineteenth century furniture and accessories such as mirrors, lamps, and prints are also available. PR: $. CC: MC, V.

SHUSHAN

Glass Shop, The
RR 1, Box 11, Stanton Road (12873)
(518) 854-7431
Hours: Tues–Sun, 9–6

One of Washington County's newest shops, it offers an outstanding collection of antique, collectible, and modern glassware. In addition to Amberina, Art Glass, cut crystal, and caramel slag, one will find pressed, Depression, milk, and Carnival glass. PR: $. CC: No.

SKANEATELES

Behind the Inn Antiques and Collectibles (MD)
4 Hannum Street (13152)
(315) 685-6542
Hours: Mon–Sat, 11–6; Sun, 12–5

Housed in a historic, two story carriage house behind the Sherwood Inn, a select group of six quality dealers offer a wide variety of china, furniture, books, jewelry, and collectibles. A Syracuse China matching service is available. PR: Affordable. CC: MC, V.

Lakeview Antiques
58 Genesee Street (13152)
(315) 685-0239
Hours: Mon–Sat, 10–5; Sun, 12–5

This shop carries a general line of collectibles, American furniture, glass, and post cards. PR: $. CC: MC, V.

White & White Antiques & Interiors, Inc.
18 East Genesee Street (13152)
(315) 685-7733
Hours: Mon–Sat, 10–5; Sun, 1–5 during the summer

These dealers offer a diverse selection of fine antiques of the 17th through the 20th century. With an emphasis on quality and a guarantee that merchandise is as represented, they offer the nicer things in areas such as American furniture, Americana, folk art, and paintings. Appraisals, consignments, restoration, and interior

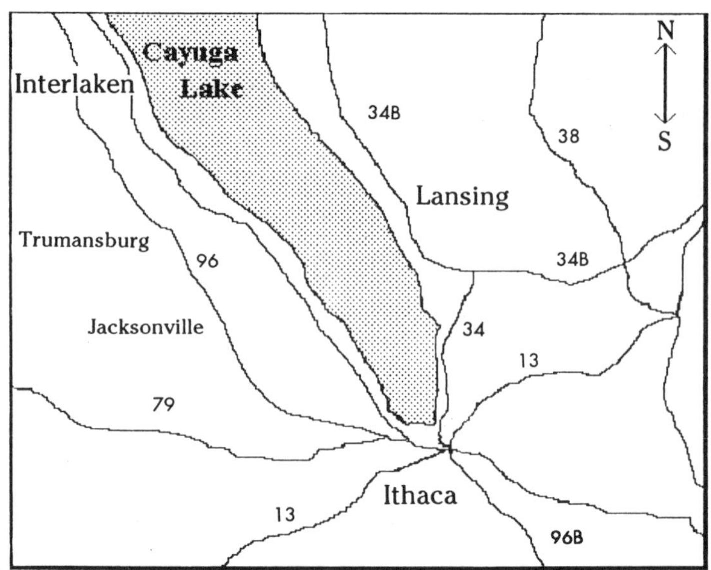

Trumansburg-Ithaca Area

design services are available. PR: $$$$$. CC: V, MC, AMEX.

SMITHVILLE FLATS

Heisler's Antique Merchantile
Main Street (13841)
(607) 656-4179
Hours: By chance or appointment

In an old country store setting, one will discover quality Americana—furniture in original finish, quilts, baskets, samplers, paintings, and similarly desirable antiques—and a few collectibles. CC: No.

Snoop Sisters
Genegantslet Road (13841)
(607) 656-7492
Hours: Open by chance or appointment

This shop contains all types of paper advertising with an emphasis on old magazine pieces, post cards, sheet music, and other items having to do with paper. CC: No.

SODUS

Past and Present Antiques
7082 Ridge Road East (14551)
(315) 483-6761
Hours: Tues–Sat, 10–5

This unique country shop offers five rooms of furniture dating from the the 1800s to the 1940s with appropriate accessories such as glass, silver, prints, and many collectibles. Appraisals and research can be done. PR: Affordable. CC: MC, V, AMEX, D.

SOUTH KORTRIGHT

Betty Brook Road Antiques
Betty Brook Road, Box 13A (13842)
(607) 538-9432
Hours: Daily 10–5

This shop contains Depression glass, refinished oak and pine furniture, lamps, costume jewelry, salt & pepper shakers, and kitchen collectibles. CC: No. LOC: Five hundred feet off the road between Hobart and Bloomfield.

SOUTH SALEM

Janice F. Strauss American Antiques

P.O. Box 354 (10590-0354)
(914) 763-5933
(914) 763-5933 fax
Hours: By appointment only

This gallery of authentic formal and country American furniture and accessories from the 18th and early 19th century places an emphasis on Queen Anne, Chippendale, and the Early Federal periods. Decorative accessories include looking glasses, fireplace equipment, and glass. All items are sold with a written guarantee. In addition, interior decorating services to create both formal and country, period and reproduction early American settings are available. PR: $$$$$. CC: No.

SOUTH WESTERLO

Country Gentleman Antiques, The

Route 401/405, P.O. Box 52 (12163)
(518) 966-5574
Hours: June–Oct 12th; Tues–Sat, 10–5 and Sun, 11–4:30
Oct 13–Dec; Fri-Sat, 10-5 and Sun, 11-4:30
Apr–May; Thur-Sat, 10-5 and Sun, 11-4:30
By appointment: (518) 966-5739, 966-5574

This shop contains a selection of furnishings with an emphasis on country, Early Victorian, Federal, and 1876 Centennial. In addition to decorative smalls, china, glass, folk art, paintings and prints, this shop features smaller scale furniture for decorating flexibility. PR: $$$$$. CC: No.

SPENCERTOWN

Art & Antique Co. of Spencertown

Route 203, Box 143 (12165)
(518) 392-4445, 392-4442 evenings
Hours: Fri & Mon, 1–5:30; Sat–Sun, 11–5:30 or by appointment

In a 7,000 square foot shop, fine paintings, sculpture, prints, Americana, antique firearms, furniture, Oriental rugs, and Shaker are offered. Dealers are always welcome. PR: $$$$. CC: Yes.

SPRINGFIELD CENTER

Bobbi Von Dehmlein Antiques

Route 80, Box 428 (13468)
(315) 858-0232
(315) 858-0232 fax
Hours: Mon–Sun, 10–5

Established in 1983, this shop specializes in antiques for collectors and interior decorators by featuring majolica, Staffordshire figures, decorative furniture, and accessories. Appraisals can be done. LOC: One mile south of Route 20 on Route 80 going toward Cooperstown or ten miles north of Cooperstown on Route 80.

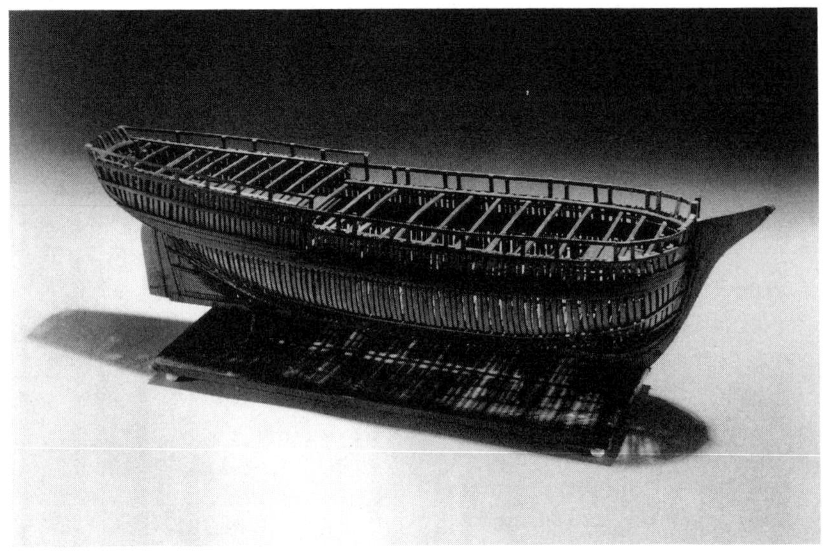

A British Dockyard Framing model, ca 1780, 1/4" scale. Originally these models were used by the Royal Dockyards to document and experiment with construction techniques. *(Courtesy North Star Galleries, New York City)*

STAMFORD

Uncle Alan's Antiques & Oddities
RD #1, Box 156, Route 23
(12167-9601)
(607) 652-7236
Hours: By chance or appointment

Specializing in eclectica, this shop offers an interesting selection of lighting, advertising, pottery, Arts and Crafts, small furniture, games, puzzles, medical and barber shop collectibles, mirrors, lighters and cigarette paraphernalia, clocks, and bottles. PR: $. CC: No.

STANFORDVILLE

Tin Rabbit, The
RR 1, Box 507 (12581)
(914) 868-7524
Hours: By appointment only

This dealer specializes in country antiques in old paint and in as found condition plus folk art and decorative smalls. PR: $200+

STAATSBURG

Archatrive
13 Reservoir Road (12580)
(914) 889-8144
Hours: By appointment only

This business specializes in deconstructionist antique furniture and decoratives using antique and period architectural elements in a new context including beds, tables, cabinetry (kitchen, bathroom, etc.), and lighting. Original painted colors and surfaces can be developed and enhanced. Design services for commercial and domestic projects, furniture reproduction, home restoration, display materials, and prop rentals are also offered. CC: No.

STONE RIDGE

Myron Cohen Antiques
4034 U.S. Highway 209 (12484)
(914) 687-7019
Hours: By chance or appointment

This shop contains a wide variety of antiques and collectibles including lighting, clocks, dolls, copper, brass, pottery, glass, and memoribilia. Lamp repair and restoration are available.

Stone Ridge Antiques (MD)
Intersection of Route 209 & 213 (12484)
(914) 687-7400 (shop), 687-9031 (office)
Hours: Wed–Sun, 11–5; Mon & Tues by appointment or chance

Fifteen dealers bring together the eclectic, the unusual, and the funky. One will find primitives, painted pine furniture, collectibles, textiles, cupboards, fine toys, quilts, pottery, photographs, china, and glassware. PR: $$. CC: No.

Things Antiques
4127 U.S. Highway 209 (12484)
(914) 687-4577
Hours: Fri–Tues, 10–5
or by appointment

Country furniture, architectual artifacts, lighting, and outdoor furnishings are featured at this shop. CC: No.

Thumbprint Antiques
209 Tongore Road (12484)
(914) 687-9318
Hours: Tues–Sun, 12–5

Located in a barn, this business offers quality antiques such as furniture, china, glass, and silver. Woodstock Lampshades are stocked. An appraisal service is available. PR: $$$. CC: MC, V.

SUFFERN

North Hill Antiques
P.O. Box 455 (10901)
(914) 357-4484
Hours: Closed Shop

Doing only mail order and shows, this business specializes in early American silver with a particular emphasis on regional makers. CC: No.

SYRACUSE

Antique Underground (MD)
247 West Fayette Street (13202)
(315) 472-5510
Hours: Mon–Sat, 10–6; Sun, 12–5

Located in a massive underground complex in the heart of Syracuse's revival district, 20 dealers offer a large and constantly changing array of American antiques and collectibles from the 18th century up to the 1950s. In addition, appraisals, lectures, repair and restoration, shipping, and prop rentals are available. PR: $$. CC: MC, V, AMEX, D.

Dacia of New York, The Vintage Furniture Shop
2416 Court Street, Route 298
(13208-1951)
(315) 455-2651
Hours: Mon–Sat, 10–5

This shop contains fully refinished wood furniture from the 1800s to the 1950s along with a general line of antiques and collectibles. The workmanship and finish of all wood furniture is guaranteed. Appraisals, caning, furniture and clock repair and restoration, lamp repair and rewiring, and furniture stripping are done. PR: $$. CC: MC, V, AMEX, D.

Dalton's American Decorative Arts
1931 James Street (13206)
(315) 463-1568
(315) 463-1615 fax
Hours: Mon–Sat, 10–5
or by appointment

This is a full service shop for the Arts & Crafts collector. In addition to offering Mission furniture by major and minor manufacturers, this shop also handles a complete line of accessories. Upholstery and restorations can be done. Specialized since 1980, the dealers understand proper restoration techniques. CC: MC, V, AMEX, D.

Second Hand Rose
827 East Genesee Street (13210)
(315) 474-4515
Hours: Tues–Sat, 11–6

This shop has men's and women's vintage clothing, fine household linens, textiles, and small decorative items. In addition to appraisals and costume rentals, restoration, and cleaning, this shop also does costuming for period theater and parties. PR: $. CC: MC, V.

Syracuse Antique Exchange (MD)
1629 North Salina Street
(13208)
(315) 471-1841
Hours: Mon–Sat, 10–5;
Sun, 12–5

Located in a large, restored 19th century warehouse, this eight dealer co-op features American and European furniture, decorative arts, paintings, sculpture, china, crystal, and lighting devices and fixtures.

TARRYTOWN

Bittersweet Antiques (MD)
37 Main Street (10591)
(914) 332-9832
Hours: Tues–Sun, 12–5:30

Located in a 19th century historical row house, the co-op of 13 dealers offers a wide range of merchandise such as oak, pine, and painted furniture; country primitives; textiles; pottery; cameras; pens; Victorian furnishings; wicker; linens; hooked rugs; decorative smalls; and 1930s to 1950s merchandise.

North Castle Antiques
28 Main Street (10591)
(914) 631-1112
Hours: Tues–Sun, 12–5

In addition to offering an eclectic selection of furniture, this shop also has an interesting selection of jewelry. CC: No.

Piacente
38 Main Street (10591)
(914) 631-4231
Hours: Thur–Sat, 12–5
or by appointment

Fine clothing, textiles, and accessories including a large selection of alligator handbags, luggage, and smalls fill this shop. There is also a selection of small furniture and painted furniture. CC: No.

Remember Me Antiques
9 Main Street (10591)
(914) 631-4080
Hours: Tues–Sun, 11–5

This shop specializes in 19th and 20th century furniture and appropriate accessories such as lamps, art, pewter, silver, and architectural items. Collectibles and other interesting items can also be found. PR: $$. CC: No.

Sam Said...Antiques
80 South Broadway (10591)
(914) 631-3368
Hours: Thur–Sun, 12–5; other days by appointment or video mail order

Established in 1986, this funky and eclectic shop contains folk art curiosities, offbeat decorative accessories, rustic and distressed furniture, and textiles. PR: $. CC: No. LOC: One mile north of NYS Thruway at the intersection of Franklin Street and Broadway.

Schmul Meier, Inc.
23 Main Street (10591)
(914) 332-1310
Hours: Thur–Sat, 11–5

This shop offers a wide range of fine furniture and quality decorative accessories. This business is also located in New York City. PR: $$. CC: Yes.

Tarrytown Antique Center (MD)
25 Main Street (10591)
(914) 631-9710
Hours: Tues–Sun, 11–5

Quality antiques and collectibles which include china, jewelry, paintings, prints, furniture, and kitchenware are offered by more than 20 dealers. CC: No.

TIVOLI

Country Cottage Antiques
3322 Route 9G (12583)
(914) 757-5005
Hours: By chance or appointment, shows, and mail order

Established in 1988, this shop specializes in early pottery, majolica, Flow Blue, Royal Dalton, yellow ware, and glassware. PR: $$. CC: No.

J.S. Clark & Co.

Broadway (12583)
(914) 757-5671
Hours: Weekends, best to call

In addition to emphasizing 19th century American furnishings and decorations, this dealer also carries lighting fixtures, textiles, and both architectual and garden elements. CC: No.

White Clay Kill Antiques

3278 Route 9G (12583-5509)
(914) 757-3041
Hours: Fri–Sat, 10–5; Sun, 12–5 or by appointment

Located in a Victorian house, this shop has a general line of antiques and collectibles. CC: No.

TOMKINS COVE

Shades of the Past

Route 9W (10986)
(914) 942-0209
Hours: Fri–Mon, 1–5; and by chance or appointment

This shop carries cut-and-pierced lampshades, old lamps, stringed instruments, books, and a general line of vintage goods and collectibles. Courses in lampshade making are given. In addition, lamp repairs, lampshade supplies, and custom made shades are available. Consignments and want lists are accepted. There is also a mailing list service. CC: MC, V. LOC: Two miles north of Stony Point, take Palisades Parkway Exit 15.

TRUMANSBURG

Collection, The

9-11 Main Street, Route 96 North (14886)
(607) 387-6579
Hours: Tues–Sun, 11–5

The Collection, the oldest antique business in Thompkins County, carries a general line of quality antiques at affordable prices. Country and formal furniture, schoolgirl samplers, early lighting, stoneware, and folk art fill this shop. Appraisals and estate settlements can be done.

Ponzi's Antiques

9838 Congress Street Extension (14886)
(607) 387-5248
Hours: Daily 9–5

This dealer specializes in 18th and 19th century furniture—painted and formal—and appropriate accessories of the period—paintings, lamps, pottery, stoneware, rugs, lighting devices, and primitives. Repair and restoration of furniture can be done. CC: MC, V, D.

UNADILLA

Ingalls Antiques
Box 168, River Road (13849)
(607) 369-2672
Hours: Daily 9–5

Established in 1958, this 2,200 square foot shop offers the varied contents of country estates. In addition to furniture in as found condition, one will discover everything from Woolworth to Tiffany. A cataloged wants list and finders service is available. CC: No.

UNIONVILLE

Rainbow Farm Antiques
Main Street, Box 591 (10988)
(914) 726-3738
Hours: Thurs–Tues, 12–5

In a former 1850s general store, one will find area settings appropriate for antiques and collectibles of the kitchen and library such as linens, rugs, furniture, china, and glass. PR: $. CC: No.

VALOIS

Raspberry Patch Antiquities
Route 414, Lake Street (14888)
(607) 546-4626
Hours: July–September;
Tues–Sat, 12–5

This shop specializes in miniatures, dolls, books, collectibles, and a variety of antiques.

VERNON

Just Like Grandma's
6541 State Route 5 (13476)
(315) 829-4593
Hours: Tues–Sat, 11–5;
Sun, 1–4 by chance

This shop specializes in restored antique stoves. Reproduction tinware and handcrafted items are available. Clock repair and chair caning can be done.

VICTORY MILLS

Black Shutters, The
80 Gates Avenue, Route 32
(12884-0092)
(518) 695-9225
Hours: January, closed;
February–March, Sat–Sun, 12–5;
April–June, Wed–Sun, 12–5;
July–August, Daily 12–5;
September–December, Wed–Sun, 12–5

Since 1964, these dealers have been selling a diverse line of antiques and collectibles in two large buildings. In addition, simple custom framing, appraisals, hooked rug instruction and supplies, and Shaker chair taping are available. A Christmas shop is also located here. PR: Low to Middle. CC: No.

WALLKILL

Wallkill River House (MD)

38 Wallkill Avenue (12589)
(914) 895-1410
Hours: Wed–Sat, 10:30–5; Sun, 10–4; Tues closed

Six dealers offer a great variety of country and Victorian antiques, decorative items, collectibles, estate and costume jewelry, glass, and linens in this shop.
PR: Very Affordable. CC: No.

WAPPINGER FALLS

Par Excellence

7 Ervin Road (12590-3805)
(914) 297-9724
(914) 298-0695 fax
Hours: By appointment

In addition to a fine line of porcelain and china, this dealer also offers estate jewelry. CC: Yes.

WARRENSBURG

Donegal Manor Antique Shop

117 Main Street (12885)
(518) 623-3549
Hours: Daily 10–6

Located behind their bed and breakfast, this shop contains a wide variety of antiques and collectibles. CC: MC, V.

Stuff & Things Antiques

Friends Lake Road (12885)
(518) 494-3948
Hours: May–October; Mon–Sat, 9–6; Sun, 12–6; other times by appointment

This shop offers a mixture of country furniture, smalls, folk art, American Indian items, and much more. Also, an unusual selection of decorative items from here and abroad is available. CC: MC, V.

Warrensburg Antiques

197 Main Street (12885)
(518) 623-2149
Hours: Mon–Sat, 9–5

Antiquarian books, country furniture, lamps, china, glass, pewter, and automobilia can be found in this shop. CC: No.

WARWICK

Accent on Oak Antiques

29 Sutton Road (10990)
(914) 986-2538
Hours: Sat–Sun, 10–5
or by appointment

Quality turn of the century oak furniture, smalls, and accessories to complement every room are found in this shop. CC: MC, V.
LOC: Travel two and seventh tenth miles from Warwick on West Street, turn right on Sutton Road.

Bearly Antiques

18 Beverly Drive (10990)
(914) 986-1996
Hours: Call ahead or make an appointment, mail order, and shows

Established in 1987, this shop specializes in bears—collectible, Steiff, North American, Gund, artist bears, and antique bears. Miniature items, small furniture,

A group of 19th century Chinese Rose Medallion porcelains. *(Courtesy of Flying Cranes Antiques, LTD, New York City)*

and Amish quilted wall hangings are also available. CC: MC, V, DC. LOC: Route 94 onto Old Ridge Road, left onto West Ridge Road, right onto Beverly Drive—look for sign.

Clocktower Antique Center (MD)
65 Main Street (10990)
(914) 986-5199
Hours: Wed–Sun, 10–5

Thirty dealers in more than 7,000 square feet of space present a diverse, quality mix of antiques and collectibles. In addition to country furniture and accessories, one will find garden accessories, fine furniture from all periods, Art Deco, cast iron, postcards, jewelry, paintings, linens, and stoneware. PR: $$. CC: MC, V.

1809 House, The
210 South Route 94 (10990)
(914) 986-1809
(914) 986-3899 fax
Hours: Sat–Sun and by appointment

This shop carries an extensive line of turn of the century, refinished oak furniture. CC: MC, V.

Grapevine Antiques
76 Foley Road (10990)
(914) 986-4700
Hours: Fri–Mon, 10–5

In addition to quality oak and pine antique furniture from the mid 19th to the early 20th century, this shop also offers decorative smalls, prints, lamps, porcelain, and Depression glass. PR: $$$. CC: No.

Victorian Treasures
21 Main Street (10990)
(914) 986-7616
Hours: Mon–Sat, 10–6; Sun, 11–4

Antique linens and laces and Victoriana are offered by this shop which is located in the town's historical district. PR: $. CC: Yes.

WATERLOO

Golden Days Antiques
36 West Main Street (13165)
(315) 539-3131
Hours: Mon–Sat, 10–5; Sun, 12–5

Located in a beautiful 1860s house, this shop has 15 rooms of mahogany, oak, country, and Victorian furniture; carnival, pattern, Depression, and other glassware; china; lamps; pottery; mirrors; and other treasures. Reproduction hardware, lamp burners and chimneys, plate stands, and Briwax are also for sale. This is one of the largest shops in the Finger Lakes Region. PR: Mid range. CC: MC, V, D.

Hobbs
39 West Main Street (13165)
(315) 539-3606
Hours: Mon–Sat, 10–4; Sun, 9–3

Occupying more than 1,600 square feet, this shop contains an eclectic mix of collectibles—early through the 1950s. One will find Victoriana, rugs, glass, jewelry, and furniture. PR: $$. CC: MC, V, AMEX.

WATKINS GLEN

Currie's Antiques
22 North Franklin Street (14891)
(607) 535-7358, shop; 535-2507, home
Hours: May 20th–December 31st, Daily 11–5; January–May 19th, Fri–Sun, 11–5 or by appointment

Established in 1979, this general country antique shop specializes in estate and costume jewelry, primitives, country furniture, glass, china, and racing automobilia. Appraisals are given, tag sales can be arranged, and connections for furniture, painting, and jewelry repair can be arranged. PR: $$. CC: No.

WAWARSING

Browsing Corner, The
Route 209, P.O. Box 234 (12489)
(914) 647-6902
Hours: By chance or appointment

Since 1978, this shop has offered academic American and European paintings of the 19th and 20th century, 19th century prints, 18th and 19th century china, 19th century furniture, and garden accessories. CC: AMEX.

Old Mine Road Antiques
P.O. Box 71 (12498)
(914) 647-6771
Hours: By appointment or by chance

In addition to carrying decorative smalls, this dealer offers unusual costume and silver jewelry featuring one of a kind originally designed pieces that are recycled from broken pieces. PR: $. CC: No. LOC: Located 150 feet off of Route 209 on a private road.

WEBSTER

From The Cutter's Wheel Antiques
649 Van Alstyne Road (14580)
(716) 671-3760
Hours: By appointment plus shows and mail order

This dealer specializes in American Brilliant Period (1880–1920s) cut glass for the beginning, intermediate, and advanced collector. CC: MC, V.

Webster Antique Group Shop, Inc. (MD)
82A East Main Street (14580)
(716) 265-3078
Hours: Tues–Sun, 10–5

Occupying 16,000 square feet and stocked by more than 100 dealers, this is the largest group shop in western New York. Merchandise is displayed in both showcases and booths. PR: $$$. CC: MC, V.

WELLSVILLE

Times Past Antiques
R. D. #2, Box 97 (14895)
(716) 593-4630
Hours: Mon–Sat, 10–5; Sun, 1–5

Established in 1985, this shop contains American oak furniture, pottery, lighting devices and fixtures, glassware, and collectibles. CC: MC, V, D, DC.

WEST HURLEY

Goosewing Antiques
183 Nissen Lane (12491)
(914) 679-9206
Hours: Open by chance or appointment

This shop has a large selection of high quality, rare, and unusual antique wood working tools and decorated stoneware. Telephone inquiries are invited. PR: $$. CC: No.

WEST PARK

Down To Earth
127 Floyd Ackert Road (12493)
(914) 384-6718
Hours: Wed–Fri, 10–6; Sat, 10–6; Sun, 11–4

This shop offers Japanese antiques and collectibles such as decorative items, scrolls, ceramics, and folk art. CC: MC, V.

WEST WINFIELD

Collins Antiques and Uniques

R.D.#1, Box 259, Millers Mills Road (13491)
(315) 822-5621
Hours: By chance or appointment day and evening

Located in an old horse barn and hop house, this unique shop contains all kinds of country and primitive antiques. In addition one will find a nostalgic assortment of gifts with antiques in wreaths; baskets; or used as the main interest point. PR: $.

Puce Goose Antiques

R. R. #2, Box 748 (13491)
(315) 822-5611
Hours: Open by chance or appointment

Since 1986, this dealer has offered personally selected country furniture, primitives, and decorative accessories tastefully arranged in an early 1800s farm house. LOC: Old Cherry Valley Turnpike (Route 20), three miles east of West Winfield.

WESTFIELD

Marketplace on Main (MD)

19-21 Main Street (14787)
(716) 326-2130
Hours: April–December, Mon–Sat, 10–5; Sun 11–5; Jan–Mar, Fri–Sun, 10–5

Twenty dealers offer a full line of antiques and collectibles that include furniture, paintings, quilts, linens, china, silver, jewelry, primitives, Oriental rugs, and vintage clothing. CC: No.

Militello Antiques

31 Jefferson Street (14787-1012)
(716) 326-2587
Hours: Daily 10–4

A Second Empire brick house is the setting for a large general line of 19th century antiques. Americana, Chinese Export porcelain, and American furniture and glass are some of the antiques that are available. This business was established in 1922. PR: $$$. CC: No. LOC: One block from North Portage, one mile from Exit 60 on the NY Thruway.

Notaro's Antiques

161 West Main Street (14787)
(716) 326-3348
Hours: By chance or appointment

In an 1870s restored barn, these dealers offer oak, cherry, and walnut furniture; primitives; wicker; and advertising items. CC: No.

Priscilla B. Nixon Antiques & Interiors

119 West Main Street (14787)
(716) 326-3511
Hours: By appointment only

Located in a carriage house for more than twenty years, this shop specializes in quality formal and country furniture, appropriate accessories, folk art, textiles, and Oriental rugs. PR: $$$. CC: No.

Saraf's Emporium (MD)
58 East Main Street (14787)
(716) 326-3590
Hours: Mon–Sat, 10–5; Sun, 1–5

Ten quality dealers offer antiques and collectibles from the 18th century to the 1950s in a wide range of specialty areas. Antique jewelry, fine furniture, toys, china, glassware, cut glass, pottery, paintings, Oriental carpets, and pictures account for only some of the items on display. PR: $$$. CC: MC, V, AMEX.

Vilardo Antiques
7303 Walker Road (14787)
(716) 326-2714
Hours: May–October, Tues–Sun, 10–5; November–April by chance or appointment

These dealers specialize in quality cherry, oak, walnut, and wicker furniture; glassware; and collectibles with a special emphasis on Victorian. PR: $$. CC: No.

W. B. Mollard Antiques
120 East Main Street (14787)
(716) 326-3521
Hours: Open daily

Lamps of all kinds (mostly oil converted), early ornaments, mirrors, Curriers and a great assortment of things before the turn of the century compliment this business' specialty areas—pattern glass and hand painted china, mostly Haviland and Bavarian.

WHITE PLAINS

James M. Labaugh
P.O. Box 177 (10603-0177)
(914) 428-9155
Hours: By appointment only and shows

Conducting business since 1972, this dealer offers the finest selection of 18th and 19th century English and Continental porcelain, pottery, silver, and decorations. China Trade porcelain is also offered. PR: $$$$$. CC: No.

WHITNEY POINT

Days Gone By (MD)
2659 Main Street (13862)
(607) 692-2713
Hours: Wed–Mon, 10–6

Located in an old country church, this shop is stocked by ten dealers who offer everything from antique furniture to collectible glass and china. PR: $$. CC: No.

Millville Antiques
Corner of Ford Hill and West Main Street (13862)
(607) 692-4430
Hours: Spring through fall, 12–6; winter by chance or appointment

Having a warm country look, this shop features furniture of the 19th century in pine, cherry, walnut, chestnut, and mahogany. Tables, chairs, stands, cupboards,

Fine Meissen yellow ground covered sugar bowl, polychrome landscapes with figures in the foreground, German, circa 1740–50. *(Courtesy James M. Labaugh, White Plains)*

dough boxes, dry sinks, commodes, desks, chests of drawers, and blanket chests in antique oil finish or original condition can be found. Accessories such as oil lamps, chandeliers, rag rugs, quilts, prints, and paintings complement the furniture.

WILLIAMSON

Kieningers from Apponaug, The
5159 Ridge Road East, R.D. 3 (14589)
(315) 589-8093
Hours: Open when home

Located in the fieldstone basement of an old farmhouse, this shop is filled with both early and late American pressed glass. PR: $. CC: No.

Nancy's Antiques
7217 Lake Avenue (14589)
(315) 589-8400
Hours: By appointment

One will find advertising trade cards, trade catalogs, and ephemera in this shop. Supplies for protecting and displaying postcards and other paper collectibles are sold. Appraisals can be given. And,

there is a search service.
CC: No.

Reflections Antiques
3239 Lake Road (14589)
(315) 589-3421
Hours: Daily by chance in the summer and weekends throughout the fall by chance

In an 1840s home on Lake Ontario, these dealers offer country furniture, primitives, 1800s quilts, and a variety of children's collectibles.
CC: No.

Yankee Peddler Bookshop
3895 Route 104 (14589)
(315) 589-2063
(315) 589-9413 fax
Hours: Mon–Wed, 10–5; Thurs–Sun, 1–5

This shop carries a large general stock of antiquarian books, prints, paintings, and photographs. In addition to book, print, and painting restoration, hand coloring, matting, and framing are available. Appraisals can be given. PR: $$$.
CC: MC, V.

WILLIAMSVILLE

Antiques Americana
5600 Main Street (14221)
(716) 633-2570
Hours: Mon–Sat, 11–5

For 18 years, this dealer has offered quality 18th, 19th, and 20th century furniture and accessories such as art, china, and porcelain. Silver clinics for replating and repairing are given every five weeks. Call for information. PR: $$$.
CC: MC, V, AMEX, D.

WINDSOR

McMurray Antiques
Route 17 Expressway East, Exit 79 (13865)
(607) 655-2053
Hours: Daily 10–5

Located in a restored 1831 home that also contains an apothecary shop and museum, this shop consists of eight rooms of quality antiques. One will discover country antiques, medical and apothecary items, bottles, stoneware, and pottery. PR: $$.
CC: MC, V.

WOODBOURNE

Andrea's Antiques
Box 83, Ulster Heights Road (12788)
(914) 434-0659
Hours: By appointment only

This shop, located on a dairy farm, specializes in silver, bronzes, and porcelain from the Art Deco period through the 19th century.

WOODSTOCK

Anatolia—Tribal Rugs and Weavings

54G Tinker Street (12498)
(914) 679-5311
Hours: Wed–Mon, 12–5
and by appointment

These dealers have been direct importers of Turkish, Bessarabian, and Caucasian Kilims since 1981. Semi-antique and antique kilims in a wide variety of sizes and prices, kilim pillows, and antique Sumak pillows are also available. PR: $$.
CC: MC, V, AMEX, D.

Cooper House Antiques

99 Tinker Street (12498)
(914) 679-7561
Hours: Fri–Sun, 12–5:30 or by appointment

Specializing in furniture of the American Arts and Crafts Movement, this shop carries pieces by such makers as Gustav Stickley, L&JG Stickley, Limbert, and Roycroft. Old hickory, pottery, Roycroft, copper, textiles, and paintings of the period are also carried. This shop has been dealing in Mission Oak since 1982. PR: $$. CC: MC, V.

Terry Ann Tomlinson

Box 203 (12498)
(914) 679-6554
(914) 679-6554 fax
Hours: By appointment only
and shows

Doing business since 1979, this dealer specializes in antique and decorative Oriental rugs and tapestries and European carpets for both the home and the collector. It is the largest selection of antique rugs in the Hudson Valley. Appraisals can be given. Oriental rug restoration is available.
CC: No.

YONKERS

Cyd Leon Antiques

720 Tuckahoe Road (10710-5240)
(914) 725-2060
Hours: By appointment only and shows

Antique, estate, and period jewelry (Retro, Art Deco, and Art Nouveau), decorative and collectible smalls and miniatures, and an eclectic selection of one of a kind quality signed pieces of silver are the specialties of this dealer. Appraisals, a finders service, and jewelry repair are available.

YORK

York Antiques

Main Street (14592)
(716) 234-2690
Hours: Sat, 11–5 and by appointment

This shop contains a distinctive collection of 19th century antiques that includes furniture, linens, glass, lighting, jewelry, textiles, and objects of art. Painting restoration can be done.
CC: No.

YORKTOWN HEIGHTS

Whittington Antiques
2160 Saw Mill River Road (10598)
(914) 962-1097
(914) 962-3686 fax
Hours: By appointment

This shop contains pre-1890 country antiques, painted American furniture, pre-1920 quilts, and textiles. In addition, interior design consultation and a finders service are available. PR: $$$. CC: AMEX (retail/full priced merchandise only).

Specialty Areas - Upstate New York

Adirondack

Advertising
Antiques & Tools of Business & Kitchen, Pound Ridge, p. 239
Curious Goods, Caledonia, p. 175
Glory Daze Antiques, Saugerties, p. 249
Ivan's Antiques & Misc., Belmont, p. 169
Lady Paydacker, Greene, p. 197
Notaro's Antiques, Westfield, p. 266
Snoop Sisters, Smithville Flats, p. 254
Thomas Jardas Antiques, Schenectady, p. 251
Wilson's Antique Services, Cortland, p. 188

American Indian
Carol's Antiques, Newark, p. 226
Collection Agency, The, Seneca Falls, p. 252
Dalton's American Decorative, Syracuse, p. 258
Grasshopper Antique Center, Madison, p. 215
Great Lakes Artifact Repository, Buffalo, p. 174
Miriam Rogachefsky Antiques, Rochester, p. 245
Muleskinner, Clarence, p. 183
Once Upon A Time, Franklinville, p. 193
Richard & Betty Ann Rasso Antiques, East Chatham, p. 181
Southside Antique Center, Inc., Oneonta, p. 231
Stuff & Things Antiques, Warrensburg, p. 262
Susan Bean of Silhouette, Rhinebeck, p. 243

Americana
Antiques At The Inn, Cuba, p. 188
Art & Antique Co. of Spencertown, Spencertown, p. 255
Barbara Zitz Antiques, Rhinebeck, p. 242
Beacon Hill Antiques, Beacon, p. 168
Black Sheep Antiques Center, Duanesburg, p. 189
Blue Stores Antiques, Germantown, p. 194
Carol's Antiques, Newark, p. 226
Cheshire Union Antique Center, Cheshire, p. 177
Chester Square Antiques, Chester, p. 182
Cider Mill Antiques, Horse Heads, p. 201
Cider Mill Antiques, Red Hook, p. 241

Antique Automobiles

Antiquities

Architectural Antiques

Barbara F. Israel Enterprises, Katonah, p. 208
Chester Square Antiques, Chester, p. 182
Day-Barb Antiques, Gilboa, p. 195
Dennis & Valerie Bakoledis Antiques, Rhinebeck, p. 243
Horsefeathers Architectural Antiques, Buffalo, p. 175
Ivan's Antiques & Misc., Belmont, p. 169
J. Gardner, Port Jervis, p. 238
J.S. Clark & Co., Tivoli, p. 260
Mad Hatter Antiques, Binghamton, p. 170
Sam Said . . . Antiques, Tarrytown, p. 259
707 Warren Street Antiques, Hudson, p. 203
Things Antique, Stone Ridge, p. 257
Vincent R. Mulford, Hudson, p. 203
Willow Parva Antiques, Pine Bush, p. 236

Art Deco

Antiques of a Rare Bird, Bedford Hills, p. 168
C&D Antiques, Amsterdam, p. 163
Chelsea Antiques, Madison, p. 215
Clinton Mill Antiques, Binghamton, p. 169
Clocktower Antiques Center, Warwick, p. 263
Cooper House Antiques, Woodstock, p. 270
Dualities Gallery, Larchmont, p. 212
Greenwillow Farm Ltd., Chatham, p. 181
Jackie's Place, Bouckville, p. 216
Maple Avenue Antiques, Elmira, p. 191
Mix, Buffalo, p. 175
Oldies But Goodies Antiques, Jefferson Valley, p. 207
Possibly Antiques, Albany, p. 161
Stone House Gallery, Saugerties, p. 250
TscHopp Stained Glass, Clarence, p. 183
Uncle Alan's Antiques & Oddities, Stamford, p. 256

Art Glass

Dimitroff's Antiques, Corning, p. 187
Kruggel Antiques, Rochester, p. 245
Vi & Si's Antiques, Clarence, p. 184

Art Nouveau

Dualities Gallery, Larchmont, p. 212
Oldies But Goodies Antiques, Jefferson Valley, p. 207
Rhinebeck Antique Center, Rhinebeck, p. 243

Baskets
Dutch House The, Claverack, p. 184
Heisler's Antique Mercantile, Smithville Flats, p. 254

Beer & Whiskey Collectibles
Owen's Collectibles, New Hartford (Utica), p. 225

Black Americana
Broadway Antiques & Interiors, Newburgh, p. 227
Maxwell's Treasures Books, Lima, p. 214

Books on Antiques
Art Book Services, Hughsonville, p. 204
Behind The Inn Antiques & Collectibles, Skaneateles, p. 253
Belknap Hill Books, Penn Yan, p. 234
Cross's Antique Center, Marathon, p. 218
Heirlooms, Delhi, p. 189
Lyrical Ballad Bookstore, Saratoga Springs, p. 247
Sarabeck Antiques, Cold Spring, p. 185

Books/Antiquarian
Abacus Bookshop, Rochester, p. 244
Antique Center at Forge Hill Village, New Windsor, p. 226
Antiques at Cedarwood, Monticello, p. 223
Antiques at Ward's Bridge, Montgomery, p. 222
Atlantis Rising, Hudson, p. 202
Belknap Hill Books, Penn Yan, p. 234
Birch Bark Bookshop, The, Potsdam, p. 238
Booktrader, Saugerties, p. 249
Calhoun's Books, Geneva, p. 194
Clinton Shops Antique Center, Montgomery, p. 222
Country Books, Greenwich, p. 197
Crossroads Country Mall, Lima, p. 213
DeSimone & Yount, Rochester, p. 245
Holiday Hill Antiques, Kingston, p. 209
Ingeborg Quitzau, Antiquarian Books, Edmeston, p. 190
Jem Shoppe, The, Madison, p. 216
Kinderhook Antique Center, Kinderhook, p. 208
Lyrical Ballad Bookstore, Saratoga Springs, p. 247
Maxwell's Treasures Books, Lima, p. 214
Mrs. Hudson's Emporium, Cold Spring, p. 185
Olana Gallery, Brewster. p. 172

Owl Pen Books, Greenwich, p. 198
Pheasant Farm, Greene, p. 197
Pierce-Archer Antiques, Bronxville, p. 174
Pink Church Antiques, The, Friendship, p. 194
Raspberry Patch Antiquities, Valois, p. 261
Serendipity II, Millport, p. 221
Shades of the Past, Tomkins Cove, p. 260
Strawberry Hill Bookshop, Pittsford, p. 237
Third Eye Antiques, Plattsburgh, p. 238
Warrensburg Antiques, Warrensburg, p. 262
Yankee Peddler Bookshop Vol II, Rochester, p. 245
Yankee Peddler Bookshop, Williamson, p. 269
Zeller's, Albany, p. 162

Bottles

Anntiques, Friendship, p. 193
Back to Granny's Day Antiques, Mohawk, p. 221
Black Smith Shop Antiques, Cambridge, p. 176
Chester Square Antiques, Chester, p. 182
Elmantiques, Katonah, p. 208
Green Acres Antique Center, Preston Hollow, p. 240
Jack & Maryellen Whistance, Kingston, p. 209
John Sideli, Chatham, p. 181
McMurray Antiques, Windsor, p. 269
Millport Mercantile, Millport, p. 221
Owen's Collectibles, New Hartford (Utica), p. 225
Stone Lodge Antiques, Bouckville, p. 216

Brass

Anthony S. Werneke Antiques, Pond Eddy, p. 238
Donald Metzker Antiques, Fairport, p. 191
Elisabeth de Bussy Inc, Pound Ridge, p. 239
Hickory Bend Antiques, Jasper, p. 207
Hob Nail Antiques, Pawling, p. 233
Janice F. Strauss American Antiques, South Salem, p. 255
Kruggel Antiques, Rochester, p. 245
Mark & Marjorie Allen, Putnam Valley, p. 240
Pierce-Archer Antiques,Bronxville, p. 174
Pig Hill Antiques, Cold Spring, p. 185

Bronzes

Andrea's Antiques, Woodburne, p. 269

Dualities Gallery, Larchmont, p. 212
Green River Gallery, Millerton, p. 220
Jenny Hall, Asian Antiques, Ghent, p. 195
Saugerties Antique Gallery, Saugerties, p. 250

Buttons
B.J. Antiques, Cuddebackville, p. 188
Board'N Batten Antiques, Olmstedville, p. 231
Buffalo's Attic, Buffalo, p. 174
Cracker Barrell, Cortland, p. 187
Necia Smith Antiques & Collectibles, Penn Yan, p. 234
Old Stuff, Saratoga Springs, p. 247
Pastimes, Ithaca, p. 206

Cameras
B.J. Antiques, Cuddebackville, p. 188
Hudson Photographic Center, Hudson, p. 202
Third Eye Antiques, Plattsburgh, p. 238

Carnival Glass

Cartoon Art

Cast Iron
Barbara F. Israel Enterprises, Katonah, p. 208
Country Antique Unlimited, Briarcliff Manor, p. 172
Fisher's Antiques, Albion, p. 162
Horsefeathers Architectural Antiques, Buffalo, p. 175
Jerry's Antique Co-op, Olean, p. 231
Kapell's Antiques, Greenport, p. 125
Old Hickory Antique Center, Bainbridge, p. 166
707 Warren Street Antiques, Hudson, p. 203

China
Angelica Antique Emporium, Angelica, p. 163
Antiques Americana, Williamsville, p. 269
Antiques at Ward's Bridge, Montgomery, p. 222
Blakes Antiques, Corning, p. 186
Bridge Street Antique Emporium, Plattsburgh, p. 238
Butter Hill Antiques, Cornwall on Hudson, p. 187
Carriage House Antiques, Leroy, p. 212
Cavern View Antiques, Howes Cave, p. 202

Chinese Export Porcelain

Circus & Amusement Park Collectibles

Clocks/Watches

Millport Mercantile, Millport, p. 221
Noah's Ark Antiques Center, Fishkill, p. 192
Olde Clocks, Gloversville, p. 196
Second Time Around Antiques, Brewster, p. 172
Sugar Loaf Antiques, Cold Spring, p. 185
Woodshed Antiques, Macedon, p. 214

Coca Cola

Samuel R. Page House, Millport, p. 221

Coin Operated Machines

Antiques of a Rare Bird, Bedford Hills, p. 168
Hickory Bend Antiques, Jasper, p. 207

Coins

Donegal Manor Antique Shop, Warrensburg, p. 262
Silversmith & Goldsmith Jewelers, The, Oneonta, p. 231
Zeller's, Albany, p. 162

Collectibles

American Flyer, Larchmont, p. 212
Annex Antiques Center, Red Hook, p. 240
Antique Alley, Chester, p. 182
Antique Center at Forge Hill Village, New Windsor, p. 226
Antique Center of Preston Hollow, Preston Hollow, p. 240
Antiques of a Rare Bird, Bedford Hills, p. 168
Assets Antiques & Collectibles, Buffalo, p. 174
Atlantis Rising, Hudson, p. 202
Avon Antique House, Avon, p. 165
Back to Granny's Day Antiques, Mohawk, p. 221
Beacon Hill Antiques, Beacon, p. 168
Bear Gulch Shop, Richmondville, p. 243
Beehive Antique Co-op, The, North Cohocton, p. 227
Behind The Inn Antiques & Collectibles, Skaneateles, p. 253
Birge Hill Farm Antiques, Chatham, p. 180
Black Smith Shop Antiques, Cambridge, p. 176
Blue Stores Antiques, Germantown, p. 194
Bob & Ginny's Treasures, Interlaken, p. 206
Boulevard Attic, Kingston, p. 209
Brockmann's Antique Center, Milford, p. 219
Brynilsen's Homestead Antiques, Rome, p. 246
C&D Antiques, Amsterdam, p. 163

Cookie Jars

Country Antiques

Mulberry Bush Antiques B&B, Durham, p. 190
Old Country Store, Greene, p. 197
Old Greenwich Hardware Antiques, Greenwich, p. 197
Old Hickory Antique Center, Bainbridge, p. 166
Opera House Antiques, Hammondsport, p. 198
O'Wagon Antiques, Greenwich, p. 198
Partridge Run Antiques, Schoharie, p. 252
Past & Present Antiques, Sodus, p. 254
Paul L. Baker Antiques, Jordanville, p. 207
Petticoat Junction Antiques, Canandaigua, p. 178
Pig Hill Antiques, Cold Spring, p. 185
Priscilla B. Nixon Antiques & Interiors, Westfield, p. 266
Proud American Shoppe, Pine City, p. 236
Ruggiero Antiques, Newburgh, p. 227
707 Warren Street Antiques, Hudson, p. 203
76 Barn, Chester, p. 182
Selective Eye Antiques, At The 1849 House, Schoharie, p. 252
Sheaf of Wheat, Cambridge, p. 176
Simply Country, Interlaken, p. 206
Southtown's Antiques, Angola, p. 164
Steele Creek Antiques, Ilion, p. 205
Stepping Stone Inn Antiques, Middletown, p. 219
Stimson's Antiques & Gifts, Lewiston, p. 213
Stuff & Things Antiques, Warrensburg, p. 262
Things Antique, Stone Ridge, p. 257
Timothy's Treasures, Madison, p. 216
Touch of Country, House of Shops, Elmira, p. 191
Tow Path House Antiques, High Falls, p. 199
Treasure Chest, The, Mohawk, p. 222
Treasure Shop, The, Saugerties, p. 251
Warner's Antiques, Belfast, p. 168
Whittington Antiques, Yorktown Heights, p. 271
Willowen Antiques, Flint, p. 192
Windy Acres Antiques, Fairport, p. 192
Wood Bull Antiques, Milford, p. 219
Woodshed Antiques The, Pine City, p. 236

Cut Glass

Dimitroff's Antiques, Corning, p. 187

Daguerreotypes

Dennis Holzman Antiques, Albany, p. 161
Hudson Photographic Center, Hudson, p. 202

Decorative Smalls

Yesteryears, Chatham, p. 182

Decoys

Paul Coon, Penn Yan, p. 234

Depression Glass

Antique Center of Preston Hollow, Preston Hollow, p. 240
Apple Tree Antiques, Greenfield Park, p. 197
Back To Granny's Day Antiques, Mohawk, p. 221
Betty Brook Road Antiques, South Kortright, p. 254
Bob & Ginny's Treasures, Interlaken, p. 206
Buffalo's Attic, Buffalo, p. 174
Days Gone By, Whitney Point, p. 267
Glass Shop, The, Shushan, p. 253
Hamilton's Antique Shoppe, Neversink, p. 225
Lady Paydacker, Greene, p. 197
Maple Avenue Antiques, Elmira, p. 191
Pink Church Antiques, The, Friendship, p. 194
Trend The, Mount Vernon, p. 225
You Want What!, Ovid, p. 233

Dolls

American Jazz, Ossining, p. 232
Antique Barn, Rochester, p. 244
Antiques Americana, Williamsville, p. 269
Eagle's Roost Antiques, Marlboro, p. 218
Jasada Antiques Inc., Ballston Lake, p. 167
Myron Cohen Antiques, Stone Ridge, p. 257
Now & Then Antiques, Nyack, p. 229
O'Wagon Antiques, Greenwich, p. 198
Raspberry Patch Antiquities, Valois, p. 261
Wilson's Antique Services, Cortland, p. 188
Ye Olde Wishin'Shoppe, Saratoga Springs, p. 247

Engravings

M.L. Baran, Binghamton, p. 170

Ephemera

Antique Alley, Chester, p. 182
Btrading Co.,Albany, p. 161
Calhoun's Books, Geneva, p. 194
Cobblestone Store, The, Bouckville, p. 215

Dennis Holzman Antiques, Albany, p. 161
Dew Drop Inn Antique Center, Cold Spring, p. 185
Gramm-O-Phone Antiques, Campbell Hall, p. 176
Great Lakes Artifact Repository, Buffalo, p. 174
Holiday Hill Antiques, Kingston, p. 209
Hopewell Antique Center, Hopewell Jct., p. 201
Ingrid Migonis Antiques, Hamilton, p. 198
Larry Gottheim Fine Photograph, Binghamton, p. 170
Mrs. Hudson's Emporium, Cold Spring, p. 185
Nancy's Antiques, Williamson, p. 268
Old Mill House Antiques, Rhinebeck, p. 243
Owl Pen Books, Greenwich, p. 198
Red Balloons, Buffalo, p. 175
Snoop Sisters, Smithville Flats, p. 254
Tom Jardas Antiques, Schenectady, p. 251
Townhouse Antiques, Hudson, p. 203
Van Deusen House Antiques, Hurley, p. 204

Firearms

Fireplace Equipment

Binder Joiner & Smith, Kinderhook, p. 208
Crown House Antiques, Chappaqua, p. 179
Fischer's Antiques, Albion, p. 162
Janice F. Strauss American Antiques, South Salem, p. 255
Kitchen Cupboard Antiques, Andover, p. 163
Pierce-Archer Antiques, Bronxville, p. 174
Yellowplush Antiques, Briarcliff Manor, p. 173

Fishing Equipment

Annex Antiques Center, Red Hook, p. 240
Cobblestone Store, The, Bouckville, p. 215
Grasshopper Antique Center, Madison, p. 215
Southside Antique Center, Inc., Oneonta, p. 231

Folk Art

Abbey's Antiques, Art & Appraisals, Bath, p. 167
American Jazz, Ossining, p. 232
Anne Smith Antiques, Saugerties, p. 248
Axtell Antiques, Deposit, p. 189
Beacon Hill Antiques, Beacon, p. 168
Bobbi von Dehmlein Antiques, Springfield Center, p. 255

Brennan Antiques, Rochester, p. 244
David Mouilleseaux, Rochester, p. 244
Dennis & Valerie Bakoledis Antiques, Rhinebeck, p. 243
Fischer's Antiques, Albion, p. 162
Grasshopper Antique Center, Madison, p. 215
John Sholl Antiques, Norwood, p. 228
J&R Ferris Antiques, Madison, p. 215
Kapell's Antiques, Greenport, p. 125
Kathy Schoemer American Antiques, North Salem, p. 228
Kitchen Cupboard Antiques, Andover, p. 163
Marna Anderson Gallery, New Paltz, p. 226
Monroe Antiques, Monroe, p. 222
Muleskinner, Clarence, p. 183
Pig Hill Antiques, Cold Spring, p. 185
Rainbow Farm Antiques, Unionville, p. 261
Red Fox Antiques, Hillsdale, p. 200
Richard & Betty Ann Rasso Antiques, E. Chatham, p. 181
Richard Romberg, Rochester, p. 245
Sam Said . . . Antiques, Tarrytown, p. 259
Stuff & Things Antiques, Warrensburg, p. 262
Suzanne Courcier/Robert W. Wilkins, Austerlitz, p. 165
Tin Rabbit, The, Stanfordville, p. 256
Tow Path House Antiques, High Falls, p. 199
Treasure Shop, The, Saugerties, p. 251
Voss Beringer, Ltd., Pound Ridge, p. 239
Webb Brennan American Antiques, Pittsford, p. 237
White & White Antiques & Interiors, Inc., Skaneateles, p. 253
Windy Acres Antiques, Fairport, p. 192

Frames

Mary Webster Frames, Binghamton, p. 170

French Antiques

Furniture/American

Alan Pereske Antiques, Lake Placid, p. 211
Alan Y. Roberts, Inc., Pound Ridge, p. 239
Anderson American Antiques, E. Chatham, p. 180
Angelica Antique Emporium, Angelica, p. 163
Anthony S. Werneke, Antiques, Pond Eddy, p. 238
Antique Alley, Chester, p. 182
Antique Barn, Rochester, p. 244

Furniture/Cherry

Furniture/Continental
Antiques and Such, Lake George, p. 211
Antiquities, Hudson, p. 202
Apple Antiques Ltd., Mt. Kisco, p. 224
Arles Ltd., Scarsdale, p. 251
Bobbi Von Dehmlein Antiques, Springfield Center, p. 255
Broadway Antiques & Interiors, Newburgh, p. 227
Dagmar's Antiques, Nyack, p. 228
Elizabeth de Bussy Inc., Pound Ridge, p. 239
Fred Hanson Antiques, New Paltz, p. 226
Irish Princess, The, Hudson, p. 203
Lou Marotta, Inc., Hudson, p. 203
Michael Kessler Antiques Ltd, Mamaroneck, p. 218
R&M Leed Antiques, Hopewell Jct., p. 201
Skevington-Back Antiques, Chatham, p. 181
Upstate Gallery Antiques, Rochester, p. 245
Willow Parva Antiques, Pine Bush, p. 236

Furniture/English
Alan Y. Roberts, Inc., Pound Ridge, p. 239
Apple Antiques Ltd., Mt. Kisco, p. 224
Irish Princess, The, Hudson, p. 203
Millbrook Antique Center, The, Millbrook, p. 220
Pierce-Archer Antiques, Bronxville, p. 174
R&M Leed Antiques, Hopewell Jct., p. 201
Rainbird, The, Pittsford, p. 237
Skevington-Back Antiques, Chatham, p. 181
Yellow Monkey Antiques, Cross River, p. 188
Yellowplush Antiques, Briarcliff Manor, p. 173

Furniture/French
Apple Antiques Ltd., Mt. Kisco, p. 224
Monroe Antiques, Monroe, p. 222
Yellowplush Antiques, Briarcliff Manor, p. 173

Furniture/Fruitwood
Carol David Antiques, Scarsdale, p. 251

Furniture/General
Alan Pereske Antiques, Lake Placid, p. 211
Ana Maria Recouso Antiques, Katonah, p. 208
Beacon Hill Antiques, Beacon, p. 168

Harvest Mill, Canandaigua, p. 178
Justin Thyme Antiques Center, Jefferson, p. 207
Marvin's, Ardsley, p. 164
Memories, Nyack, p. 229
Now & Then Antiques & Gifts, Nyack, p. 229
Oak Ridge Antiques, Lansing, p. 211
Oldies But Goodies, Elmira/Big Flats, p. 191
Old Mill Antiques, Krumville, p. 210
Page In Time, A, Saratoga Springs, p. 247
Second Time Around Antiques, Brewster, p. 172
Shades Of The Past Antiques, Orchard Park, p. 232
Two + Four Antiques, Herkimer, p. 199
Vincent R. Mulford, Hudson, p. 203
Vin-Dick Antiques, Kingston, p. 210
Webb & Brennan American Antiques, Pittsford, p. 237

Furniture/Oak

Accent on Oak Antiques, Warwick, p. 262
Antiques and Such, Lake George, p. 211
Apple Tree Antiques, Greenfield Park, p. 197
Betty Brook Road Antiques, South Kortright, p. 254
Board'N Batten Antiques, Olmstedville, p. 231
Bob & Ginny's Treasures, Interlaken, p. 206
Carriage House Antiques, Leroy, p. 212
Country Heritage Antique Center, Pine Bush, p. 235
Day-Barb Antiques, Gilboa, p. 195
Days Gone By, Whitney Point, p. 267
1809 House, The, Warwick, p. 263
Fieldstone Antiques, Lake Carmel, p. 210
Four Winds Center & Steve's Antiques, New Hampton, p. 226
Golden Days Antiques, Waterloo, p. 264
Grapevine Antiques, Warwick, p. 263
Guild Bros. Antiques, Montour Falls, p. 224
Hamilton's Antique Shoppe, Neversink, p. 225
Hoosick Antique Center Hoosick, p. 200
Justin Thyme Antique Center, Jefferson, p. 207
Lone Gable Emporium, LeRoy, p. 212
Lucky Strike A, Scarsdale, p. 251
Mad Hatter Antiques, Binghamton, p. 170
Maple Avenue Antiques, Elmira, p. 191
Marvin's, Ardsley, p. 164
McMullen Lasalle Antiques, Niagara Falls, p. 227

Furniture/Oriental

Furniture/Painted

Furniture/Pine

Sue Evans Antiques, Rome, p. 246
Timothy's Treasures, Madison, p. 216
Uncle Sam's Antiques, Clarence, p. 184
Vin-Dick Antiques, Kingston, p. 210
William A. Gustafson Antiques, p. 165
Windy Acres Antiques, Fairport, p. 192

Furniture/Victorian
Black Creek Farm, Fair Haven, p. 191
Carriage House Antiques, Leroy, p. 212
Caywood Antiques, Lodi, p. 214
Chelsea Antiques, Madison, p. 215
John Laing's Yesteryear Antiques, Hopewell Jct., p. 201
Lakeside Antique Galleries, Cazenovia, p. 179
Lucky Strike A, Scarsdale, p. 251
Mad Hatter Antiques, Binghamton, p. 170
Maple Avenue Antiques, Elmira, p. 191
Memory Lane Antiques & Collectibles, Hartsdale, p. 199
Seventy Nine Wistful Vista Ltd, Brewster, p. 172
Victoria's Garden, Morris, p. 224
Wallkill River House, Wallkill, p. 262

Furniture/Walnut
Country Heritage Antique Center, Pine Bush, p. 235
Marvin's, Ardsley, p. 164
Notaro's Antiques, Westfield, p. 266
Old Mill Antiques, Krumville, p. 210

Games & Puzzles
Southside Antique Center, Inc., Oneonta, p. 231

Garden Accessories
Alan Pereske Antiques, Lake Placid, p. 211
Barbara F. Israel Enterprises, Katonah, p. 208
Bristol Antiques, Honeoye, p. 200
Clocktower Antiques Center, Warwick, p. 263
Horsefeathers Architectural Antiques, Buffalo, p. 175
J. Gardner, Port Jervis, p. 238
J.S. Clark & Co., Tivoli, p. 260
Lou Marotta, Hudson, p. 203
Marna Anderson Gallery, New Paltz, p. 226
Millbrook Antiques Mall, Millbrook, p. 220

Glass

Golf

Holiday Collectibles

Possibly Antiques, Albany, p. 161
Strap Hinge, Pound Ridge, p. 239

Hooked Rugs

Anderson American Antiques, E. Chatham, p. 180
Antiques of Merritt, Rochester, p. 244
John & Lynn Gallo, Otego, p. 233
Kathy Schoemer American Antiques, North Salem, p. 228

Jazz Memoribilia

American Jazz, Ossining, p. 232

Jewelry

Andrea's Antiques, Woodburne, p. 269
Antiques Americana, Williamsville, p. 269
Beata Baird Antique, Hudson, p. 202
Black Sheep Antiques Center, Duanesburg, p. 189
Blakes Antiques, Cornish, p. 186
Bob & Sallie Connelly, Binghamton, p. 169
Bridge Street Antique Emporium, Plattsburgh, p. 238
Centennial Corner Antiques, Ossining, p. 232
Cider Mill Antiques, Oxford, p. 233
Country Kitchen Antiques, Oak Hill, p. 230
Cracker Barrell, Cortland, p. 187
Cyd Leon Antiques, Yonkers, p. 270
Depot Antique Gallery, The, Bouckville, p. 215
Donegal Manor Antique Shop, Warrensburg, p. 262
Early Everything, Beacon, p. 168
Frantiques, Johnson City, p. 207
Heirlooms With A Background, Cuddebackville, p. 188
Iroquois Antiques & Collectibles, Bainbridge, p. 166
Lakeside Antique Galleries, Cazenovia, p. 179
New Scotland Antiques, Albany, p. 161
Old Mine Road Antiques, Wawarsing, p. 265
Pastimes, Ithaca, p. 206
Pheasant Farm, Greene, p. 197
Phoenicia Antique Center, Phoenicia, p. 235
Regent Street Antique Center, Saratoga Springs, p. 247
Rhinebeck Antique Center, Rhinebeck, p. 243
Saugerties Antique Center, Saugerties, p. 250
Tarrytown Antique Center, Tarrytown, p. 259
Village Antique Center, Millbrook, p. 205

Jewelry/Costume

Jewelry/Estate

Kitchen Collectibles

Anntiques, Friendship, p. 193
Antiques at the Warehouse, Hammondsport, p. 198
Antique & Tools of Business & Kitchen, Pound Ridge, p. 239
Boulevard Attic, Kingston, p. 209
Country Charm Antiques, New Paltz, p. 226
Country Kitchen Antiques, Oak Hill, p. 230
Curio Cupboard/Twin Rivers Ant. & Gifts, Binghamton, p. 170
Findings Antiques, Hyde Park, p. 205
Golden Days Antiques, Waterloo, p. 264
Hayloft Antiques, Champlain, p. 179
Kelso Antiques, Pine Bush, p. 235
Lady Paydacker, Greene, p. 197
Memory Lane Antiques & Etceteras, Middletown, p. 219
Necia Smith Antiques & Collectibles, Penn Yan, p. 234
Old Country Store, Greene, p. 197
Open Door, Barker, p. 167
Rainbow Farm Antiques, Unionville, p. 261
Shedd's Antiques, Mohawk, p. 221
Silver Fox, Binghamton, p. 171
Stepping Stone Inn Antiques, Middletown, p. 219
Treasure Shop The, Saugerties, p. 251
Turn of the Century, Interlaken, p. 206
Ver-Del's, Chester, p. 182
Willow Hill Antiques, Madison, p. 217

Lace & Linen

Antiques at Ward's Bridge, Montgomery, p. 222
Behind The Inn Antiques & Collectibles, Skaneateles, p. 253
Country Kitchen Antiques, Oak Hill, p. 230
Curio Cupboard/Twin Rivers Ant. & Gifts, Binghamton, p. 170
Dickinson's Antiques, Beacon, p. 168
Dutch Mill Antiques, Allegany, p. 163
Eagle's Roost Antiques, Marlboro, p. 218
Gateway Antiques, Shokan, p. 253
Hancock Antiques, Hancock, p. 199
Heirlooms, Delhi, p. 189
Marketplace on Main, Westfield, p. 266
Mary Ann Thompson, Morris, p. 224
McMullen Lasalle Antiques, Niagara Falls, p. 227
Necia Smith Antiques & Collectibles, Penn Yan, p. 234
Patent The, Cobleskill, p. 184
Pink Church Antiques, The, Friendship, p. 194
Red Balloons, Buffalo, p. 175

Reminiscences, Campbell Hall, p. 177
Seventy Nine Wistful Vista Ltd., Brewster, p. 172
Southtown's Antiques, Angola, p. 164
Susan Bean of Silhouette, Rhinebeck, p. 243
Victorian Treasures, Warwick, p. 264
Vintage House Antique Center, Colliersville, p. 186
Wallkill River House, Wallkill, p. 262
Willowen Antiques, Flint, p. 192
Ye Olde Wishin' Shoppe, Saratoga Springs, p. 247
Yesteryears, Chatham, p. 182
York Antiques, York, p. 270

Lighting Devices & Fixtures

Anntiques, Friendship, p. 193
Axtell Antiques, Deposit, p. 189
Betty Brook Road Antiques, South Kortright, p. 254
Brewster Station Antiques & Lighting, Brewster, p. 172
Burning Lights, Saugerties, p. 249
Caywood Antiques, Lodi, p. 214
Century House Antiques, Argyle, p. 164
Cheshire Union Antique Center, Cheshire, p. 177
Cider Mill Antiques, Oxford, p. 233
Collection, The, Trumansburg, p. 260
Cooperstown Antique Center, Cooperstown, p. 186
Curio Cupboard/Twin Rivers Ant. & Gifts, Binghamton, p. 170
Donald Naetzker Antiques, Fairport, p. 191
Doyle Antiques, Hudson, p. 202
Fed-On Antiques, Saugerties, p. 249
Gatehouse, The, Morris, p. 224
Gloria Paul Antique, Nyack, p. 229
J.S. Clark & Co., Tivoli, p. 260
Jackie's Place, Bouckville, p. 216
Lucky Strike Antiques, Scarsdale, p. 251
McMullen Lasalle Antiques, Niagara Falls, p. 227
Millville Antiques, Whitney Point, p. 267
Mission Oak Antiques, Rochester, p. 245
Mix, Buffalo, p. 175
Myron Cohen Antiques, Stone Ridge, p. 257
Oak Ridge Antiques, Lansing, p. 211
Oldies But Goodies, Elmira/Big Flats, p. 191
Old Mill Antiques, Krumville, p. 210
Sarabeck Antiques, Cold Spring, p. 185
Shades of the Past Antiques, Orchard Park, p. 232

McMurray Antiques, Windsor, p. 269

Militaria

Art & Antiques Co. of Spencertown, Spencertown, p. 255
Bath Antiques, Bath, p. 167
Cheritree Antiques, Oak Hill, p. 230
J&R Ferris Antiques, Madison, p. 215
Noah's Ark Antique Center, Fishkill, p. 192

Miniatures

Bearly Antiques, Warwick, p. 262
Carol's Antiques, Newark, p. 226
Cyd Leon Antiques, Yonkers, p. 270
Priscilla B. Nixon Antiques & Interiors, Westfield, p. 266
Raspberry Patch Antiquities, Valois, p. 261
Ver-Del's Collectibles, Chester, p. 182
White Lion Antiques, Patterson, p. 233

Miniatures/Art

James William Lowery, Baldwinsville, p. 166

Mirrors

Archatrive, Staatsburg, p. 256
Bayberry House, Gloversville, p. 195
Carol David Antiques, Scarsdale, p. 251
Chelsea Antiques, Madison, p. 215
Circus Barn Antiques/Chairs Upstairs, Friendship, p. 193
Crown House Antiques, Chappaqua, p. 179
Delores Rogers Murphy Antiques, Clinton Corners, p. 184
Janice F. Strauss American Antiques, South Salem, p. 255
Mary Webster Frames, Binghamton, p. 170
Old Mill Antiques, Krumville, p. 210
Old Time Trappings, McGraw, p. 218
Pheasant Hill Antiques, Homer, p. 200
Pine Woods Antique Shop, Bouckville, p. 216
Savannah Antiques, Hudson, p. 203
Wall Street Antiques, Kingston, p. 210

Movie Memorabilia

Marilyn in Monroe, Monroe, p. 222

Musical Instruments

Chatsworth Auction Rooms, Mamaroneck, p. 217

Nautical/Marine

Needlework

Oriental Arts

Oriental Carpets

Paintings

Artemis Gallery, North Salem, p. 228
Audree Bryce Chase's Collector's Corner, Pittsford, p. 236
Bob & Sallie Connelly, Binghamton, p. 169
Brennan Antiques, Rochester, p. 244
Browsing Corner, The, Wawarsing, p. 264
Butter Hill Antiques, Cornwall on Hudson, p. 187
Calico Quail Antiques & Bed & Bkfst, Mabbettsville, p. 214
Chelsea Antiques, Madison, p. 215
Clinton Mill Antiques, Binghamton, p. 169
Collection Agency, The, Seneca Falls, p. 252
Country Gentleman Antiques, The, South Westerlo, p. 255
Dagmar's Antiques, Nyack, p. 228
David Mouilleseaux, Rochester, p. 244
Doyle Antiques, Hudson, p. 202
Dualities Gallery, Larchmont, p. 212
Fischer's Antiques, Albion, p. 162
Gloria Paul Antique, Nyack, p. 229
Grasshopper Antique Center, Madison, p. 215
Green River Gallery, Millerton, p. 220
Guest House, The, Bronxville, p. 173
Hancock Antiques, Hancock, p. 199
Heisler's Antique Mercantile, Smithville Flats, p. 254
Ingrid Migonis Antiques, Hamilton, p. 198
Jack & Maryellen Whistance, Kingston, p. 209
Jenkinstown Antiques, New Paltz, p. 226
Kapell's Antiques, Greenport, p. 125
Kiplings Treasures & Antiquities, Canandaiqua, p. 178
Lakeside Antique Galleries, Cazenovia, p. 179
Lawrence P. Kohn, Hudson, p. 203
Marketplace on Main, Westfield, p. 266
M. L. Baran, Binghamton, p. 170
Millbrook Antique Mall, Millbrook, p. 220
New Scotland Antiques, Albany, p. 161
Oak Ridge Antiques, Lansing, p. 211
Old Red Mill, Bergen, p. 169
Post Road Gallery, Larchmont, p. 212
Rags and Rarities, Irvington-on-Hudson, p. 206
Remember Me Antiques, Tarrytown, p. 259
Rensselaerville Antiques, Rensselaerville, p. 242
Rondout Art and Antiques, Kingston, p. 210
Saugerties Antique Center, Saugerties, p. 250
Seymour June House Art Antiques, Fayetteville, p. 192

Antiques at Cedarwood, Monticello, p. 223
Arles Ltd., Scarsdale, p. 251
Bettiques, Rochester, p. 244
Bloomingsburg Antique Center, Bloomingsburg, p. 171
Brickwood Antiques, Gloversville, p. 196
Browsing Corner, The, Wawarsing, p. 264
Carol David Antiques, Scarsdale, p. 251
Cavern View Antiques, Howes Cavern, p. 202
Centennial Corner Antiques, Ossining, p. 232
Country Cottage Antiques, Tivoli, p. 259
Dagmar's Antiques, Nyack, p. 228
DeWitt Hotel Antiques, Oak Hill, p. 230
Dora Landey Antiques, Scotts Corners, Pound Ridge, p. 239
Elayne's Antiques, Nyack, p. 229
Foxfire, Ltd., Hudson, p. 202
Gateway Antiques, Shokan, p. 253
Hyde Park Antiques Center, Hyde Park, p. 205
Irish Princess, The, Hudson, p. 203
James K. Van Dervort Antiques, Delmar, p. 189
James M. Labaugh, White Plains, p. 267
Jenkinstown Antiques, New Paltz, p. 226
Jenny Hall, Asian Antiques, Ghent, p. 195
Jill Fenichell, Gilbertsville, p. 195
John Laing's Yesteryear Antiques, Hopewell Jct., p. 201
Michael Kessler Antiques Ltd, Mamaroneck, p. 218
Oldies But Goodies Antiques, Jefferson Valley, p. 207
Old Mill Antiques, Krumville, p. 210
Old Time Trappings, McGraw, p. 218
Par Excellence, Wappinger Falls, p. 262
Paul L. Baker, Jordansville, p. 207
Pug Crossing Antiques, Bronxville, p. 174
Reminiscences, Campbell Hall, p. 177
Rhinebeck Antique Center, Rhinebeck, p. 243
Riverbend Antiques Center, Marathon, p. 218
Roberta Stewart Antiques, Cambridge, p. 176
Route 104 Antiques Center, Ontario, p. 232
Touch of Country, House of Shops, A, Elmira, p. 191
Trend, The, Mount Vernon, p. 225
Van Deusen House Antiques, Hurley, p. 204
Village Antique Center, Millbrook, p. 220
Vi & Si's Antiques, Clarence, p. 184
Webster Antique Group Shop, Inc., Webster, p. 265

Postcards

Pottery

Cider Mill Antiques, Red Hook, p. 241
Claudia Kingsley Quilts & Antiques, Malden Bridge, p. 217
Clinton Mill Antiques, Binghamton, p. 169
Cobblestone Store, The, Bouckville, p. 215
Country Antique Unlimited, Briarcliff Manor, p. 172
Country Cottage Antiques, Tivoli, p. 259
Cracker Barrell, Cortland, p. 187
Dew Drop Inn Antique Center, Cold Spring, p. 185
Elizabeth de Bussy Inc., Pound Ridge, p. 239
Gatehouse, The, Morris, p. 224
James M. Labaugh, White Plains, p. 267
Jan's Early Attic, Bloomfield, p. 171
Jerry's Antique Co-op, Olean, p. 231
Jill Fenichell, Gilbertsville, p. 195
John and Lynn Gallo, Otego, p. 233
Justin Thyme Antique Center, Jefferson, p. 207
Kathleen Seibel Antiques, Catskill, p. 179
Kruggel Antiques, Rochester, p. 245
Lake Placid Antique Center, Lake Placid, p. 211
Lorraines Antiques, Mamaroneck, p. 218
Madison Inn Antiques, Madison, p. 217
Maracek & Wood Antiques, Alfred, p. 162
McMurray Antiques, Windsor, p. 269
Millport Mercantile, Millport, p. 221
Nine Caroline Antiques, Saratoga Springs, p. 247
Old Hickory Antique Center, Bainbridge, p. 166
Old Mill Antiques, Krumville, p. 210
Old Stuff, Saratoga Springs, p. 247
Olean Antique Center, Olean, p. 231
Saraf's Emporium, Westfield, p. 267
Silver Fox, Binghamton, p. 171
Times Past Antiques, Wellsville, p. 265
Townhouse Antiques, Hudson, p. 203
Tow Path House Antiques, High Falls, p. 199
Village Antique Center, Millbrook, p. 220
Vintage Antique Center, Leroy, p. 213
Wilson's Antique Services, Cortland, p. 188

Poster

Primitives

Antiques at the Warehouse, Hammondsport, p. 198

Tin Rabbit, The, Stanfordville, p. 256
Treadwell Farm Enterprises, Binghamton, p. 171
Treasure Shop, The, Saugerties, p. 251
Wagonjack and Holly Cobbles Antiques, Fairport, p. 192
William A. Gustafson Antiques, Austerlitz, p. 165
Wood Bull Antiques, Milford, p. 219
Woodshed Antiques, Macedon, p. 214
Woodshed Antiques, The, Pine City, p. 236

Prints
Abacus Bookshop, Rochester, p. 244
Antiques of Merritt, Rochester, p. 244
Browsing Corner, The, Wawarsing, p. 264
Butter Hill Antiques, Cornwall on Hudson, p. 187
Calico Quail Antiques & Bed & Bkfst, Mabbettsville, p. 214
Clinton Mills Antique Center, Binghamton, p. 169
Country Books, Greenwich, p. 197
Crown House Antiques, Chappaqua, p. 179
David Mouilleseaux, Rochester, p. 244
DeSimone & Yount Booksellers, Rochester, p. 245
English Garden Antiques & Interiors, Saugerties, p. 249
Foxfire, Ltd., Hudson, p. 202
Gatehouse, The, Morris, p. 224
Green River Gallery, Millerton, p. 220
Guest House, The, Bronxville, p. 173
Heritage Hill Antiques, Lake Placid, p. 211
Kiplings Treasures & Antiquities, Canandaiqua, p. 178
Lorraines Antiques, Mamaroneck, p. 218
Lucky Strike Antiques, Scarsdale, p. 251
Lyrical Ballad Bookstore, Saratoga Springs, p. 247
Mary Ann Thompson, Morris, p. 224
Old Stone House Antiques, Saugerties, p. 250
Past & Present Antiques, Sodus, p. 254
Pine Woods Antique Shop, Bouckville, p. 216
Rensselaerville Antiques, Rensselaerville, p. 242
Rondout Art and Antiques, Kingston, p. 210
Seventy Nine Wistful Vista Ltd., Brewster, p. 172
Steele Creek Antiques, Ilion, p. 205
Third Eye Antiques, Plattsburgh, p. 238
Touch of Country, House of Shops, A, Elmira, p. 191
Uncle Alan's Antiques & Oddities, Stamford, p. 256
Zeller's, Albany, p. 162

Quilts

Quimper

Radios

Railroadiana

Salt Dips
Old Stone House Antiques, Saugerties, p. 250

Samplers
Collection, The, Trumansburg, p. 260
Donald Naetzker Antiques, Fairport, p. 191
Heisler's Antique Mercantile, Smithville Flats, p. 254

Scientific Instruments
B.J. Antiques, Cuddebackville, p. 188
J&R Ferris Antiques, Madison, p. 215
William A. Gustafson Antiques, Austerlitz, p. 165

Sculpture
Artemis Gallery, North Salem, p. 228
Barbara F. Israel Enterprises, Katonah, p. 208
M.L. Baran, Binghamton, p. 170
Post Road Gallery, Larchmont, p. 212
Rondout Art and Antiques, Kingston, p. 210
Syracuse Antiques Exchange, Syracuse, p. 258
Terry Seldon Calhoun/Fifth Estate, Pelham, p. 234

Shaker
Art & Antique Co. of Spencertown, Spencertown, p. 255
Black Shutters, The, Victory Mills, p. 261
Greenwillow Farms Ltd., Chatham, p. 181
Maria C. Brooks Antiques, Delmar, p. 189
Red Fox Antiques, Hillsdale, p. 200
Richard & Betty Ann Rasso Antiques, E. Chatham, p. 181
Suzanne Courcier/Robert W. Wilkins, Austerlitz, p. 165

Sheet Music
Open Door, Barker, p. 167
Wall Street Antiques, Kingston, p. 210

Silver
Alfred's Antiques, Circleville, p. 182
Andrea's Antiques, Woodburne, p. 269
Antiques at Ward's Bridge, Montgomery, p. 222
Arles, Ltd., Scarsdale, p. 251
Bayberry House, Gloversville, p. 195
Bettiques, Rochester, p. 244
Black Bear Antiques, Plattsburgh, p. 238

Blake's Antiques, Corning, p. 186
Carriage House Antiques, Leroy, p. 212
Dagmar's Antiques, Nyack, p. 228
Deacon's Bench Antiques The, Penn Yan, p. 234
Dew Drop Inn Antique Center, Cold Spring, p. 185
Fanny Doolittle, Patterson, p. 233
Frank Hoxie Jeweler, Cortland, p. 187
Gloria Paul Antique, Nyack, p. 229
Hyde Park Antiques Center, Hyde Park, p. 205
Jackie's Place, Bouckville, p. 216
James M. Labaugh, White Plains, p. 267
Lakeside Antique Galleries, Cazenovia, p. 179
Mad Hatter Antiques, Binghamton, p. 170
North Hill Antiques, Suffern, p. 257
Regent Street Antique Center, Saratoga Springs, p. 247
Route 104 Antiques Center, Ontario, p. 232
Sarabeck Antiques, Cold Spring, p. 185
Saugerties Antique Annex, Saugerties, p. 250
Saugerties Antique Gallery, Saugerties, p. 250
Seymour June House Art Antiques, Fayetteville, p. 192
Silversmith & Goldsmith Jewelers, The, Oneonta, p. 231
Southtowns Antiques, Angola, p. 164
Stimson's Antiques & Gifts, Lewiston, p. 213
Thumbprint Antiques, Stone Ridge, p. 257
Village Antique Center, Millbrook, p. 220
Vin-Dick Antiques, Kingston, p. 210
Vi & Si's Antiques, Clarence, p. 184

Soda Fountain Collectibles
Collectors' Showcase, Greene, p. 196
Hickory Bend Antiques, Jasper, p. 207

Sporting Equipment
Bristol Antiques, Honeoye, p. 200

Staffordshire
Bobbi Von Dehmlein Antiques, Springfield Ctr, p. 255
Dora Landey Antiques, Scotts Corner, Pound Ridge, p. 239
Foxfire, Ltd., Hudson, p. 202

Stained Glass
Angelica Antique Emporium, Angelica, p. 163

Stamps
Btrading Co., Albany, p. 161
Zeller's, Albany, p. 162

Stoneware
Barbara Zitz Antiques, Rhinebeck, p. 242
Cider Mill Antiques, Oxford, p. 233
David Davis Antiques, Rensselaer, p. 242
Edward & Judith Keiz Antiques, Hurleyville, p. 205
Frog Hollow Shop, The, Cooperstown, p. 186
Glass Shop, The, Shushan, p. 253
Golden Eagle Antiques, New Lebanon, p. 225
Goosewing Antiques, West Hurley, p. 265
Mad Hatter Antiques, Binghamton, p. 170
Mark Twain Country Antiques, Elmira, p. 191
McMurray Antiques, Windsor, p. 269
Olean Antique Center, Olean, p. 231
Paul Coon, Penn Yan, p. 234
Paul L. Baker Antiques, Jordanville, p. 207
Pine Woods Antique Shop, Bouckville, p. 216
Two + Four Antiques, Herkimer, p. 199

Television Collectibles
Collectors' Showcase, Greene, p. 196
Marilyn in Monroe, Monroe, p. 222

Textiles
Anatolia-Tribal Rugs & Weavings, Woodstock, p. 270
Antiques at Cedarwood, Monticello, p. 223
Antiques of Merritt, Rochester, p. 244
At Home Antiques, Phoenicia, p. 234
Audree & Bryce Chase's Collector's Corner, Pittsford, p. 236
Beata Baird Antique, Hudson, p. 202
Binder Joiner & Smith, Kinderhook, p. 208
Black Shutters, The, Victory Mills, p. 261
Buy-Gone Days, Montgomery, p. 222
Clocktower Antique Center, Warwick, p. 263
Dutch House, The, Claverack, p. 184
Gateway Antiques, Shokan, p. 253
Granny's Attic, Saugerties, p. 250
Hancock Antiques, Hancock, p. 199
Heir-loom House Antiques, Canandaigua, p. 178

Tools

Toys

Buy-Gone Days, Montgomery, p. 222
Heirlooms, Delhi, p. 189
K&K Quilteds, Hillsdale, p. 199
Marilyn in Monroe, Monroe, p. 222
Mary Ann Thompson, Morris, p. 224
Memory Lane Antiques & Collectibles, Hartsdale, p. 199
Piacente, Tarrytown, p. 259
Pink Church Antiques, The, Friendship, p. 194
Red Balloons, Buffalo, p. 175
Second Hand Rose, Syracuse, p. 258
Skillypot Antique Center, Kingston, p. 210
Susan Bean of Silhouette, Rhinebeck, p. 243
Sweetcheeks, Binghamton, p. 171
Ye Olde Wishin' Shoppe, Saratoga Springs, p. 247
York Antiques, York, p. 270

Weather Vanes
Dennis & Valerie Bakoledis Antiques, Rhinebeck, p. 243
John Sideli, Chatham, p. 181
Marna Anderson Gallery, New Paltz, p. 226
Old Mill Antiques, Krumville, p. 210

Wicker
Antiques at the Warehouse, Hammondsport, p. 198
Golden Eagle Antiques, New Lebanon, p. 225
Lady Paydacker, Greene, p. 197
Miriam Rogachefsky Antiques, Rochester, p. 245
Notaro's Antiques, Westfield, p. 266
Steele Creek Antiques, Ilion, p. 205
Strap Hinge, Pound Ridge, p. 239
Vilardo Antiques, Westfield, p. 267
Wiccopee Antiques, Inc., Hopewell Jct., p. 201

Yellow ware
Bristol Antiques, Honeoye, p. 200

ANTIQUE DEALERS AND CO-OP MANAGERS PLEASE SEE PAGE 342

Services - Upstate New York

Note: Some of the categories below have no shops listed under them; the categories have, however, been included for the sake of completeness and to indicate that at present no shops in this region provide these services.

Appraisals

Abacus Bookshop, Rochester, p. 244
Abbey's Antiques, Art, & Appraisals, Bath, p. 167
Alan Pereske Antiques, Lake Placid, p. 211
American Jazz, Ossining, p. 232
AnaMaria Recouso Antiques, Katonah, p. 208
Anthony S. Werneke Antiques, Pond Eddy, p. 238
Antique Underground, Syracuse, p. 257
Antiques at Ward's Bridge, Montgomery, p. 222
Art & Antique Co. of Spencertown, Spencertown, p. 255
Artemis Gallery, North Salem, p. 228
Beacon Hill Antiques, Beacon, p. 168
Belknap Hill Books, Penn Yan, p. 234
Black Bear Antiques, Plattsburg, p. 238
Black Shutters, The, Victory Mills, p. 261
Bob & Sallie Connelly, Binghamton, p. 169
Brennan Antiques, Rochester, p. 244
Brickwood Antiques, Gloversville, p. 196
Broadway Antiques & Interiors, Newburgh, p. 227
Btrading, Albany, p. 161
Buffalo's Attic, Buffalo, p. 174
Buy-Gone Days, Montgomery, p. 222
Calhoun's Books, Geneva, p. 194
Carder Steuben Glass Shop, Corning, p. 187
Carol's Antiques, Newark, p. 226
Cavern View Antiques, Howes Cave, p. 202
Cheritree Antiques, Oak Hill, p. 230
Collection Agency, The, Seneca Falls, p. 252
Collection, The, Ithaca, p. 206
Crown House Antiques, Chappaqua, p. 179
Currie's Antiques, Watkins Glen, p. 264
Cyd Leon Antiques, Yonkers, p. 270
Dacia of New York, Syracuse, p. 258
Dagmar's Antiques, Nyack, p. 228
Dalton's American Decorative, Syracuse, p. 258

Past and Present Antiques, Sodus, p. 254
Paul Coon, Penn Yan, p. 234
Praiseworthy Antiques, Guilford, p. 198
Pricilla B. Nixon Antiques & Interiors, Westfield, p. 266
R&M Leed Antiques, Hopewell Jct, p. 201
Rader's Antiques, Holcomb, p. 200
Rags and Rarities, Irvington-on-Hudson, p. 206
Red Fox Antiques, Hillsdale, p. 200
Rensselaerville Antiques, Rensselaerville, p. 242
Richard & Betty Ann Rasso Antiques, E. Chatham, p. 181
Richard Romberg, Rochester, p. 245
Robert Herron Antiques, Austerlitz, p. 165
Sarabeck Antiques, Cold Spring, p. 185
Savannah Antiques, Hudson, p. 203
Second Hand Rose, Syracuse, p. 258
Seymour June House Art & Antiques, Fayetteville, p. 192
Shades of the Past Antiques, Orchard Park, p. 260
Silversmith & Goldsmith Jewelers, The, Oneonta, p. 231
Skevington-Back Antiques, Chatham, p. 181
Stimson's Antiques & Gifts, Lewiston, p. 213
Stone House Gallery, Saugerties, p. 250
Sue Evans Antiques, Rome, p. 246
Sullivan's Antiques & Collectors Items, North Troy, p. 228
Susan Bean of Silhouette, Rhinebeck, p. 243
Suzanne Courcier-Robert W. Wilkins, Austerlitz, p. 165
Terry Ann Tomlinson, Woodstock, p. 270
Thumbprint Antiques, Stone Ridge, p. 257
Vi & Si's Antiques, Clarence, p. 184
Vin-Dick Antiques, Kingston, p. 210
Ward's Antiques, Auburn, p. 164
Webb & Brennan, Pittsford, p. 237
White & White Antiques & Interiors, Skaneateles, p. 253
William A. Gustafson Antiques, Austerlitz, p. 165
Wilson's Antique Services. Cortland, p. 188
Woodshed Antiques, Macedon, p. 214
Woolf's Den Antiques, Larchmont, p. 212
Yankee Peddler Bookshop Vol II, Rochester, p. 245
Zeller's, Albany, p. 162

Authentication

Audree & Bryce Chase's Collector's Corner, Pittsford, p. 236
DeWitt Hotel Antiques, Oak Hill, p. 260

Dimitroff's Antiques, Corning, p. 187
Green River Gallery, Millerton, p. 220
Jill Fenichell, Gilbertsville, p. 195
R&M Leed Antiques, Hopewell Jct, p. 201
Richard & Betty Ann Rasso Antiques, E. Chatham, p. 181
Richard Romberg, Rochester, p. 245
Seymour June House Art & Antiques, Fayetteville, p. 192
Suzanne Courcier-Robert W. Wilkins, Austerlitz, p. 165
Webb & Brennan American Antiques, Pittsford, p. 237

Book Binding & Restoration

Belknap Hill Books, Penn Yan, p. 234
Yankee Peddler Bookshop, Williamson, p. 269
Yankee Peddler Bookshop Vol II, Rochester, p. 245

Cabinetry

Good Trade Farm. Friendship, p. 193
William A. Gustafson Antiques, Austerlitz, p. 165

China & Pottery Restoration

Behind the Inn Antiques & Collectibles, Skaneateles, p. 253
Hopewell Antique Center, Hopewell Junction, p. 201
Memory Lane Antiques & Collectibles, Hartsdale, p. 199
Oldies But Goodies Antiques, Jefferson Valley, p. 207

China Matching Service

Clock Repair & Restoration

Bath Antiques, Bath, p. 167
Bob & Sallie Connelly, Binghamton, p. 169
Country Clocks, Cold Spring, p. 185
Crown House Antiques, Chappaqua, p. 179
Dacia of New York, Syracuse, p. 258
Just Like Grandma's, Vernon, p. 261
Marvin's Antiques & Refinishing Ctr, Ardsley, p. 164
Memory Lane Antiques & Coillectibles, Hartsdale, p. 199
Olde Clocks, Gloversville, p. 196
Second Time Around Antiques, Brewster, p. 172

Consignments

Antique Center at Forge Hill Village, New Windsor, p. 226
Antique Center of Preston Hollow, Preston Hollow, p. 240

Suzanne Courcier-Robery W. Wilkins, Austerlitz, p.165
Tow Path House Antiques, High Falls, p. 199
Vintage House Antiques Center, Colliersville, p. 186
Voss Beringer, Ltd., Pound Ridge, p. 239
White & White Antiques & Interiors, Skaneateles, p. 253
William A. Gustafson Antiques, Austerlitz, p. 165
Willowen Antiques, Flint, p. 192
Woolf's Den Antiques, Larchmont, p. 212

Crystal & Glass Restoration
Noah's Ark Antique Center, Fishkill, p. 192

Display Material
Archatrive, Staatsburg, p. 256

Doll Repair
Early Everything, Beacon, p. 168
Wilson's Antique Services, Cortland, p. 188

Electric Train Repair

Finders Service
AnaMaria Recouso Antiques, Katonah, p. 208
Anthony S. Werneke Antiques, Pond Eddy, p. 238
Antique Center at Forge Hill Village, New Windsor, p. 226
Art & Antique Co. of Spencertown, Spencertown, p. 255
Belknap Hill Books, Penn Yan, p. 234
Black Bear Antiques, Plattsburgh, p. 238
Brewster Station Antiques & Lighting, Brewster, p. 172
Cyd Leon Antiques, Yonkers, p. 270
Dalton's American Decorative, Syracuse, p. 258
David Davis Antiques, Rensselaer, p. 242
DeSimone and Yount Booksellers, Rochester, p. 245
Gramm-O-Phone Antiques, Campbell Hall, p. 176
Heritage Hill Antiques, Lake Placid, p. 211
Ingalls Antiques, Unadilla, p. 261
Ingeborg Quitzau, Antiquarian Books, Edmeston, p. 190
Kathy Schoemer American Antiques, North Salem, p. 228
Kinderhook Antique Center, Kinderhook, p. 208
Maxwell's Treasures Books, Lima, p. 214
Memory Lane Antiques and Etceteras, Middletown, p. 219
Nancy's Antiques, Williamson, p. 268

Oak Ridge Antiques, Lansing, p. 211
Olana Gallery, Brewster, p. 172
Shades of the Past, Tomkins Cove, p. 260
Stone House Gallery, Saugerties, p. 250
Strawberry Hill Bookshop, Pittsford, p. 237
Whittington Antiques, Yorktown Heights, p. 271
William A. Gustafson Antiques, Austerlitz, p. 165
Woodshed Antiques, Macedon, p. 214

Fixtures

Frame Repair & Restoration
Calico Quail Antiques and B&B, Mabbettsville, p. 214
Mary Webster Frames, Binghamton, p. 170
Silver Fox, Binghamton, p. 171

Furniture Refinishing
Antique Palace Emporium, Inc., Liberty, p. 213
Black Creek Farm, Fairhaven, p. 191
Brockmann's Antique Center, Milford, p. 219
Chelsea Antiques, Madison, p. 215
Dacia of New York, Syracuse, p. 258
Good Trade Farm, Friendship, p. 193
Guest House, The, Bronxville, p. 173
Guild Brothers Antiques, Montour Falls, p. 224
Holiday Hill Antiques, Kingston, p. 209
Hoosick Antique Center, Hoosick, p. 200
Lone Gable Emporium, Le Roy, p. 212
Maple Avenue Antiques, Elmira, p. 191
Marvin's Antiques & Refinishing Ctr, Ardsley, p. 164
Notaro's Antiques, Westfield, p. 266
Old Greenwich Hardware Antiques, Greenwich, p. 197
Oldies But Goodies, Elmira, p. 191
Once Upon A Time Country, Franklinville, p. 193
Proud American Shoppe, Pine City, p.236
Randallville Mill Antiques, Florida, p. 193
Sarabeck Antiques, Cold Spring, p. 185
Saugerties Antique Annex, Saugerties, p. 250
Semmel Antiques, Naples, p. 225
76 Barn, Chester, p. 182
Touch of Country, House of Shops, A, Elmira, p. 191
Village Antique Center, Millbrook, p. 220

Furniture Repair & Restoration

Furniture Reproduction

Glass Matching Service
Iris Cottage Antiques, Canaan, p. 177
Kieningers from Apponaug, The, Williamson, p. 268

Hardware
Cheritree Antiques, Oak Hill, p. 230
Findings Antiques, Hyde Park, p. 205
Golden Days Antiques, Waterloo, p. 264

Hooked Rug Repair & Restoration

Home Restoration
Archatrive, Staatsburg, p. 256
Cheritree Antiques, Oak Hill, p. 230
DeWitt Hotel Antiques, Oak Hill, p. 230
Howard Bliss Antiques, Schenectady, p. 251
Janice F. Strauss American Antiques, South Salem, p. 255
Jenkinstown Antiques, New Paltz, p. 226
Once Upon A Time Country, Franklinville, p. 193
Praiseworthy Antiques, Guilford, p. 198
76 Barn, Chester, p. 182
Voss Beringer, Ltd., Pound Ridge, p. 239
White & White Antiques & Interiors, Skaneateles, p. 253

Jewelry Repair
Assets Antiques & Collectibles, Buffalo, p. 174
Cyd Leon Antiques, Yonkers, p. 270
Frank Hoxie, Cortland, p. 187
Heritage Hill Antiques, Lake Placid, p. 211
Hopewell Antique Center, Hopewell Junction, p. 201
Memory Lane Antiques & Collectibles, Hartsdale, p. 199
Midtown Antiques, Binghamton, p. 171
New Scotland Antiques, Albany, p. 161
Page in Time, A, Saratoga Springs, p. 247
Silversmith & Goldsmith Jewelers, Oneonta, p. 231
Village Antique Center, Millbrook, p. 220
Yellow Shed Antiques, Mahopac, p. 217
Zeller's, Albany, p. 162

Lamp Repair & Restoration
Angelica Antique Emporium, Angelica, p. 163
Antique Center at Forge Hill Village, New Windsor, p. 226
Brewster Station Antiques & Lighting, Brewster, p. 172

Green River Gallery, Millerton, p. 220
Jenkinstown Antiques, New Paltz, p. 226
Lawrence P. Kohn, Hudson, p. 203
Noah's Ark Antique Center, Fishkill, p. 192
Rondout Art and Antiques, Kingston, p. 210
Stone House Gallery, Saugerties, p. 250
Yankee Peddler Bookshop Vol II, Rochester, p. 245
Yankee Peddler Bookshop, Williamson, p. 269
York Antiques, York, p. 270

Pewter Repair & Restoration
Noah's Ark Antique Center, Fishkill, p. 192

Phonograph Repair
American Flier, Larchmont, p. 212
For Your Listening Pleasure, Binghamton, p. 170
Gramm-O-Phone Antiques, Campbell Hall, p. 176
Midtown Antiques, Binghamton, p. 171

Piano & Organ Repair

Prop Rentals
AnaMaria Recouso Antiques, Katonah, p. 208
Antique Center of Preston Hollow, Preston Hollow, p. 240
Antique Underground, Syracuse, p. 257
Antiques at Ward's Bridge, Montgomery, p. 222
Archatrive, Staatsburg, p. 256
Buffalo's Attic, Buffalo, p. 174
DeWitt Hotel Antiques, Oak Hill, p. 230
Horsefeathers Architectural Antiques, Buffalo, p. 175
Kinderhook Antique Center, Kinderhook, p. 208
Kipling's Treasures & Antiques, Canandaigua, p. 178
Marilyn in Monroe, Monroe, p. 222
Noah's Ark Antique Center, Fishkill, p. 192
Rondout Art and Antiques, Kingston, p. 210
Sarabeck Antiques, Cold Spring, p. 185

Quilt Repair & Restoration
K & K Quilted, Hillsdale, p. 199

Radio Repair and Restoration
American Flyer, Larchmont, p. 212
For Your Listening Pleasure, Binghamton, p. 170

New Scotland Antiques, Albany, p. 161

Research

Antiques at Ward's Bridge, Montgomery, p. 222
DeWitt Hotel Antiques, Oak Hill, p. 230
Green River Gallery, Millerton, p. 220
Iris Cottage Antiques, Canaan, p. 177
Jill Fenichell, Gilbertsville, p. 195
John and Lynn Gallo, Otego, p. 233
Maracek & Wood Antiques, Alfred, p. 162
Oak Ridge Antiques, Lansing, p. 211
Past and Present Antiques, Sodus, p. 254
Rondout Art and Antiques, Kingston, p. 210

Silver Matching Service

Memory Lane Antiques & Collectibles, Hartsdale, p. 199

Toy Repair & Restoration

Wicker Repair - Chair Caning, Rush, Taping

Black Creek Farm, Fairhaven, p. 191
Black Shutters, The, Victory Mills. p. 261
Black Smith Shop Antiques, Cambridge, p. 176
Butter Hill Antiques, Cornwall-on-Hudson, p. 187
Circus Barn Antiques . . . , Friendship, p. 193
Country Store Antiques, E. Chatham, p. 180
Curio Cupboard, Binghamton, p. 170
Dacia of New York, Syracuse, p. 258
Dickinson's Antiques, Beacon, p. 168
Early Everything, Beacon, p. 168
Guild Brothers Antiques, Montour Falls, p. 224
Just Like Grandma's, Vernon, p. 261
Lone Gable Emporium, Leroy, p. 212
Marvin's Antiques & Refinishing Ctr, Ardsley, p. 164
Millbrook Antique Mall, Millbrook, p. 220
Page in Time, A, Saratoga Springs, p. 247
Semmel Antiques, Naples, p. 225
Stimson's Antiques & Gifts, Lewiston, p. 213
Wiccopee Antiques, Inc, Hopewell Jct, p. 201

Last Minute Replies

CHAMPLAIN

Wagenshot Antiques and Collectibles
683 Prospect Street (12919)
(518) 298-3451
Hours: Daily 10-6 by appointment or chance

On two floors, one will find a general line of antiques. Furniture, linens, pottery, quilts, penny rugs, kitchen collectibles, and loomed rugs are offered. PR: $

COLD SPRING

Solomon's Mine
93 Main Street (10516)
(914) 737-5071
Hours: Fri-Sun, 12-5 or by appointment

This store carries a general line of antiques and collectibles such as games, toys, advertising, all types of glass, Art Pottery, jewelry, cast iron, folk art, and furniture. CC: No.

NEW CITY

Borghis Garofalo
418 North Little Tor Road (10956)
(914) 634-8274
Hours: By appointment only

In addition to offering some decorative items and accessories, this dealer specializes in 18th and 19th century American and European furniture, paintings, folk art, and architecturals. PR: $$$$$. CC: No.

NEW YORK CITY

David Air Marine Art & Artifacts
8 Beach Street (10013)
(212) 925-7876
Hours: By Appointment

The finest quality vintage ship and boat models, paintings, prints, nautical instruments and some fishing equipment are offered by this dealer. In addition to accepting consignments, appraisals, restoration, display cabinets, rentals are available. PR: $$$$$. CC: No.

Exclusive Art Ltd.
818 Broadway (10003)
(212) 674-1814
Hours: Mon-Sat, 9:30-5:30

This shop specializes in Impressionist paintings and high quality 18th and 19th century furniture and works of art. PR: $500+. CC: No.

Imperial Oriental Art
760 Madison Avenue, 2nd floor
(10021)
(212) 717-5383
(212) 249-0333 fax
Hours: Mon-Sat, 11-6

Chinese, Japanese, and Korean ceramics and works of art are the specialty areas of this business. An appraisals service is offered. PR: $2,000+. CC: MC, V.

ROSLYN

House of Antiques & Fine Art
1040 Northern Boulevard
(11576)
(516) 484-8383
Hours: Daily 10-5:30

This business buys and sells high quality 18th and 19th century furniture and works of art, especially Impressionist paintings. PR: $500+. CC: No.

ATTENTION

Antique Dealers & Co-op Managers

If you would like to be listed in the next edition of *Antiquing New York*, please write or call:

John L. Michel
Columbia University Press
562 West 113th Street
New York, NY 10025
(212) 666–1000, ext. 7137

Being listed in the guide is complimentary

and

If you would like to have a picture in *Antiquing New York* that is representative of the antiques you regularly carry, please submit a 5 x 7 or 8 x 10 professional quality black & white photograph with an appropriate caption. The pictures cannot be returned, but, if selected, they will be included free of charge. Submissions should be sent to John L. Michel at the above address.

Index